Mapping Canada's Music

Helmut Kallmann, ca. 1997, wearing his Order of Canada insignia; on the shelf over his left shoulder: *Encyclopedia of Music in Canada*, first and second editions, and several volumes of *The Canadian Musical Heritage*. *Photograph © Government of Canada. Reproduced with the permission of the Minister of Public Works and Government Services Canada (2012). Source: Library and Archives Canada's website, http://www.collectionscanada.gc.ca/.*

Mapping Canada's Music
Selected Writings of Helmut Kallmann

John Beckwith and Robin Elliott, editors

Wilfrid Laurier University Press acknowledges the support of the Canada Council for the Arts for our publishing program. We acknowledge the financial support of the Government of Canada through the Canada Book Fund for our publishing activities. Funding provided by the Government of Ontario and the Ontario Arts Council. This work was supported by the Research Support Fund.

Library and Archives Canada Cataloguing in Publication

Title: Mapping Canada's music : selected writings of Helmut Kallmann / John Beckwith and Robin Elliott, editors.
Names: Kallmann, Helmut, author. | Beckwith, John, editor. | Elliott, Robin, 1956- editor.
Description: Includes bibliographical references and index.
Identifiers: Canadiana 2024035852X | ISBN 9781771126687 (softcover)
Subjects: LCSH: Kallmann, Helmut. | LCSH: Music—Canada—History and criticism.
Classification: LCC ML205 .K315 2024 | DDC 780.971—dc23

Cover design by Blakeley Words+Pictures. Cover image: musical excerpt from *Le Papillon*, Op. 18, étude for solo piano (1874), by Calixa Lavallée (1842–1891). Text design by James Leahy.

© 2024 Wilfrid Laurier University Press
Waterloo, Ontario, Canada
www.wlupress.wlu.ca

This book is printed on FSC recycled paper and is certified Ecologo. It is made from 100% post-consumer fibre, processed chlorine free, and manufactured using biogas energy.

Printed in Canada

Every reasonable effort has been made to acquire permission for copyrighted material used in this text, and to acknowledge all such indebtedness accurately. Any errors and omissions called to the publisher's attention will be corrected in future printings.

No part of this publication may be reproduced, stored in a retrieval system, or transmitted, in any form or by any means, without the prior written consent of the publisher or a licence from the Canadian Copyright Licensing Agency (Access Copyright). For an Access Copyright licence, visit http://www.accesscopyright.ca or call toll free to 1-800-893-5777.

Contents

List of Illustrations   vii
Preface and Acknowledgements   ix

Helmut Kallmann: A Brief Biography   1
Helmut Kallmann and Canadian Music   17

Selected Writings of Helmut Kallmann (*indicates material which has not been previously published)

1 *Studying Music at a Canadian University, 1946–1949 (1949)   27
2   Canadian Music as a Field for Research (1950)   35
3   The New *Grove's*: Disappointment to Canada (1955)   39
4   Introduction, from *A History of Music in Canada 1534–1914* (1960)   43
5 *Joseph Quesnel's *Colas et Colinette* (1963)   49
6   Music Library Association Digs Up Our Musical Past (1966)   61
7   James Paton Clarke, Canada's First Mus.Bac. (1970)   65
8   The Music Division of the National Library: The First Five Years (1975)   79
9   The Canadian League of Composers in the 1950s: The Heroic Years (1984)   87
10 The Making of a One-Country Music Encyclopedia: An Essay after an Encyclopedia (1994)   103
11 Music in the Internment Camps and after World War II: John Newmark's Start on a Brilliant Canadian Career (1995)   125
12 *Franz Schubert in Canada: A Historical Survey of Performance, Appreciation, and Research (1996)   149

Contents

13 Taking Stock of Canada's Composers from the 1920s to the
    Catalogue of Canadian Composers (1952) (1996)   167
14 *A Selection of Correspondence (1949/1966/1992)   183
15 Mapping Canada's Music: A Life's Task (1997)   189
16 The Matter of Identity (2001)   217
17 *At Home with the Kallmanns: A Schöneberg Family in the 1930s
    (1992/2001)   223

List of Helmut Kallmann's Writings   263
Index   277

List of Illustrations

The illustrations appear on pages 137–47.

1. The Kallmann family, Berlin, 1936
2. The 1933–34 "Quinta" class of the Hohenzollern Gymnasium, Berlin
3. HK's map of the family's Berlin apartment
4. HK's *Abgangszeugnis* (Leaving Report), Private School of the Jewish Community, 7 June 1939
5. Sketches by HK of Internment Camp 1, Île aux Noix, QC, 1943
6. HK in 1997, with censored letter from internment camp
7. Gordon Jocelyn and HK on their graduation day, Toronto, 1949
8. HK in the CBC Music Library, Toronto, 1955
9. Posed portrait, December 1960
10. a. Ruth and Helmut Kallmann with friends in Germany, 1962
    b. Ruth Singer Kallmann, Berlin, 1962
11. Launch of the *Encyclopedia of Music in Canada*, Toronto, November 1981
12. HK with Music Division staff, 1987
13. HK on his sixty-seventh birthday, 7 August 1989
14. Editorial committee, Canadian Musical Heritage Society, 1989
15. Addressing the Ottawa meeting of IAML, 17 July 1994
16. A reunion of ex-internees, 13 May 2000
17. Traute Weinberg and Helmut Kallmann, December 2004

Preface and Acknowledgements

It was in October 2011 that we first had the idea to honour Helmut Kallmann's contributions to Canadian music research by assembling a collection of his writings. After his death from kidney failure at the age of eighty-nine on 12 February 2012, the book assumed the added significance of serving as a memorial to his life's work. We have chosen seventeen of his writings for this collection—five of them are published here for the first time and twelve were previously published, though many of these appeared in sources that are not easily accessible at present. Almost all deal with some aspect of Canadian music; included are reviews, autobiographical reflections, research articles, a reception history, and reminiscences of several major Canadian music publications and projects with which Kallmann was involved.

Helmut Kallmann's daughter, Liora Salter, kindly gave us free and full access to his personal archive—some fifty boxes of books and periodicals, and four filing cabinets full of his writings. We thank her for her support of this venture, including permission to publish these writings and reproduce the illustrations. Shelley Zhang, a recent graduate of the Bachelor of Music program at the University of Toronto, was an efficient, diligent, and astute research assistant who typed and formatted all of the articles. Dawn Keer graciously loaned copies of photos from her University of Alberta thesis, an invaluable study of Kallmann's career. At Library and Archives Canada, Ottawa, Richard Green and Florence Hayes provided background information on the work of the department which Kallmann initiated. Kathleen McMorrow contributed her knowledge and experience in making the index.

At Wilfrid Laurier University Press, we thank the director, Brian Henderson, for his swift acceptance of our proposal for this book, and the acquisitions editor, Ryan Chynces, for seeing it through to completion.

Preface and Acknowledgements

James Leahy was the expert copy editor of the book, and we are grateful to him for the care and attention that he devoted to this task. We also wish to thank the four anonymous external reviewers, whose comments were thoughtful, detailed, and well informed; the book has benefited greatly from the insights of these careful readers.

We feel especially fortunate to have received financial assistance from a number of sources towards the preparation and publication of this book. The (US) Music Library Association chose it as the 2013 recipient of the Carol June Bradley Award; the Michael and Sonja Koerner Charitable Foundation and the Institute for Canadian Music, University of Toronto, provided further generous funding. We view these gestures of support as symbolic of the enduring value of Kallmann's life and work.

—J.B., R.E.

Helmut Kallmann: A Brief Biography

The Faculty of Music representative on the editorial committee of *Torontonensis 1949*, the yearbook published by the Students' Administrative Council of the University of Toronto, is listed as "Helmut Kallman," an early example of a misspelling of his surname that later became widespread. Kallmann's photo is fifteenth in alphabetical order in the Faculty of Music's 1949 graduating class of twenty-eight. The group is historically significant as the first graduating class of the Bachelor of Music program in School Music (later, Music Education), inaugurated in 1946. Each photo carries a name and two lines of identification—the student's special undergraduate activity or function, followed by his/her future plans. Kallmann's entry reads: "Music Reviewer for *The Varsity*; To Study More Music and Be Useful." In Montreal, years later, Kallmann recalled this last phrase when he accepted the 2007 Friends of Canadian Music Award. Writing about music, constantly studying music, and being in myriad ways a *useful* member of society: it reads like an advance description of his long career.

Most of his fellow students enrolled to qualify as public-school music specialists. Such was not Kallmann's ambition, but he was steered to the then-new program because it promised a full range of instruction and its staff was young and eager, compared to the established "General Music" degree program of the Faculty. Richard Johnston, one of his professors, recalled years later: "He was quiet. He was shy ... He was also very bright ... If I ever dared to ask him a question ... he always had the answer and he was always correct.... [W]henever he opened his mouth to say anything he had something worth listening to."[1] He was already a competent pianist (while at the University of Toronto he completed the Grade X examination of the Royal Conservatory of Music in piano), and the course offered him a wider knowledge of music, including other instruments. A program of the student concert band, conducted by another professor, Robert Rosevear, lists Kallmann as percussionist and librarian,[2] and by graduation he became a reliable performer on the French horn. But his favourite subject was music history. An assessment of his experience, his professors, and his fellow students, written at the end of his program, is reproduced here for the first time (see page 27). This frank account of the state of postsecondary studies in music in Canada at the time might appear arrogant except that he prepared it only for himself.

He was not quite twenty-seven when he graduated, but by no means the oldest member of his class: many had enrolled in 1946 on veterans' grants, having interrupted their studies to serve in the Second World War. Few even of those who saw battle action overseas had had their young lives disrupted to the same extent as Kallmann.

Helmut Max Kallmann was born on 7 August 1922 in Berlin. His father, Arthur, was a lawyer and keen amateur musician; his mother, Fanny, a social worker. He had one sister, Eva, who was one year older (b. 20 March 1921). In a major essay of his retirement years, also given its first publication here (see page 223), Kallmann describes his family and school life in 1930s Berlin, noting his fondness for his piano studies with his father and his childhood habit of making lists (for example, cataloguing the city's public transit system, or compiling, with a school friend, his own "Köchel" of Mozart compositions)—presaging perhaps the adult librarian and historian. Jewish and leftist, the Kallmanns were unusually vulnerable to the increasingly cruel persecutions imposed by the Nazis after 1933. Arthur Kallmann gradually lost his professional standing and his livelihood. Towards the end of Helmut's high-school studies, and only a couple of months before the outbreak of war, he was chosen to join the *Kindertransport*, set up by a refugee committee in London to take younger members of Jewish families to safety in England.

In London, deprived of contact with his family, quarantined at first with other rescued children because of a suspected illness, and having only the consolation of a limited opportunity to continue music study, in May of 1940 Kallmann found himself rounded up with other German citizens during a national panic over the apparent likelihood of invasion by Hitler's forces. They were labelled "enemy aliens" and first imprisoned at Huyton Alien Internment Camp in the Liverpool suburbs, then on the Isle of Man, and finally (as panic deepened into hysteria) prepared for internment in British overseas locations.[3] At the Greenock docks, near Glasgow, several ships were headed to Canada, and one to Australia: internees were not permitted to choose. Kallmann was assigned to the *Sobieski*, a refurbished Polish liner, with more than 1,000 other men aged sixteen to sixty, heading for the uncertainty of prison life in a new country, Canada. Few political or military figures of the time, whether British or Canadian, saw the flawed logic of branding these individuals as "enemies" when the huge majority were refugees of Nazi Germany, Jews and others, whose knowledge of Nazism was more immediate than that of the Allied authorities. In the confusion, they were imprisoned alongside actual prisoners of war. The internment policies lasted only for a short period, but the internees' lives were suspended in many cases for almost the whole duration of the war.

Arriving at Quebec City on 15 July 1940, Kallmann spent a few weeks in a camp near Trois-Rivières while the Canadian government hastily converted a former labour camp at Ripples (about twenty-five kilometres east of Fredericton, NB) to house them. It was at this "Camp B" that he spent the next year, guarded by members of the veterans' militia. The camp's population (some 700 men) was a varied one—in age, educational status, and political and religious persuasion. Work parties dug ditches and helped clear forestland in the area; professional chefs managed to prepare some favourite foods, and the orthodox Jewish contingent observed its dietary restrictions; lectures, concerts, and theatrical performances were arranged; a library was organized. A democratic pattern emerged, with elected "spokesmen" to maintain order at each of the four large billeting huts and to negotiate during disputes (of which there were several). The obligatory camp uniform featured a red stripe down the trouser seam and a large red circle (like a target) on the back of the jacket.

One piano was available for the dozen or so pianists, professional and amateur, in the camp. Kallmann took his turn practising and spent many hours studying scores and historical writings. Peter Ball, a friend in the United States, sent him Paul Henry Lang's monumental *Music in Western Civilisation*, newly published, a work he regarded as a breakthrough discovery. Again prophetic is the citation he received when awaiting transfer to another camp (he was not yet nineteen):

> Dear Mr. Kallmann,
> At the occasion of the breaking up of our camp we should like to express to you our gratitude and admiration for the way in which you managed the camp library. With best wishes for a brighter and happier future,
> Yours sincerely,
> [signed] A. Ebel, Camp Spokesman; A. Rosenberg, Education Department[4]

The camp in New Brunswick was scheduled to be rebuilt, to house a growing number of actual war prisoners. Many of the original internees had been released, and some returned to Britain to enlist in the Allied forces there. Kallmann and others were transferred in mid-1941 to a camp at Farnham in the Eastern Townships area of Quebec ("Camp A"). In January 1942 he was moved again to the nearby Sherbrooke camp ("Camp N"), and while there he completed an external examination of McGill University in harmony and counterpoint. Internees who were sponsored in Canada, for example by a potential employer, were eligible for release. Kallmann's special skills, as a student of music history and librarianship, had only a slight hope of meeting employment opportunities in wartime Canada, and as a result he was one of the last internees to be released. He remained in Camp N for over half a year, and when it was disbanded he spent the winter of 1942–3 in yet another camp ("Camp I") at Île aux Noix near the Quebec/Vermont border. In the summer of 1943, his aptitude for mathematics (not music) brought him to the attention of an accountancy firm in Toronto, and he was released with the prospect of a clerk's position with them. He was twenty-one and for four years had endured this severe loss of freedom. At first he had communicated fitfully with his parents and his sister in Germany, but gradually the contact was broken, and he was never to see them again. In his essay "At Home with the Kallmanns" (see page 223), he recounts how, after the war, he pieced together the tragic story of their fate.

In Toronto, the local branch of the National Refugee Committee arranged contacts and helped him find inexpensive clothes, and his fellow internee John Newmark suggested lodging (see the essay about camp life and the start of Newmark's Canadian career, page 125). On the recommendation of Arnold and Maria Walter, he registered for piano lessons with Naomi Adaskin and later with Greta Kraus. Walter, a transplanted Austrian, taught music at Upper Canada College and the Royal Conservatory, and eventually became a nationally prominent figure in post-secondary music education. Other new friends included Barker Fairley and Humphrey Milnes, professors of German at the University of Toronto. Kallmann's job entailed a good deal of travel around the city to assist with audits, and this introduction to Toronto he found satisfying, although the work itself was routine and mechanical. In January 1944 he found more agreeable and challenging employment, at Coles Books, then a fixture at the corner of Yonge and Charles Streets. From lowly clerk's duties—sweeping the floor, pricing the bargain-table books—he gradually assumed more responsibility and was intrigued by the chance to learn about the publishing world; he remained in this job for over two years. He shared rooms in the west end at the Shuster home; his landlady (HK described her as "a Jewish mama with a big heart"),[5] the mother of the renowned comedian Frank Shuster, was delighted to find a tenant who would play her piano. He completed Ontario university-entrance qualifications at this time, and in 1946 he became a naturalized Canadian citizen. When he felt ready to apply for admission to degree studies in music, it was Arnold Walter who suggested the university's new School Music course.

While Kallmann pursued his academic program, several extracurricular involvements broadened his sense of the shape his future career might take. Another recent European émigré, the conductor Heinz Unger, started a non-professional community orchestra, and Kallmann played a few seasons in the horn section. He contributed concert reviews to the student newspaper, *The Varsity*. Most strikingly, when he chanced upon a reference to the German-Canadian Theodore Molt's 1825 visit to Beethoven in Vienna, the discovery served as the epiphanic start of his lifelong investigation of Canada's musical past (as he recounts in his essay "Mapping Canada's Music," page 189). Soon after his graduation, he was in correspondence with Willi Apel (see page 183) about Canadian representation in the *Harvard Dictionary of Music*, of which Apel was the editor, and was regularly being described by his dean, Sir Ernest MacMillan, as *the* person to consult on the topic of music in Canada.

Kallmann exhibited an extraordinary curiosity and vision that led him to explore the country's hitherto-hidden musical past and also to map and organize the missing infrastructure in its musical culture. The older repertoire needed to be gathered and preserved; channels for professional communication needed to be stimulated or created; the documentation tools (scores, reference sources) needed to be assembled. He soon turned his attention to each of these tasks.

In describing his early life in Berlin, Kallmann notes that recording family occasions with a camera was not considered or even approved. But he later became a keen photographer and found a historian's satisfaction in capturing with the camera as well as in words the scenes and events he experienced, and the people he met. In addition he developed skill at pencil sketching, as illustrated in his drawings of his internment camp surroundings (see page 140). To improve his technique, he attended a workshop at the Doon School of Fine Arts near Kitchener, Ontario, in the early 1950s, where one of his fellow students was the young R. Murray

Schafer, then undecided whether to launch a career in art or in music.[6] They became good friends and later collaborators.

Though gaining recognition for his writing and research, he went for nearly a year without salaried employment after leaving university. Then in June 1950 he joined the CBC Toronto music library as a clerk. The position was ideal for him, despite the initially low pay. He was again in a challenging situation collecting and cataloguing music, and regularly in touch with active musicians at a time when CBC Radio placed great emphasis on live performance and the commissioning of new works. Day by day he expanded his knowledge and resourcefulness, as library users demanded everything from the second-oboe part of the *Unfinished Symphony* to "Melancholy Baby" in E flat. He was scarcely a month into the job when a new edition of the CBC's 1947 *Catalogue of Canadian Composers* was proposed, and he was assigned to edit it. In "Taking Stock of Canada's Composers" (see page 167), he records how he used this opportunity to examine, for the first time in such depth, the country's legacy of composed music—a remarkable effort that was not at first taken seriously.

The CBC library remained his base for twenty years. He revamped its cataloguing system, judiciously expanded its holdings, and in 1962 succeeded Erland Misener as head. He used holiday leave periods to travel to other parts of Canada in order to meet other librarians and music scholars and investigate local archives for what evidence they might yield of earlier musical events, practices, and personalities. His contribution of a historical preface to the Canadian Music Council's publication *Music in Canada*[7] and his substantial entry "Kanada" in volume 7 of the monumental German-language reference work *Die Musik in Geschichte und Gegenwart*[8] together represented a kind of dry run for the book-length historical study his accumulated findings were pointing to; in 1960 it appeared: *A History of Music in Canada 1534–1914*. The starting date was that of Cartier's arrival in southern Labrador, at which, according to contemporary accounts, music was heard; the closing date of 1914 was chosen, Kallmann said, so as to avoid making historical judgments or predictions on events still in progress. "Mapping Canada's Music" outlines the *History*'s evolution and reception, and the volume's introduction (see page 43) is Kallmann's statement of its approach and raison d'être.

His contacts with other music librarians, notably Jean Lavender and Ogreta McNeill in Toronto and Lucien Brochu in Quebec City, persuaded Kallmann of the need for a national organization that would facilitate communication within the profession, initiate common ventures, and serve as a collective public voice. In 1955–56 the Canadian Music Library Association (CMLA) came into being, with McNeill as the first president. Kallmann himself later served as president for two terms and launched several of the association's early projects and publications. At the inception of the International Association of Music Libraries (IAML) in the early 1950s, he corresponded with its officials and coordinated Canadian contributions to IAML's RISM (Répertoire international des sources musicales) series. Later such duties were assumed by the CMLA, which became the Canadian national wing of IAML in 1971. Canadian representatives, including Kallmann, have attended the biennial gatherings of the international group, and these have been held in Canada on two occasions (1994, Ottawa, and 2012, Montreal). In 1971 the Canadian organization was reconstituted as the Canadian Association of Music Libraries. In 2000, in tribute to his long and active service, CAML named its Canadian-music research award the Helmut Kallmann Award.

Kallmann was regularly associated during his Toronto years with the Canadian League of Composers (founded in 1951), acting as its unofficial (and unpaid) archivist and editing (without acknowledgement and again probably without compensation) its fifty-eight-page *Catalogue of Orchestral Music* in 1957. (For his views of the League's early years, see page 87). In addition to his role in promoting new music, Kallmann sought outlets for the revival of earlier compositions by Canadians, as his research revealed more and more of them. With the newly founded Ten Centuries Concerts in 1962, he persuaded programmers to mount performances of several Canadian scores from the past, among them Joseph Quesnel's *Colas et Colinette* (see page 49), the curious battle piece *The Siege of Quebec* by Franz Koczwara, and a selection of shorter pieces, popular and serious, by Toronto composers of the nineteenth and early twentieth centuries. As a special CBC project in the buildup to the 1967 centenary of Confederation, he produced in 1965 a cycle of thirteen radio broadcasts entitled *The Music of Canada*, choosing the programs and collaborating with the writer James Bannerman on the scripts. Presented from Toronto, the series was later repeated with French-language scripts in Montreal.

An active, independent person, committed to many projects and organizations, but always shy and deliberate, Kallmann had a wide circle of friends in his Toronto years. He formed a close friendship with Ruth Singer, a native of Toronto whom he had met in 1951. With her background in theatre, interior design, and sculpture, she shared his artistic interests. "They must have seemed an unlikely combination: a dark-haired actress with large green eyes and a younger man so shy he would drop his head whenever someone from outside the world of music addressed him."[9] She is credited with helping him overcome his shyness in public situations, where he often had to give formal speeches. In 1955 they married and set up an apartment with Singer's daughter Liora ("Lynn") from a previous marriage. The happy bond was to last thirty-seven years, until Ruth's death in 1993. Kallmann enthusiastically took on the role of father to Liora (now Liora Salter) and later grandfather to her three children. He and Ruth invested in a piece of the wild landscape of the Muskoka Lakes area north of Toronto, living in a tent there for several weeks every summer.

Helmut Kallmann was a frequent contributor to and editorial-board member of the *Canadian Music Journal* throughout its lively and too-short existence (1956–62). His 1958 report, "The Percy Scholes Collection: Nucleus for a National Music Library"[10] is of unexpected significance in his life story. He had been in correspondence with the National Librarian in Ottawa, W. Kaye Lamb, drawing attention to the availability of the large accumulation of books, music, and research files of the English musical scholar Percy A. Scholes and urging the National Library of Canada (NLC) to bid for it. When Kaye acted on this advice and the Library acquired the Scholes papers, Kallmann persuaded the CBC and the *Journal* to sponsor a short visit to Ottawa so that he could inspect the collection and report on it. Scholes, whose *Oxford Companion to Music* was one of Kallmann's first English-language purchases in his clerking days at Coles, was a writer with wide knowledge and a mission to bring musical culture to the largest popular audience. His collection included 3,000 books on music, complete editions of several European masters, 450 vocal scores of operas and oratorios, forty music periodicals in complete sets, and eighty music dictionaries in various languages; the clippings, pictures, and files on musical topics filled 600 boxes and over 3,000 folders. One may well regard Scholes as a sort of professional role model for Kallmann. For example, Scholes's elaborate investigation of the history of the English anthem "God Save the King"[11] has a counterpart in Kallmann's lifelong attention to the origins and reception history of Lavallée's "O Canada." Although acquired in the late 1950s, the Scholes collection was not catalogued until many years later;[12] meanwhile, in 1970, the National Library, under Lamb's successor Guy Silvestre, decided to establish a separate Music Division and appointed as its first chief—Helmut Kallmann.

His move to Ottawa to take on this new responsibility was a classic case of the right person in the right job at the right time. Although confident, Kallmann was conscious that he lacked the professional qualification of a degree in library science. On his recommendation, two expert associates joined the Division, the music librarian Maria Calderisi and the musicologist Stephen Willis. He also persuaded a former CBC colleague, Edward G. Moogk, an authority on historical discography, to come aboard. On the death of the Canadian composer Healey Willan in 1968, the Library had acquired a second huge collection consisting of his library and personal papers, and on Kallmann's initiative a public exhibit was organized, the first of many which he arranged and for which he introduced the catalogue. His description of the division's first five years (see page 79) draws attention to the policy of acquiring such collections of the country's leading musical figures.[13]

In 1970, the joint meeting in Toronto of two major US professional associations, the American Musicological Society and the College Music Society, provided an opening for a discussion by Canadian teachers, students, and researchers on the future of Canadian-music studies. Kallmann delivered the keynote address. The following year his alma mater, the University of Toronto, presented him with an honorary degree, LL.D. (Doctor of Laws). He commented that he had always imagined as a young man that his only degree would be an honorary one, and observed that the degree, being in law, was the same as his father's.

Writing assignments continued to occupy him. Having criticized the fifth edition of *Grove's Dictionary of Music and Musicians* for its neglect of Canada (see page 39), he now found himself asked not only to supply entries on a dozen or more Canadian musicians for the proposed *New Grove*, but also to serve as one of three members of an advisory committee for Canadian content, the others being Keith MacMillan and John Beckwith. A still larger responsibility and demand on his time arose shortly after his appointment to the National Library. As he relates in "Mapping Canada's Music" (see pages 203–4) the Toronto publisher and philanthropist Floyd Chalmers stimulated a plan for a national music reference work, and Kallmann was asked to be its senior editor. The project was one he had envisioned ever since the publication of his *History*. The National Library agreed to a time-share scheme, offices were set up in Toronto, Montreal, and Ottawa, and the plan was put into action with two associate editors, Kenneth Winters and Gilles Potvin. At the start no one could have predicted how long the *Encyclopedia of Music in Canada* would take to complete (as Winters was fond of noting, many of the topics had never previously been researched); it eventually appeared only after ten years, in late 1981 in English and early 1983 in French. At close to 1,100 triple-columned pages, the English edition was the largest volume produced up to that time by the University of Toronto Press. Devoting a comprehensive reference work to the music of one country was a novel idea; similarly novel was the idea of treating all kinds of music, whether traditional, popular, or "cultivated": most standard music encyclopedias of the day concentrated on the "cultivated" repertoire and its creators. Sales exceeded everyone's expectations, and Kallmann was shortly occupied with planning for a second edition, which appeared in an even larger single-volume form in English in 1992 and in French the following year, this time in a three-volume boxed set. Kallmann reflected on his experiences with the *Encyclopedia of Music in Canada* in the article "The Making of a One-Country Music Encyclopedia" (see page 103).

The 1970s and 80s were decades of expansion in the Music Division of the NLC. Kallmann summarized its development in a report on the first five years, reproduced here (see page 79) and later in a full description in 1987, the year of his retirement.[14] From the initial half-dozen acquisitions of the archives of senior musicians, the holdings grew by 1988 to include "95 major and 280 smaller archival collections"[15]—several of which were the subject of National Library exhibitions, often curated by Kallmann. To the jazz and popular-music collection of recordings and sheet music, already substantial, were added archives of leading Canadian performers and composers in those fields. Kallmann's retirement was marked by his appointment as a member of the Order of Canada (awarded 1986, invested 1987), by a special "Canadian" number of the IAML journal, *Fontes artis musicae*,[16] and by a Festschrift in his honour.[17]

The 1990s saw the establishment of greatly enlarged premises for the national libraries of Britain and France, reflecting the growth and preservation needs in those countries. In Canada, successive governments of the time moved in a contrary direction, looking for economies and imagining the savings that new technology appeared to promise. Kallmann's successor, S. Timothy Maloney, when he left the position in 2002, was not replaced. In 2004 the NLC and the Public Archives were merged into Library and Archives Canada, the Music Division as such was dissolved, and large parts of its collection were placed in storage across the Ottawa River in Gatineau—an inevitable move that however made them less accessible than formerly. There were drastic staff reductions, and limitations were imposed on acquisitions of new materials. While Kallmann's long and patient work in building up the Library was still visible, in 2012 the former Division's existence as a national depository for music appeared seriously threatened.

As well as noting the need for a national music encyclopedia, Kallmann had often observed the lack of a publication series of highlights from the national repertoire of published music: where, he would ask, was the Canadian equivalent to the *Denkmäler* or *Monumenta* collections of other countries? In 1981 the young composer Clifford Ford felt the same need when teaching Canadian music history at Dalhousie University in Halifax and started an organized effort to produce such a series. Kallmann became chairman of the editorial board of the Canadian Musical Heritage Society / Société du patrimoine musical canadien, and an active participant in the production of twenty-five volumes in the next two decades. Each volume had a principal editor, but all board members received copies of pieces under consideration for their comments prior to the final selection. Kallmann himself was principal editor of volumes 8 (*Orchestral Music I*) and 22 (*Piano Dances and Marches*). The first of these gave him the opportunity to edit and write about the orchestral output of nineteenth-century composers such as Couture and Lucas, with which he was already familiar; the second drew on his appreciation for casual and functional music of the past, often addressed to amateurs. In assembling that volume, he sight-read at his piano several hundred early Canadian sheet-music compositions. On publication, volume 8 created a mild controversy when a reviewer revealed that the Overture in F by Antoine Dessane (1826–73) was in fact an orchestral overture by the French composer of *Giselle* and other ballet and opera scores, Adolphe Adam (1803–56). The manuscript bore no composer's name but was discovered in a Quebec archive together with other Dessane works: to have argued that it was by Dessane was, Kallmann said, "an honest mistake," and a correction slip was subsequently circulated with the volume. In reviewing a choral manuscript by Dessane for another volume in the *CMH* series, Kallmann had noted, "I am suspicious whether this is really his composition," and guessed it might turn out to be by Cherubini.[18] Dessane, a capable musician, may have had the innocent habit to copy out scores that interested him; however, in the case of the Overture, Kallmann's doubts were not roused.

With his growing reputation as an encyclopedist and historian and his position at the National Library, Kallmann was often called on to address professional, musical, or educational organizations. Sometimes these talks were worked up into publications. He also lectured regularly at Carleton University beginning in 1975 as a part-time faculty member; his association with the university continued (as an adjunct research professor) after his retirement.

The Kallmanns enjoyed travels to remote parts of Canada and twice to Germany, where Ruth Kallmann joined in his reunions with surviving old friends. In the 1980s she endured two battles with cancer and underwent treatment for other ailments. During her long illness, Kallmann had to attend conferences and meetings in other centres but always stipulated that he would have to return to Ottawa by nightfall. Her death on 14 July 1993 was a sad blow.

Kallmann was always writing, either in response to some publication project or simply to resolve a research puzzle for himself, whether musical, political, or humanitarian. In early years he spent long preparation time on a Canadian instrument inventory and a bibliography of Canadian folk music resources; later, he wrote a dozen and a half entries on musical notables for the *Dictionary of Canadian Biography* and many times that number for other reference works both national and international, each requiring patient assembly and checking. When other writers were assigned, their work often borrowed heavily from Kallmann's: of two histories of Canadian music published in the 1980s, 20 per cent of the citations on early historical phases in the first are from his 1960 *History*; in the other the figure is 50 per cent.[19] Nor were his topics always musical or always Canadian: for example, in response to an article on world politics in the twentieth century[20] he produced several drafts of a critique in four or five carefully reasoned pages, which remained unpublished. In his retirement years he edited, published, and distributed ten issues of a newsletter about the activities and whereabouts of surviving internees, and he was a principal organizer for a number of reunions and renewed exchanges. He devoted extensive research and correspondence to his family history, both in Canada and on his several visits to Berlin and other centres in Germany. His detailed and factual account of his Berlin childhood and his parents' fate (see page 223) was circulated privately in both German and English, and he contributed a short essay on his sense of national identity (see page 217), which elicited considerable positive reaction in letters from readers.[21]

His retirement allowed him time for other musical pursuits. He played chamber music with various Ottawa groups (a trio, a quintet). A longtime hobby was tracking down what he called "melodic similarities." Noting that the Second World War hit song "We're Going to Hang Out the Washing on the Siegfried Line"[22] began with precisely the same melodic contour as the third fugue (in C-sharp major) of Bach's *Well-Tempered Clavier*, written over two hundred years previously, he pondered whether such affinities were always mere coincidence. His files contained jottings of several thousand examples, some dating back to his teen years. In the 1990s he delivered two talks on this preoccupation and wrote over fifty pages of commentary for a proposed book, never completed.

In the lonely years after Ruth's death, he renewed a friendship with Traute Weinberg, a Berliner and widow of his fellow internee Bernd Weinberg, and she was his companion from 2000; in 2005 they moved together to a retirement home in Bell's Corners, west of Ottawa. He donated his Nordheimer grand piano to the home's lounge and continued to enjoy playing on it.[23] Having lived with diabetes for many years, he experienced symptoms of kidney failure in 2011. He passed away on 12 February 2012, about six months short of his ninetieth birthday.[24] Traute died from pneumonia seven months later.

His massive life accumulation of papers, largely unsorted at this writing, includes mostly musical items but also items on history, politics, and other topics, as well as files of often lengthy correspondence with family, friends, and colleagues in Canada, the US, and Europe.[25] In the records of the *EMC* and the *CMH,* the signature "HK" on numerous memos is a reminder of his long and patient devotion to those projects. As a youth he hoped to be "useful": but "useful," to describe such a career, is a grotesquely inadequate term.

NOTES

1 Quoted in Dawn L. Keer, "Helmut Kallmann: An Account of His Contributions to Music Librarianship and Scholarship in Canada" (unpublished MLIS thesis, University of Alberta, 1991), 41. Based on interviews with HK and those who knew him, this thesis is the most complete account of his life to 1991. It is one of three major sources of information for this biographical chapter, together with HK's archival papers and our personal knowledge of him. Keer also prepared a profile on HK for the CBC Radio program *Ideas*, broadcast on 20 April 1995; a transcript is available from http://www.cbc.ca/ideas/IDEAS-Catalog.pdf.
2 Program for the inaugural concert of the Conservatory Symphonic Band, director Robert Rosevear, on 16 April 1947 (among HK's archival papers).

3 Among those interned at the same time as HK was the music theorist Hans Keller, who was released before being sent overseas and so stayed on in Britain; see Alison M. Garnham, *Hans Keller and Internment: The Development of an Émigré Musician 1938–48* (London: Plumbago, 2011).
4 The original document, in English, dated 19 June 1941, is reproduced in Keer, "Helmut Kallmann," 31.
5 Ibid., 37
6 Ibid., 5, 71.
7 Helmut Kallmann, "Historical Background," in *Music in Canada*, ed. Ernest MacMillan (Toronto: University of Toronto Press, 1955), 10–31.
8 Helmut Kallmann, "Kanada," in *Die Musik in Geschichte und Gegenwart*, vol. 7 (Kassel and Basel: Bärenreiter Verlag, 1958), 499–507.
9 Liora Salter, private communication, 14 June 2012.
10 *Canadian Music Journal* 2/3 (Spring 1958), 43–45.
11 Percy A. Scholes, *God Save the King! Its History and Its Romance* (London: Oxford University Press, 1942).
12 See Maria Calderisi, "An Unsung Treasure at the National Library of Canada: The Percy A. Scholes Collection," *Fontes artis musicae* 41/1 (January-March 1994), 53–65.
13 The most famous acquisition was of the Glenn Gould papers and memorabilia in 1983; see HK's "The Glenn Gould Fonds of the National Library of Canada: From Acquisition to Exhibition," *GlennGould* 6/2 (Fall 2000), 72–74. Katie Hafner, *A Romance on Three Legs: Glenn Gould's Obsessive Quest for the Perfect Piano* (New York: Bloomsbury, 2008), 4–7, tells the story of HK's role in the acquisition of Gould's favorite Steinway piano, CD318.
14 "The Music Collection of the National Library of Canada," *Fontes artis musicae* 34/4 (Oct./Dec. 1987), 174–84.
15 Figures from Library and Archives Canada staff.
16 *Fontes artis musicae* 34/4 (October/December 1987); this issue also marked the achievement of HK's colleague Maria Calderisi in becoming the first Canadian to serve as the President of IAML, 1986–89.
17 John Beckwith and Frederick A. Hall, eds., *Musical Canada: Words and Music Honouring Helmut Kallmann* (Toronto: University of Toronto Press, 1988).
18 From a "master sheet" dated 15 March 1994 in the *Canadian Musical Heritage* files of the Kallmann Fonds, Library and Archives Canada.
19 The first history is Clifford Ford, *Canada's Music: An Historical Survey* (Agincourt, ON: GLC Publishers, 1985); the second is Timothy J. McGee, *The Music of Canada* (New York: W.W. Norton, 1985).
20 John Lukacs, "The End of the Twentieth Century," *Harper's Magazine* (January 1993), 39–46. It is uncertain whether HK's essay was intended for publication.

21 As verified by the editors in a file that is part of HK's personal archival papers.
22 1939; words and music by Jimmy Kennedy and Michael Carr.
23 The piano was a reconditioned instrument manufactured by the prominent Canadian firm A. and S. Nordheimer. Coincidentally, a descendant of the family, Gerry Nordheimer, had been a colleague of HK's in the CBC Music Library.
24 Obituaries of Kallmann include: James Adams, "Helmut Max Kallmann: Spirited from Nazi Germany as a Teen, He Became Canada's Doctor of Music," *Globe and Mail,* 25 February 2012, S10; [John Beckwith], "A Tribute to Helmut Kallmann 1922–2012: Reflecting on the Achievements of the Original Canadian Musicologist and Music Librarian," Canadian Music Centre Ontario Region *Notations* 19/1 (Fall 2012): 8–9; Robin Elliott, "Helmut (Max) Kallmann," *The Bulletin of the Society for American Music* 38/3 (Fall 2012), 82; Shelley Page, "Canada's First Great Music Historian: Refugee from Nazi Oppression Spent Time in Internment Camps," *Ottawa Citizen*, 4 March 2012, B5. A dedicated number of *CAML Review/Revue de l'ACBM* 40/2 (August 2012) titled "Special Issue: Honouring Helmut Kallmann" includes a brief biography and tributes from friends and colleagues.
25 The collection has been accessioned by Library and Archives Canada in Ottawa, where it will be available to future researchers.

Helmut Kallmann and Canadian Music

The past thirty years have witnessed an enormous growth in the volume of writings on Canadian music—thanks in no small measure to the influence of the *Encyclopedia of Music in Canada* (1981) / *Encyclopédie de la musique au Canada* (1983), which Helmut Kallmann co-edited—but there have not yet been many historiographical studies. The fundamental precepts and guiding ideas of Canadian music studies, the development of the field from its origins to the present day, the nature of its institutional frameworks and of its shifting preoccupations—all these topics and more remain to be explored in greater depth.[1] When the measure of Canadian music studies in the twentieth century is taken, Kallmann will loom large as a pioneering figure and a predominating presence. His influence has been truly national in scope and has been exerted both through his publications (in the first order, his book *A History of Music in Canada 1534–1914*, and the two editions of the *Encyclopedia of Music in Canada*; see the Appendix for a complete list of his writings), and also via the institutions within which he worked and which he helped to create (notably the Music Division of the National Library of Canada, the Canadian Music Library Association, and the Canadian Musical Heritage Society).[2]

As an immigrant to the country, Kallmann brought an outsider's curiosity and perspective to bear on his research into the musical life of Canada. He was part of a wave of mid-century émigré musicians who collectively exerted an enormous impact on the country's musical life.[3] If he was subjected to any prejudice, discrimination, or anti-Semitic invectives in the course of his education and professional career, he was silent on the matter. The markedly anglophile cast of musical life in English Canada gradually gave way during the 1940s to a more cosmopolitan outlook, one in which those who would have been viewed as "outsiders" previously were now free to exercise their career with fewer constraints. John Weinzweig, who was nine years older than Kallmann and a native-born Canadian, was the recipient of anti-Semitic slights on occasion, beginning in grade school and continuing into his university years in the 1930s and beyond.[4] He was one of the first Jewish music students at the University of Toronto. By the time Kallmann enrolled in the undergraduate music program at the same university in the 1940s, there were more Jewish students, among them Jack Kane, Hans Gruber, and Victor Feldbrill, all of whom went on to distinguished careers in music. Jewish immigrant musicians, including Istvan Anhalt, Boris Berlin, Walter Homburger, Otto and Walter Joachim, Oskar Morawetz, John Newmark (see pages 125–35), Charles Reiner, and Heinz Unger, among many others, numbered among the leading figures in Canada's postwar musical life. Kallmann was part of a distinguished and accomplished group of immigrant musicians whose contributions had a vital influence upon virtually every aspect of musical life in Canada.

Kallmann's native language was German, and on occasion he wrote about Canadian music for German-language publications, notably his work for the authoritative reference work *Die Musik in Geschichte und Gegenwart*. The vast majority of his research, however, was published in his second language. He was fluent in English but remained somewhat self-conscious about his ability as a prose stylist and was grateful for the assistance of editors whose native language was English. He did not publish original research in French, though he read the language fluently and could converse in French to some degree. His entire career was spent in the employment of two leading national institutions, the CBC and the National Library of Canada, and notwithstanding his own trilingualism, he was attuned to the importance of bilingualism to Canada's cultural and musical identity. He paid special attention to historical figures whose careers had taken place in Quebec—Joseph Quesnel (see pages 49–60), Theodore F. Molt, and Calixa Lavallée among them—and some of his most important work arose out of research that he conducted in various archival collections in Quebec. Nevertheless, his network of professional associations spread across the entire country.

Kallmann's work as a scholar and librarian was born out of a passionate attachment to music as sound. His primary instrument was the piano. A keen amateur performer, he loved nothing more than to explore the classical solo, duet, and chamber music repertoire at the keyboard. While he had an intense and abiding interest in the processes and techniques of composition, he did not compose music himself, aside from technical and pastiche exercises completed as part of his music studies. Similarly, while he had a solid grasp of music theory, advanced analytical skills were not part of his education. In his archival papers are many pages of notated music examples from works of the great composers, written out in a neat and fluent hand. Many but by no means all of these notations arose out of a lifelong curiosity about melodic similarities. Other examples arose out of a wish to record on paper striking melodic ideas or harmonic progressions in works that were of particular interest to him. The knowledge that he gained of the great masterpieces of the European repertoire in this way was impressively broad and deep.

The music that Kallmann loved most of all was that of the leading composers of the classical era (Mozart, Schubert, and Beethoven above all), and he wrote fine reception histories about the introduction and spread of their music in Canada (his work on Schubert appears here in print for the first time; see pages 149–65). During the formative years of his education, music scholarship was primarily concerned with examining the work of the great European composers and with filling in knowledge about the historical antecedents of the common repertoire, extending from Bach back through the early baroque, Renaissance, and medieval eras. If Kallmann had begun his university music studies a bit later, or if music scholarship as a discipline had taken root in Canada earlier, he might have become a musicologist.[5] He was always careful to distinguish between music history and musicology as disciplines; in his mind, the former was primarily concerned with documentation and narrative, the latter with value and interpretation. His career path led him to become a music librarian and music historian, and he was largely self-taught in both disciplines. The choice of these two fields was a logical outcome of his chosen area of specialization.

In embracing Canadian music as his field, he quickly realized two basic truths. In the first place, he saw that what was urgently needed was the preservation of ephemeral materials that were widely dispersed, little valued, and mostly obscure. This was the work of a music librarian. In the second place, in the absence of a Mozart or Beethoven in the world of Canadian music, his research would not call upon the resources of musicology (as it was then understood), with its focus on the great works of the European repertoire. Rather, his work would lie in the field of music history and would require the patient piecing together of a narrative account about how people of all classes and eras, and of widely differing interests and abilities, had found music to be meaningful to their lives.

To begin with, Kallmann read everything of any importance that had previously been written on the subject of Canadian music. Indeed, much of this earlier work we now know about primarily through Kallmann's attention to it in his own publications. It is in this sense that he was a pioneering figure in the field of Canadian music studies: he shed light on what had been accomplished, and then he methodically set about to extend the dimensions of the field, both chronologically and geographically. Few writers before Kallmann had any idea about the true extent or the precise nature of historical precedents in Canada for the musical events they were describing, and in addition their horizons did not extend much beyond their own immediate surroundings. It fell to Kallmann in his own contributions to supply both historical depth and a truly nationwide perspective on Canadian music.

As a new Canadian curious about his adopted country, Kallmann took every opportunity to get to know the lay of the land. Vacations were spent travelling to archives across the country and interviewing those knowledgeable about the musical life of their region. From the mid-1950s onwards, his work with the Canadian Music Library Association enabled him to make contact with like-minded members across the country and to mobilize large-scale research projects (see "Music Library Association Digs Up Our Musical Past," pages 61–64). Without historical ties of his own to any particular region of Canada, he became the ideal unbiased observer. He was keenly interested in unearthing information about the historical development and the particular qualities of each musical region in the country.

The national scope of his research interests was facilitated by the fact that his entire career was spent in the employment of two of the leading national cultural organizations, the CBC and the National Library of Canada. The CBC Toronto music library was the central music collection for the entire corporation. As head of the library from 1962 onwards, Kallmann had constant contact with the various CBC branch libraries and with leading musicians from each part of the country. His work as the inaugural chief of the Music Division of the National Library of Canada was the culmination of his career as an outstanding music librarian. Starting virtually from scratch, he established operating procedures and a collections policy that resulted in the creation of a cultural resource of inestimable importance (see his report on the Music Division's first five years of activities on pages 79–86).

The fact that Kallmann's career was spent largely outside of academia (his only university appointment was a part-time one and it came late in his career) was, in retrospect, a blessing in disguise. Canadian university music departments were largely dominated by US and European musicians who typically gave short shrift to Canadian music studies, to the extent that they even considered the field at all. Canadian music courses were not introduced in universities until the mid-1960s and were not widespread until the 1980s. The few musicologists who wrote about Canadian music during this period did so, at least initially, as a sideline; their graduate training had been entirely in the field of European music.[6] Paradoxically, then, Kallmann's interest in Canadian music research may actually have been facilitated, rather than hampered, by the fact that he did not pursue graduate studies in music and that his professional career was largely non-academic.

Although university music departments were not encouraging research on Canadian music during Kallmann's formative years, the University of Toronto Press (UTP) did take an early and decisive interest in the field. Marsh Jeanneret became the director of UTP in 1953, just two years after the Massey Report had outlined the blueprint for the postwar development of Canadian cultural life. The report's nationalist tone resonated with Jeanneret; under his leadership (to 1977), UTP supplied intellectual leadership for the development of postwar Canadian cultural identity with projects such as the *Dictionary of Canadian Biography* and the *Canadian Annual Review* (both begun in 1959).[7] Writing about another UTP project of this era, J. Russell Harper's *Painting in Canada: A History* (published in 1966), Anne Whitelaw asserts that it "subscribed to many of the ideological and intellectual sentiments of the period: a conscientious attention to Canada's regional and linguistic diversity, a commitment to the development of narratives of national becoming to benefit contemporary generations, and a strong belief in the ability of culture to ensure the maintenance of an independent nation-state."[8] Much the same could be said of Kallmann's work, including his two major projects with UTP: *A History of Music in Canada 1534–1914* and the *Encyclopedia of Music in Canada* (*EMC*).

The first Canadian music project undertaken by UTP under Jeanneret's direction was *Music in Canada* (1955), a collection of essays edited by Sir Ernest MacMillan. MacMillan had been one of Kallmann's professors at the University of Toronto and asked his former pupil to supply a historical preface for the collection.[9] It was also MacMillan who recommended Kallmann to UTP as the person to write a history of music in Canada; the resulting monograph appeared in 1960.[10] *EMC* was begun in 1970 when Jeanneret was still director, but was not completed until 1981, four years after he had retired. Kallmann has told the story of the creation of the encyclopedia in detail (see "The Making of a One-Country Music Encyclopedia," pages 103–24). Notwithstanding Kallmann's own narrowly circumscribed musical interests, *EMC* is impressively broad in its treatment of the country's musical life. For Kallmann, the need to make *EMC* as comprehensive and inclusive as possible overrode his own personal interests and inclinations. Mark Miller, who was responsible for the jazz and pop content for both print editions of *EMC*, stated: "I have to say, respectfully, that I don't think Helmut ever quite 'got' jazz; more than once he asked me if there was a score that he could follow ... But he understood the importance of having *EMC* embrace all musics. *EMC* was that much more valuable for it, and Canada has been that much richer for *EMC*."[11]

Kallmann's writings cover a diverse range of topics, styles, and genres, and were intended for several different categories of readership. The present collection gives an idea of the scope of his output, including as it does history, historiography, reportage, reviews, correspondence, and autobiographical reflections. Kallmann certainly did produce peer-reviewed academic articles, such as his essays on James Paton Clarke (see pages 65–77) and on the Canadian League of Composers (see pages 87–102). But because he worked outside of academia, he was under no pressure to concentrate exclusively on this type of writing. Two of his major projects, *A History of Music in Canada* and *EMC*, each sold thousands of copies and found a widespread readership outside of academic circles. It was Kallmann's achievement to write according to the strictest scholarly standards but with the broadest readership in mind. He always strove for accuracy, and his writings are consistently backed up by sound and thorough documentation. Whether writing a short book review or editing an encyclopedia, he brought the same dedication to the task at hand. Different though his publications may appear to be on the surface, at heart they are all motivated by the same urge to document, to explain, and to bear witness to the importance of music.

Richard Crawford begins his historiographical study of American music by noting that "a tradition of historical study progresses, in the sense in which E.H. Carr has defined historical progress, by transmitting the knowledge and experience of one generation of scholars to the next."[12] Kallmann would certainly have agreed with this quotation, and in his autobiographical essay "Mapping Canada's Music" (see page 207), he himself cited E.H. Carr's book *What Is History?* as a strong influence on his own ideas about historical writing. Kallmann did his part to ensure that the wisdom of previous researchers would be made available to his contemporaries and to future generations, by his comprehensive investigation and documentation of early written sources on Canadian music. With this selection of his writings, we hope to achieve the same result for Kallmann's own scholarship.

NOTES

1   A succinct overview of scholarship on Canadian music is the section "Canada as Subject Matter for Musicological Study," in HK's article "Musicology" in the *Encyclopedia of Music in Canada*. Two pioneering historiographical studies are Gordon E. Smith, "Dualité dans l'historiographie musicale canadienne," *Les Cahiers de l'ARMuQ* 13 (May 1991), 29–37, and Beverley Diamond, "Narratives in Canadian Music History," in *Canadian Music: Issues of Hegemony and Identity*, ed. Beverley Diamond and Robert Witmer (Toronto: Canadian Scholars' Press, 1994), 139–71; reprinted with minor changes in *Taking a Stand: Essays in Honour of John Beckwith*, ed. Timothy J. McGee (Toronto: University of Toronto Press, 1995), 273–305.

2   The National Library of Canada and the Public Archives of Canada merged in 2004 to become Library and Archives Canada; there is no longer a distinct Music Division, though the collection HK built up for the National Library remains perhaps his most tangible legacy. The Canadian Music Library Association became the Canadian Association of Music Libraries in 1971, with "Archives and Documentation Centres" added to the organization's name in 1992. The Canadian Musical Heritage Society (CMHS) was founded in 1982 and by 1999 had published a 25-volume anthology containing some 1,500 works of historical Canadian music composed before 1950. The CMHS initiated various other projects, including a database and several recordings, but ceased operations in 2003.

3   For an overview of this issue, see Paul Helmer, *Growing with Canada: The Émigré Tradition in Canadian Music* (Montreal and Kingston: McGill-Queen's University Press, 2009).

4   See John Beckwith, "Weinzweig as I Knew Him," *Weinzweig: Essays on His Life and Music*, ed. John Beckwith and Brian Cherney (Waterloo, ON: Wilfrid Laurier University Press, 2011), 369.

5   HK completed his music studies at the University of Toronto in 1949; the first courses in musicology were not offered until five years later, with the appointment of the US musicologist Harvey Olnick in 1954.

6   For example, George Proctor's PhD thesis (1960) was on the Baroque composer and violinist Nicola Matteis Sr., Carl Morey's (1965) was on the operas of Alessandro Scarlatti, and Elaine Keillor's (1976) was on the

7   eighteenth-century Alsatian keyboard teacher and composer Leontzi Honauer. All three scholars went on to become best known for their publications in the field of Canadian music.

7 See chapter 10, "Major Editorial Projects," in Marsh Jeanneret, *God and Mammon: Universities as Publishers* (Toronto: Macmillan of Canada, 1989), 167–87. HK contributed to both projects, writing eighteen biographies for the *DCB* and writing reports on music for the *Canadian Annual Review* for the years 1968, 1969, and 1970.

8 Anne Whitelaw, "To Better Know Ourselves: J. Russell Harper's *Painting in Canada: A History*," *Journal of Canadian Art History* 26/1–2 (2005), 8–33; the quoted passage is from p. 11.

9 Helmut Kallmann, "Historical Background," in *Music in Canada*, ed. Ernest MacMillan (Toronto: University of Toronto Press, 1955), 10–31.

10 HK's *A History of Music in Canada 1534–1914* may have inspired UTP to commission a similar work on Canadian art history. Whitelaw (p. 12) notes that Jeanneret wrote to the Canada Council late in 1960 (just after HK's book had been published) with a proposal for a "definitive history of Canadian art." The original idea was that it be a collection of essays edited by Alan Jarvis, but when Jarvis failed to meet his deadlines, the project was turned over to J. Russell Harper, who ended up writing the entire book himself.

11 Mark Miller, in a tribute delivered on the occasion of "Remembering Helmut Kallmann," a memorial event held at the Faculty of Music, University of Toronto, on 10 April 2012. The tribute was published as "The Gentlest of Gentlemen," *CAML Review / Revue de l'ABCM* 40/2 (August 2012): 16–17.

12 Richard Crawford, "Cosmopolitan and Provincial: American Musical Historiography," in *The American Musical Landscape: The Business of Musicianship from Billings to Gershwin* (Berkeley, Los Angeles, and London: University of California Press, 1993), 3. Crawford is referring to chapter 5, "History as Progress," from Edward Hallett Carr's *What Is History?* (London: Macmillan, 1961).

Selected Writings of Helmut Kallmann

1
Studying Music at a Canadian University, 1946–1949

This typescript was completed on 29 November 1949—shortly after HK graduated as part of the first cohort of the BMus degree in School Music (i.e., music education) at the University of Toronto. He juxtaposes here an idealized conception of music studies at the university level with the rather more mundane and superficial course of study that he had just completed. The professors he critiques are Richard Johnston, Robert Rosevear, Leo Smith, Healey Willan, and S. Drummond Wolff. The dean, unnamed here, was Sir Ernest MacMillan. A curious omission in the discussion of the faculty members is Arnold Walter, with whom HK studied music history and who three years later would succeed MacMillan as the head of the Faculty of Music. Of the fellow students he discusses, three went on to highly distinguished careers in music: the music educator Kenneth Bray, the choral conductor Elmer Iseler, and the jazz performer, composer, and arranger Jack Kane. Also enjoying notable careers in music were the flutist Keith Girard and the musicologist Jaroslav Mráček. Other students mentioned by name are Leonard Dunelyk, Wallace Laughton, William Marwick, Bertram Turvey, and Eldred Winkler, who all became secondary-school music teachers, and William Girvin, Gordon Jocelyn, and Reid MacQuarrie. All were in School Music classes graduating between 1949 and 1951, except for Girard, who was in the General BMus class of 1951. HK ends this essay by observing that his words are intended for a readership fifty years in the future—a date that as of this writing is over a dozen years in the past. Reading the essay now, one is struck by how dated much of it seems—LP recordings were brand new then, Schoenberg was still alive, etc. But while many superficial aspects of music studies in the university are radically different now, some of the basic assumptions HK makes—for example, that students and faculty must be passionate about music and excel in their given fields—remain valid and as yet aspirational rather than fully realized.

The faculty of music of a university—more advanced modulation and transposition—a comparison of different theories of voice training—professors of music—advanced clef reading. How impressive all that sounds. Here is the idea I used to have of a university—an idea, which I still hope to find realized some day. The *students*: people who argue among themselves about the relative merits of Lasso and Palestrina, who discuss whether the latest Stravinsky work is aesthetically sound, who campaign for or against some modern composition, by means of booing or letters to the editor; the *professors*: people whose duty it is to know every last theory and discovery in their specialized field, who rearrange their course from year to year according to the latest findings, who all the time carry on some active research about Binchois's style or Loewe's ballads; the *dean*: a man who co-ordinates all this research, presides over it, who talks with the professors about specialized questions, like the 6-4 chord in Weber, but in all cases a man who is from morning to night steeped in musical knowledge. The *syllabus* in every subject comprises the highest, most difficult, most complete subject matter—for if the professionals are not trained at university, what higher institution is there? In other words, if the man who can talk for hours about Dufay has not got his knowledge from the university, where else can he have it from? Thus the syllabus should teach *all* about a particular subject. This is the place where there is no simplifying as in high school, no talking down as in a public lecture, no evading the most difficult [issues], because there is no higher level of learning above it. The syllabus, however, does not include the complete knowledge about music; it selects a few items, different ones each year. Thus a form professor would one year lecture for ten weeks on the variation in the Italian baroque, and another year on the chorale prelude of Bach's predecessors—also in ten lectures. All surveys of music history, outlines of form have naturally been completed before the student entered university.

Of course this description is idealized. There is no need to tell me that musicians with a thorough knowledge of Dufay are not needed here, that no students would be willing to sit through ten lectures on the early prelude. No need to tell me that the university is young, the country is young, the students come to university without any cultural background (very often), that the finances are poor, and that the tasks are much more practical. Of course this is true. There are excuses. But once in a while one likes to measure reality against the ideal. How can one improve reality without having some ideals to compare it with?

Of course the three years have been enjoyable. They have been profitable too. And things are being improved. What then is the state of affairs?

The *students* usually enter university with a good performing ability, with no lack of talent, but with more or less abject lack of familiarity with musical literature and of thinking about music from an aesthetic or philosophical point of view. Some may have come in touch with some modern movement in music, others know well the literature of one particular instrument, and still others are general exceptions. But only rarely do they talk about a Brahms symphony when they sit at lunch. Hardly ever do they get together at home to play some records or chamber music. Those things are not for the professionals—there are the amateurs, the musical snobs, the record collectors etc.—who, though often unable to read music, are the ones who have violent arguments about Schoenberg's concepts of beauty, about Stokowski's transcriptions and the like, not the musicians. The students are far too business-minded: they will sit down to play a Beethoven sonata if it is for a concert, they will listen to a Bach concerto if the teacher has made them do so, but not from their own inclination. I know there are reasons—they have families to keep up, they have homework to do—but that is not what I am concerned with here. One cannot blame the students, however, for a lack of desire to learn, for narrow-mindedness or complacency. They admit far too willingly that they know nothing about music—which is not usually true—they always *wished* they had time to listen to records, etc. Meanwhile, of course things have improved with the new record facilities and the record assignments. The professors are now doing a lot to ensure that the students get a knowledge of musical literature.

The *professors*, like the students, are of various kinds. They are all good musicians and know a lot, but some of them lack that spirit of responsibility and discipline that the ideal professor should have and that seems to exist in the Faculty of Arts. Johnston and Rosevear are conscious of all the shortcomings in the Faculty of Music and are doing much to remedy them. They are modern and experts in their fields. *Rosevear* is very musical, but not an inspiring personality or conductor. He is not an aesthetic thinker; one could not imagine him discussing whether the Brahms First or Second [Symphony] is the better. His taste is excellent though and his teaching conscientious and correct to the last detail. As the years go on he may become somewhat pedantic; he tries to be humorous but the jokes never come off very effectively. Some things he tends to let slip, e.g., the big classes which start late, etc. *Johnston* should be given a larger scope, so that he could make better use of his wonderful knowledge; he should have more time to teach literature of music instead of mere theory. He is more methodical than it appears, but he plans things that often do not materialize, like the madrigal singing, the cantata concert, and the jazz outline. As a music enthusiast he can hardly be surpassed. Some musicians think that enthusiasm is amateurish. I doubt that. Of course, *Willan* (Healinsky Willansky) may know a lot, may have known more in former days, and is an old and perhaps tired man of almost seventy. But he should not teach history. He may be good in out-of-date counterpoint, but his talking about music history is that of a practical musician who has read a lot of musical storybooks and is able to talk about it. But he does not appear to have any acquaintance with historical methods, musicology, and the like. By the way, actually he never talks about music history. He reads his history out of a book which he himself considers second-rate and intersperses anecdotes which are more or less off the point. When he does make some remarks of his own about a composer, they seem to come rather because he happens to have made that particular observation than because it is essential. Altogether, compared with the ideal of a history professor, this is a caricature. Leo *Smith's* classes demand more respect. That one cannot understand his speech is not a criticism of the man.[1] His material is very neatly organized and presented so that one can take [it] down almost word for word. His knowledge is great too. In writing he is a master of style and he has much of the gentleman about him. But his manner of presentation is somewhat inadequate. He reads almost every point off his notes, and if he has not brought the right sheet of notes he will present something outside the present topic. After a few weeks he is bound to go over the same subject again. As a matter of fact, his syllabus is organized in such a way that he starts with a bird's-eye view, then gives a general survey, then a detailed description, and when that is finished in February, he starts all over again for the fourth time. In this way one never gets deep into any subject. But the main criticism is that he teaches history, not music. The student gets the neatest descriptions of a composer's style without ever having an idea of how the music sounds. Once in a while Leo writes a few bars of something on the blackboard and lets the class sing it, but that wastes a lot of time. Besides, one occasionally has the impression that he has not digested [the] more modern theories in history, such as discarding biological analogies (the birth of, the father of, the growth of, etc.) or modern explanation—only to find him quote some recent history of music the next day.

The *dean* does not teach himself and perhaps his mistake is that of being too liberal and generous. Of course every professor should be completely on his own as far as method, views, and details of syllabus go, but the dean should be responsible that every teacher is expert in his subject. That a man like Willan teaches history, even if only once a week, or Drummond Wolff form is not admissible. Apparently the attitude prevails that history and form are mere side subjects that any musician at all can teach. And, of course, no organized research is carried on. The faculty as such does not publish historical findings (or enter into them in the first place) or encourage research. Of course no professor should ever teach a matter that he has not investigated for himself instead of just quoting textbooks. He should be his own textbook, perhaps not in harmony or clarinet-playing, but certainly in history and form, where he must have definite views about the fugue or the romantic era, or else not be a professor. See Willan and Wolff, who just read out other people's ideas and get paid for it. There should be a subject, let us say baroque opera, on which every member of the faculty works, and the findings about which are published at the end under the supervision of the dean. And the students would be enrolled in minor aspects of the project.

Drummond *Wolff*, incidentally, is a teacher of form, who admits he sees no sense in analyzing music and that he does not know anything about form nor cares to.

The *syllabus* looks fine. But if you are through with it, you find that you had one little try at everything, one exercise of a few bars in rearranging, one in orchestration, half a page of notes on radio technique. Ideally speaking, one would expect that if somebody has studied a thing he knows it; we, however, just got an inkling of everything. That the syllabus still conforms basically to the outdated British pattern is another point. Subjects like music literature, aesthetics, psychology, style should be part of a music faculty.

A few words must be said about the students. Who is a real musician? What makes a real musician? Talent? Not alone. The fact that you earn a living by it? Some students seem to think so. Love of music? Knowledge? Judgment? I do not know. Perhaps it is the urge to go on out of one's own will to investigate more and more unknown music. The hunger, the curiosity for more of that wonderful thing, music. Certainly there must be a combination of many of these things. However, [the person] who misses a special radio concert because he had to do homework; who never has any curiosity to play over at home a Beethoven sonata that the professor speaks about in his lecture; who cannot quote a single theme from a Brahms symphony is not a real musician, no matter how well he can keep time or recognize chords. Thus our list must be short. Iseler, no doubt, is a real musician, if for no other reason than for the very good one that music interests him more than anything else and that he is enthusiastic about it, like Johnston, at any time of the day. One must have a little bit of the child's attitude that would rather miss supper than abandon his favourite toy. Bray is a good musician, except that he has too many responsibilities that keep him away from it. He is certainly the best as far as practical musicianship goes. Dunelyk is a man with a real soul for music. So is Jocelyn; however music is only one of several absorbing passions with him. Of Laughton one might say that he *has* been a good musician, namely at the time when he accompanied, had a real technique, and played the piano. But it looks as if he will let his piano playing slip more and more and will become more of an administrator than a musician. Already now he is one of those who say, the time when my fingers *were* in good shape, when I *used to have* the time to play through the Beethoven symphonies. A real musician always looks for improvement, he has always time for Beethoven symphonies, there never *was* a time when. MacQuarrie and Winkler are two more musicians. It is hard to form a judgment about the people in the other years. Few of them seem to have a musical culture, an independent urge to investigate music. They have too much of a "piano lesson" attitude: "Look what piece my teacher gave me to practise for the next month." They seem to be talented performers but somewhat ignorant in music. Iseler has been mentioned as an exception. Girvin is another one with a genuine interest in music. Perhaps Marwick, Kane, Girard, Turvey. Mráček, again, has the attitude of a real musician, perhaps not enough content in his knowledge yet to be outstanding. That is all.

Altogether then, the observer who expects music students to know half of *Tristan* by memory, to discuss Schoenberg at lunch, to play Schumann trios in their spare time will be glad if he finds a professor who would do that.

This essay has dealt with the course [of studies] only from the point of view of the B course.[2] It should not be forgotten that there are severe financial handicaps, that Willan is good in counterpoint and has a reputation for his knowledge of church music. But my purpose is not to point out the handicaps, just as I am not blaming anybody, except where it is a neglect of responsibility. This is more of a document to be read in fifty years when the Faculty has matured a little more.

NOTES

1. Kallmann is likely referring here to the fact that Smith was notoriously soft spoken. [*Ed.*]
2. The intended meaning is that the essay deals only with the new School Music program of undergraduate music studies at the University of Toronto ("the B course"), and not the older General undergraduate music program. [*Ed.*]

2
Canadian Music as a Field for Research

This is HK's earliest published article. In the three years prior to this publication, he had written a number of reviews that appeared in the University of Toronto student newspaper *The Varsity*, but the article from 1950 reprinted here provides the first evidence that he had begun recently ("about a year ago") to research the musical life of Canada in a systematic way. Already at this early stage, he had seized upon a fundamental truth about Canadian music studies: that the research must extend beyond a focus on musical artworks to consider all of the ways that people have found music to be meaningful in their lives. The last two paragraphs lay out a research agenda which would occupy HK for the rest of his life. But it would take him just ten years to advance from the compilation and sifting of source materials to the creation of a comprehensive narrative account of the history of music in Canada, which he achieved in his pioneering book *A History of Music in Canada 1534–1914*, published by University of Toronto Press in 1960.

After composers have established their styles, theorists come to codify their methods, and once the musical life of a country has got under way, historians appear to record and appraise its course.

Is there a need today for research into the musical past of Canada? In composition we have hardly reached a point yet which would mark the end of a definite period with its own coherent stylistic traits, but

---

Royal Conservatory of Music of Toronto *Monthly Bulletin* (March 1950), 2

composition is only the crowning of many phases of a nation's musical activity: the enjoyment, study and discussion of music, music-making and creative endeavors. Musical life in Canada is richer and older than is generally assumed. Too often people write and speak as though music had not existed in Canada thirty or forty years ago. Performances and experiments are labelled "first in Canada" that may have had forerunners in a long forgotten time. A knowledge of our musical past would put the present into a clearer perspective and enable us to look into the future more assuredly. Besides, writers on music in Canada are handicapped by the lack of a comprehensive body of readily available factual material. This is all the more the regrettable since the outside world is fast becoming aware of Canada as a nation and also of her music.

About a year ago I started in my spare time to find out for myself about music in this country. The more material I dug up the more fascinating the subject became and the greater a need for further research was revealed. I soon decided that hasty conclusions must be avoided and that a thorough framework of facts and dates is the first task. The printed source material is quite large but is at times hard to discover. While there are some fifteen books in the University of Toronto Library on the music of Latin America, for example, not a single volume in the library is devoted entirely to a survey of the music of Canada. However, there are a number of folksong collections, biographies, volumes of essays and pamphlets. The *Dictionnaire biographique des musiciens canadiens* of 1935 is useful but unfortunately ignores the fact that Canada extends west of the Ottawa River. There have been over a dozen musical periodicals in Canada but some can only be read in libraries in New York or Washington, D.C. Valuable surveys of composition have been made by Augustus Bridle (1929), Léo-Pol Morin (1930), Sir Ernest MacMillan (1942), Leopold Houlé (1946) and others. General outlines can be found in the *Encyclopedia of Canada* (Leo Smith, 1936) and in the *Encyclopédie Grolier* (Eugène Lapierre, 1947).[1] Apart from those dealing with folksong research, most articles are confined to personal recollections and observations. Often dates are very unreliable. There was, for example, only one Mme Albani, the famous Canadian prima donna, yet the year of her birth is given as 1847, 1848, 1851 and 1852. 1847 is probably correct.

Often material is found where it is least expected. Reading through a collection of letters I noticed that a composition, if only a short canon, was written for a Canadian by no less a composer than Beethoven. Theodore Molt, a Quebec musician of German origin visited Beethoven in 1825 and asked him for a souvenir for his "homeward journey of 3000 hours." Organist of Quebec Cathedral, Molt wrote some of the earliest musical primers in Canada (1828 and 1845) and attempted a collection including Canadian songs. It would be interesting to know more about this adventurous man.[2]

Much of the material has little more than statistical interest, but there are surprises too. It is certainly odd that the first instrument mentioned in Toronto's history is one of the rarest: the bassoon. The time is around 1818. And our fighters for the opera might like to know that in a few years, in 1953, we approach in Toronto the 100-year mark in the history of opera—and its intermissions.[3]

When one day the material is sifted and a history of music in Canada is narrated, factors of geography and migration have to be observed. Comparisons with other arts in Canada, with music in the US and in the countries of our ancestors have to be drawn. The writer has to be fair to all the musical centres and national groups in Canada, [and] admit shortcomings as well as stress achievements. But above all music has to be seen as a phase of a people's social and cultural life. The relationship of the building of musical life in a newly settled country to the building of the country as a whole would in itself be an interesting sociological study.

Ultimately then, the question is, what meaning did music have in the life of the people of Canada at various stages of history? The great individual achievements with which conventional histories are pre-occupied are only the highest expression of this meaning. Research into our musical past could help us to understand where we have come from, where we stand, and can point the direction in which we may go.

NOTES

1   Publications referenced in this paragraph, in order, are: Soeurs de Sainte-Anne, *Dictionnaire biographique des musiciens canadiens* [2nd ed.] (Lachine, QC: Mont-Sainte-Anne, 1935); Augustus Bridle, "Who Writes Our Music?" *Maclean's* (15 December 1929), 20, 30, 32, and/or "Composers among Us," *Yearbook of the Arts in Canada*, ed. Bertram Brooker (Toronto: Macmillan, 1929), 133–40; Léo-Pol Morin, *Papiers de musique* (Montreal: Librairie d'action canadienne-française, 1930); Ernest MacMillan, "Musical Composition in Canada," *Culture* 3 (1942): 149–54; Léopold Houlé, "Nos compositeurs de musique," *Royal Society of Canada: Proceedings and Transactions*, series III, vol. 40 (May 1946), 51–59; Leo Smith, "Music,"

The Encyclopedia of Canada, ed. W. Stewart Wallace, vol. 4 (Toronto: University Associates of Canada, 1936), 363–72; Eugène Lapierre, "Canada: musique," *Encyclopédie Grolier*, ed. J.-B. McDonnell and Edmond Labelle (Montreal: La Société Grolier, 1947), 532–35. [*Ed.*]

2 HK subsequently wrote about Molt on many occasions, including biographical entries in *Encyclopedia of Music in Canada* (1981, 1992) and *New Grove Dictionary of Music and Musicians* (1980, 2001). The autograph manuscript of the canon that Beethoven wrote for Molt was acquired, as part of the Lawrence Lande fonds, by the National Library of Canada in 1979 while HK was chief of the Music Division. [*Ed.*]

3 HK means the history of opera performance rather than composition; specifically, the reference is to a fully staged production of Bellini's *Norma* with orchestra and chorus given at the Royal Lyceum Theatre in Toronto on 8 July 1853, which was the first grand opera to be presented in the city. The performance was given by Luigi Arditi's Artists' Union Italian Opera Company, which was based in New York. [*Ed.*]

3
The New Grove's: *Disappointment to Canada*

The first edition of *Grove's Dictionary of Music and Musicians* appeared in four volumes between 1878 and 1889. The fifth edition, published in 1954, was the most substantial revision up to then of this standard reference work, and was reprinted five times up to 1975. By the time HK wrote this review in 1955, he was an experienced musical lexicographer himself, having edited *Catalogue of Canadian Composers*, published by the CBC in 1952. HK's catalogue was clearly not consulted by Blom for the fifth edition of *Grove's*. But the review seems to have been noticed. When a supplementary volume to the fifth edition of *Grove's* was published in 1961, most of the errors in the existing articles that HK notes below were corrected; however, new articles on Canadian music were not plentiful. The lacunae and misinformation about Canadian music that HK notes in this review would prove to be the norm for subsequent international reference works on music, as detailed in two later articles by John Beckwith.[1]

The long expected and much-needed fifth edition of *Grove's Dictionary of Music and Musicians* has appeared (Macmillan, $110). Its nine volumes present a completely revised and newly-set edition, doing away with the two separate supplemental volumes, which made the use of the old edition so impractical.

Announcement of a new edition had raised the hope that note would be taken, among other developments, of the great changes in musical

---

Saturday Night (12 March 1955), 25

geography which have occurred in the last twenty or thirty years. There has been an unprecedented migration of musicians from Central Europe; the folk music of remote countries has been collected and studied; countries such as Australia, Canada, and Israel have been written on the musical map.

As far as Canada is concerned, the new edition is a bitter disappointment. To thousands of people in Canada and abroad, who in decades to come will turn to *Grove's* as a standard musical reference, the work, excellent features though it possesses, will be next to useless in answering specific questions or giving a broad picture of music and musicians in Canada.

To begin with, there is no entry under Canada. True, editorial policy—regrettably enough—seems to have excluded articles on countries. Yet Australia and Israel, for example, have been treated in special articles, and it would have been fitting to have included Canada, which has done poorly in other musical reference books (with the notable exception of Thompson's *International Cyclopedia*).[2] Articles on Canadian musical institutions, such as Les Festivals de Montréal, the [Toronto] Mendelssohn Choir, the National Film Board (as a user of film music), the CBC, the Toronto Symphony Orchestra, or even the old Hart House String Quartet, all of international reputation, are omitted altogether.

On the other hand, there is an interesting article on the folk music of Canada, written by the foremost authority on Canadian folklore, Dr. Marius Barbeau. There are also entries under some two dozen Canadian composers and performers. Included among these are some of the most prominent musicians of our past: Calixa Lavallée, prolific nineteenth-century composer; Lynwood Farnam, organist; Augustus Vogt, founder of the Toronto Mendelssohn Choir; Frederick Herbert Torrington, once the musical tsar of Toronto; and Joseph Vézina, pioneer bandmaster and conductor of Quebec. The choice of living musicians may be questioned. Newcomers to *Grove's*, such as Alexander Brott, Ettore Mazzoleni and Heinz Unger, all deserve the honour, but appear to have been included because they happen to be known in England.

It was the privilege of Eric Blom, the new edition's editor, to judge the relative importance of musical affairs in different countries. What is unforgivable in a work of this kind, however, is that many of the Canadian biographies are inaccurate and quite out-of-date. Thus the article on Ettore Mazzoleni ("conductor and composer") brings us to the mid-1930s. Shortly after 1929 Mazzoleni was appointed at the Toronto Conservatory as "lecturer in musical history and conductor of the Conservatory Orchestra." There is not a word stating that he has been principal of the Conservatory since 1945, nine years before *Grove's* publication date. It is mentioned that Mazzoleni (incidentally, he does not consider himself a composer) has been guest conductor in Montreal, but his far more significant position as associate conductor of the Toronto Symphony Orchestra (1942–1948) is ignored. Nor are we told that Mazzoleni gave up his position at Upper Canada College in the 1930s.

Other articles, too, abound in statements about appointments without mentioning the termination of these offices. Douglas Clarke has not been conductor of the "Montreal orchestra" for about a decade and Healey Willan gave up his position at St. Paul's Church in Toronto long before *Grove's* went into its *third* edition, and that as vice-principal of the Toronto Conservatory in 1936. The name of the church of St. Mary Magdalene, which has been made famous through Willan's work there since 1921, does not even appear. He "conducts the Tudor Singers"—a group disbanded at the outbreak of World War Two. It should be well-known to English musicians that Sir Ernest MacMillan has conducted the Mendelssohn Choir since 1942, that he is chairman of the Canadian Music Council, and that he was Dean of the Faculty of Music at the University of Toronto from 1926 until 1952.

Many other dates are inaccurate. Willan's opera *Deirdre* dates from 1946, not 1937.[3] In the article on Lavallée—not revised from the old edition in spite of the publication of a biography by Eugène Lapierre[4]—the order of events is turned upside down. Lavallée did not make his debut as soloist at the Paris Conservatory in 1860 as he did not study in Paris until 1873. His efforts to organize a music school in French Canada date from *before*, not *after* 1881, because in 1880 he moved to the United States for the remainder of his life. After stating that *O Canada* was written in 1887, this article refers the reader to one on National Anthems, where the date is given correctly as 1880.

The preparation of a work of such gigantic proportions as *Grove's Dictionary* requires that articles be assembled years before the date of publication. But for this very reason it ought to have been possible to set up a mechanism by which each contributor was obliged to report additions and corrections to his articles right up to the time of proof-reading.

In a few instances, question marks are printed instead of the place of birth or the date of death. These facts could have been discovered easily in many cases or by consulting other reference books in which they do appear. Is it beneath the dignity of dictionary-makers to compare and consult other dictionaries? A scholarly enterprise is not only permitted, but duty-bound to take note of the results of similar projects. Was it the same pride that prevented the editor and his contributors (few of whom are Canadians) to check their information with the Canadians about whom they wrote? Surely the Canadian Music Council, the CBC, the conservatories did not turn down requests for information? A splendid opportunity to supply musical information about Canada has been missed.

NOTES

1. John Beckwith, "About Canadian Music: The P.R. Failure," *Musicanada* 21 (July-August 1969), 4–7, 10–13; expanded and reprinted in *Music, The AGO and RCCO Magazine* 5/3 (March 1971), 33–37, 56, and "A 'Failure' Revisited: New Canadian Music in Recent Studies and Reference Works," in *Hello Out There! Canada's New Music in the World, 1950–85*, ed. John Beckwith and Dorith Cooper, CanMus Documents 2 (Toronto: Institute for Canadian Music, 1988), 114–23; both essays are reprinted in *Music Papers: Articles and Talks by a Canadian Composer 1961–1994* (Ottawa: Golden Dog, 1997), 35–49 and 111–21. [*Ed.*]
2. Oscar Thompson, ed., *The International Cyclopedia of Music and Musicians*, 6th ed., rev. by Nicholas Slonimsky (New York: Dodd, Mead, 1952). After Thompson's death in 1945, responsibility for this reference work passed on to Nicholas Slonimsky from the fourth (1946) through eighth (1958) editions. Slonimsky was a legendary musical lexicographer and engaged in extensive correspondence with music scholars in many countries, including Canada, to ensure that his biographical entries on musicians were up to date, accurate, and authoritative. [*Ed.*]
3. *Deirdre* was composed between September 1943 and May 1945, and was premiered in a CBC studio production in Toronto on 20 April 1946. [*Ed.*]
4. Eugène Lapierre, *Calixa Lavallée, musicien national du Canada* (Montreal: Granger Frères, 1936); a second edition appeared in 1950 and a third edition would be issued in 1966. The first edition of this biography would have been available to H.C. Colles, the editor of the fourth edition of *Grove's* (1940); that edition, though, was a reprint of Colles's third edition (1927) with some corrections, rather than a reworked new edition. [*Ed.*]

4
Introduction, from A History of Music in Canada 1534–1914

In his essay "Mapping Canada's Music" (see pages 189–215) HK outlines the sequence of events that led from his first compilation of random notes on Canadian music in 1948 to the appearance of *A History of Music in Canada* in 1960. The manuscript of the *History* was submitted in 1958 and published in 1960; the book was reprinted in paperback in 1969 and reissued with a list of amendments in 1987. In its two printings it sold approximately 6,000 copies before going out of print in 1995. The book is foundational to Canadian music studies in the same way that John Russell Harper's *Painting in Canada: A History* (University of Toronto Press, 1966) is to Canadian art history. Despite HK's statement that his goal was to tell "what actually happened" (alluding to Leopold von Ranke's "wie es eigentlich gewesen"), his approach aligns not with the grand tradition of European historical writing, with its concentration on great figures and decisive events, but rather with a distinctly New World approach to music history. In this Introduction, HK lays out astute ideas about historical narrative which were to exercise a considerable influence on subsequent writers of Canadian music history; indeed he foreshadows here some of the main leitmotifs in North American music historiography of the second half of the twentieth century.

The aim of this book is the description of music at various stages of Canadian history and of the meaning it held in the life of the Canadian people. To entitle this description a "history of music" requires an unorthodox

---

A History of Music in Canada 1534–1914 (Toronto: University of Toronto Press, 1960), 3–7; republished by permission of University of Toronto Press

approach, for customarily musical history relates the sequence of great composers and changing styles of composition and endeavours to demonstrate the continuity and cohesion of musical effort throughout a defined period and locale whereby mature nations assume a distinct musical character and unity. In Canada, these conditions do not yet prevail. To appreciate the fascination of the subject, one has to define musical history in different terms: such a history must deal with the planting of seeds rather than the harvesting of the fruits of a thousand years of civilization. The record of music in Canada's first three centuries takes as its subject not creative giants who determine the course of world music history but humble musicians who instil a taste for their art among pioneers preoccupied with establishing the physical and economic foundations of a new nation; instead of mirroring the entertainment of the *élite* in the world's musical capitals, it reflects the musical pastimes and aspirations of the many; and instead of noting the changing styles which express the spirit of the age and nation, it deals with the collecting and assimilating of traditional forms from outside sources. In short, the record is concerned more with social than with artistic aspects of music.

The social aspects of music are complex from the beginning: we find that even in its relatively short history music has held a great variety of meanings in the life of Canadians. To some it has been a means to implant, express and strengthen religious beliefs; to others an amusement contrary to the teachings of the church. Under varying circumstances and needs it has been regarded as a companion to daily labour and play; a pastime for idlers and dreamers; a career to be discouraged for moral and economic reasons; a social asset for daughters of the well-to-do; the expression of patriotic feeling; or a comfort in a life full of physical hardship and monotonous drudgery. Many examples for these sometimes contradictory values will be cited throughout the book.

In his search for elements of continuity and cohesion, the student of music in early Canada again finds it difficult to satisfy traditional criteria. The growth of music has been uneven in time and space, just as immigration and exploration have been spread over three centuries. Beginning at a time before Bach, Couperin, Handel and Purcell were born, music has been introduced to various regions of Canada from various mature countries, each with its own social and religious traditions, and it has been nourished with the help of vastly different mechanical means. Folk song, transmitted orally from generation to generation, and Roman Catholic liturgical music were brought to the wilderness of New France by

Introduction, from *A History of Music in Canada 1534–1914*

French peasants and missionaries in the seventeenth century; folk music also found a home in the fishing and farming communities of the Anglo-Saxon settlers on the Atlantic coast. Secular concert music and Protestant choral singing were introduced with the help of the printed page about the end of the eighteenth century to the small towns in the eastern part of Canada by the Loyalist immigrants from the United States, the British and the German bandmasters in their regimental bands. A hundred years later immigrants from many different countries entered Canadian cities and the western frontier districts, carrying with them a variety of musical skills in the folk, popular and sophisticated idioms; at the same time the dissemination of music was aided by the introduction of railways and steamships which enabled star artists and opera troupes to travel on an extensive scale, and by such devices as the phonograph, the player-piano and, a little later, radio.

These technological aids to the spread of music were of special importance as they helped to balance geographical factors which retarded the formation of a unified cultural life. A vast but thinly populated territory is not an encouragement to the exchange of artists and the sharing of musical resources and experiences. On the contrary, very often closer cultural links were established with nearby American cities than with Canadian cities a few thousand miles away, as likely as not speaking a different language, and separated by mountains, rivers and primeval forests.

It follows from the preceding observations that it is impossible to speak of music in Canada as an autonomous organism growing from primitive origins (after all, the origins were more highly developed than the offshoots!) through infancy and adolescence to adulthood. What convenient chapter headings these stages of development would make (although after reading W.D. Allen's *Philosophies of Music History*, American Book Company, 1939, one hesitates applying such biological terms to the music of any country or civilization!). It would be absurd to try to trace a chain of influence from the liturgical chants of the French Récollet and Jesuit missionaries to the choral societies of Upper Canada; or from the compositions of Dessane and Couture to those of a generation or so later. When Quebec and Halifax could look back over a century of organized musical activity, Vancouver and Winnipeg were struggling new outposts.

This isolation and interruption of musical effort is revealed not only in the comparison of different regions of Canada but often within one and the same city. Many cities have an old and distinguished record in the cultivation of music and have produced brilliant musicians, but too often the impact of each new wave of immigrants, of each new generation of Canadian-born music students returning with the latest techniques and aesthetic gospels from Paris or Leipzig, swept aside the teaching and views of the older Canadian generation. The impact from outside as well as the insufficiency of patronage and shifting population made it difficult to establish permanent institutions or home-grown "schools" of composition.

Unity in Canada's musical history, therefore, is found less in chronology, locale and musical repertoire than in the ever present themes of transplantation, assimilation and search for identity which will be traced throughout this book. The following chapters will describe what music was received in Canada, how it was accepted, and how Canadians began to make their own creative contribution to music.

The selecting of material and apportioning of space reflect to some degree the success with which material was obtained from or about various cities, provinces or historical periods, by means of printed literature, investigation in archives, correspondence or interviews. A more important criterion for selection was the need to record names of musicians and musical organizations and document events (assembled for the first time in form of a book) without degenerating into a mere catalogue of the countless available data. Fortunately the example of a few cities or careers usually serves to illustrate the essential features in many others; conversely those sections of the book which are preoccupied with the necessary registration of facts contain observations of general pertinence. The choice of examples and the thoroughness of treatment had to be determined according to both intrinsic musical value and historical interest. Description of a colourful pioneer like Frederic Henri Glackemeyer, Bishop John Medley, or David Willson helps to characterize a whole musical era; on the other hand, the careers of many erudite European-trained musicians of the late nineteenth century, more distinguished but also more routine, can be sketched adequately in summary form.

The most problematic task in selecting from the raw material is the search for a clear view of basic developments, uncluttered by an abundance of discursive asides and facts for facts' sake. But desirable though it is, clarity of structure must not be made an end in itself, if it is not inherent in the subject-matter. Space must be given to a variety of themes and topics. Altogether the first book on Canada's musical history should emphasize description rather than evaluation according to a preconceived point of view. The foremost aim must be to make the facts available, to tell "what actually happened" and to let events speak for themselves. For this

Introduction, from *A History of Music in Canada 1534–1914*

reason the application of extraneous critical standards is kept to a minimum: the historian would miss the point of his task if he examined early Canadian concert life simply to show how primitive it was in comparison with music in London or Paris, or how wonderful it was because it took place in a frontier setting.

Although it is hoped that the many factors involved in selecting and proportioning material have been evenly balanced, a definitive judgment of composition and other individual achievements can be gained only under far more advanced conditions of archival collections and when the subject becomes one of wider discussion and research. Only then will it be possible in many cases to penetrate beyond the statistical and biographical facts of a musician's career and bring to life his personality, his aesthetic views, his human qualities, his working methods, his hopes and disappointments. Some musicians, little known now, may gain in stature; others may have received undue emphasis here, because their life happens to be particularly well publicized and documented.

A word about the scope of this book. Being concerned mainly with the European heritage in Canada, it does not attempt to deal with Indian and Eskimo music. The social role of folk song is described and the names of many songs are mentioned in passing, but for the survey of Canadian folk music literature and its musical analysis readers are referred to the articles written as introductions to the song collections of Marius Barbeau, Ernest Gagnon, Helen Creighton, Elisabeth Bristol Greenleaf, Grace Yarrow Mansfield, Richard Johnston, Edith Fowke and others.

For a thorough discussion of developments in the mid-twentieth century readers may turn to the book *Music in Canada*, edited by Sir Ernest MacMillan (Toronto, 1955) and to other sources listed in the Bibliography. While this literature will help in an understanding of the contemporary scene, the specific aim of this book will be fulfilled if it helps to enlarge consciousness of a part of Canadian history which is not as well-known as it deserves; if it revives and preserves the memory of many a worthy, though forgotten musician; and if it contributes to the understanding of the preparations, problems and processes involved in establishing music in colonial surroundings.

Editors' postscript: On 30 May 1989, Beverley Cavanagh (now Beverley Diamond) presented a research paper titled "Narratives in Canadian Music History" at the annual meeting of the Canadian University Music Society, held that year at

Laval University in Quebec City.[1] The paper is a critical study of historiographical methods in Canadian music history textbooks by Clifford Ford, Timothy McGee, and HK (his *History*). Ten days later Diamond sent a copy of her paper to HK, inviting him to comment on it. HK read the paper closely and in reply sent Diamond a five-page, single-spaced letter on 21 February 1990, outlining the influences which led him to write the *History*. These included: the role of his parents in shaping his world view, his innate propensity for map-making (both literal and figurative), educational influences, his experiences during the war years, the example of specific scholars (P.H. Lang, Arnold Walter, W. Dwight Allen, Edwin H. Carr, Erich Doflein, Joseph Kerman), and finally the nature of the sources that were available at the time for writing about Canadian music. As HK noted in his letter, "I make no claim to having read all the important music histories or having made a profound study of the philosophies of musical historiography ... Perhaps one of these years I shall refine these notes and write a long paper on my understanding of musical history."

NOTE

1 The paper was subsequently given at a meeting of the Sonneck Society [now the Society for American Music] and ARMuQ (Association pour l'avancement de la recherche en musique du Québec) [now SQRM, Société québécoise de recherche en musique] held in 1990 in Toronto, and was subsequently revised and published as "Narratives in Canadian Music History," in *Canadian Music: Issues of Hegemony and Identity*, ed. Beverley Diamond and Robert Witmer (Toronto: Canadian Scholars' Press, 1994), 139–71; reprinted with minor changes in *Taking a Stand: Essays in Honour of John Beckwith*, ed. Timothy J. McGee (Toronto: University of Toronto Press, 1995), 273–305.

5
Joseph Quesnel's Colas et Colinette

The French émigré Joseph Quesnel was known as a prosperous businessman and French-language literary figure in post-Conquest Montreal, but his musical accomplishments were not investigated before HK's 1952 visit to the Archives du Séminaire, Quebec City, where he examined the vocal scores of two stage pieces with words and music by Quesnel. HK described Quesnel's musical activities and opinions at length in his *A History of Music in Canada 1534–1914* (1960), and once referred to Quesnel as one of three émigré composers in Canada's past whose stories had especially sparked his curiosity as a researcher—the others being Theodore Molt from Germany and James Paton Clarke from Scotland. With the inauguration in 1962 of Toronto's Ten Centuries Concerts, by R. Murray Schafer and several other young composers, HK's suggestion of a realization of Quesnel's first musical comedy, *Colas et Colinette*, became a reality. The revival was featured on the opening concert in the organization's second season, 6 October 1963, conducted by Godfrey Ridout, who had completed the score and composed an overture based on some of its themes. For the Ten Centuries program booklet, HK wrote this unusually full background essay. The work was well received, broadcast on both English and French CBC Radio networks in 1965, and mounted by CBC Television in Montreal in 1969. An LP recording of excerpts appeared in 1968 (RCI 234), and the publisher Gordon V. Thompson brought out a piano/vocal score of Ridout's restoration in 1974; for both HK provided a historical preface based on his original essay. Recognized as one of the earliest original music theatre works composed in North America, *Colas* enjoyed further stagings

---

Program Note for Ten Centuries Concerts, 6 October 1963

in half a dozen other centres in the 1970s and 1980s. Quesnel's *Lucas et Cécile* was revived in concert and stage versions in the 1990s in a restoration by John Beckwith, published in 1992 by Doberman/Yppan, Quebec City.

Introducing Mr. Quesnel

How old is Canadian opera? An article in *Opera in Canada* early last year began with this pronouncement: "Canadian Opera has just come of age! It is in its twenty-first year."[1] The writer, John Adaskin, was referring to Healey Willan's *Transit through Fire* which he had had a hand in commissioning for the CBC in 1941. In the *Encyclopedia Canadiana* the late Colin Sabiston identified the beginning of professional opera performance with the Montreal Opera Guild (1941). Why foreshorten historical perspective so severely? The Montreal Opera Company (1910–13) was a professional ensemble; a serious operatic work, *Torquil* by Charles Harriss, was published and performed at the turn of the century; and even earlier, in 1889, Oscar Telgmann's military opera *Leo, the Royal Cadet* had the first of a reputed 150 performances. Other light operas of that period could be cited. Instead, leaping backwards to the known beginnings of Canadian opera, let me tell the story of M. Joseph Quesnel.

If his name suggests nothing to you but a frontier town in British Columbia's Cariboo district you are merely on a side line, not on the wrong track. The town was named after Jules Maurice Quesnel, a fur-trader who accompanied Simon Fraser on his famous journey down the Fraser River in 1808. He later returned to Lower Canada and, like his brother Frédéric Auguste, served as a member of the Legislative Assembly. Jules Maurice had no doubt inherited his spirit of adventure from his father Joseph (1749–1809),[2] a native of Saint-Malo in France.

Marked by his family for a naval career, Joseph had sailed to Madagascar, Pondicherry [in former French India], Brazil and other exotic destinations before he came to Canada at the age of thirty. His arrival here was an adventure in itself. Quesnel commanded a ship which was carrying provisions and munitions to the American revolutionaries when a British frigate captured the vessel off the coast of Nova Scotia. Quesnel was taken to Halifax. Even though he had been on a mission to help the enemy, his sympathies with republicanism were not deep enough to prevent him from seeking and being granted citizenship in Canada.

Later he explored the Mississippi Valley and, as documents reveal, he intended to visit Philadelphia in 1786 and England two years later.

Meanwhile Quesnel had become head of a family, having married a Canadian girl. He settled down to the quiet life of a village merchant in Boucherville, near Montreal. His adventures did not cease, but they were less peripatetic. Quesnel was a man of versatile education, intimate with the classics of French literature; he was an able actor and violin player. Moreover he possessed creative talent and better than competent craftsmanship both in literature and music. The artistic faith of this newcomer who wrote and composed in the loneliness of the raw country deserves admiration. Yet perhaps the very lack of creative writing in Canada stimulated his efforts: no works are known to have been written [by him] before his arrival. "A gentleman of cheerful temperament and nice tastes who was happy in promoting the happiness of other people" (Notman, 1868),[3] he did not attempt the heights of Parnassus but aimed to amuse and entertain and knew how to promote these aims in theatre and literature.

Quesnel relates in his autobiographical poem "Épître a M. Généreux Labadie,"[4] written a quarter of a century later, that his first artistic concern on his arrival (in 1779) was the pitiful state of music. To improve matters, he composed a piece of Christmas music for church. Intending to please everybody he gave it "lively and slow, gay, sweet and pathetic" sections, it bristled with "flats, naturals and sharps," indeed it represented his very best effort. Alas, the music caused a small riot: it was decried as "dance music" and "the noise of demons fighting in the organ loft." Appreciated by only a few friends, he abandoned "the sterile field" of composition. An autobiographical poem is hardly meant to be a dictionary account and according to one early historian Quesnel did in fact produce more music, including orchestral symphonies, chamber music and sacred vocal pieces.[5] (Some scores were left at Montreal's Notre Dame Church but they are said to have been thrown into the fire during an overzealous housecleaning.)

Quesnel then began to focus his attention on theatre. This art had suffered a long eclipse in New France after a proposed performance of Molière's *Tartuffe* was suppressed by pontifical mandate in 1694. Its revival came only after the British conquest when officers organized amateur performances of both French and English plays and when troupes of actors and entertainers began to tour the cities of North America. Halifax, Montreal and Quebec each had less than 10,000 inhabitants. Yet there was a small minority of well-bred French Canadians, British officers and Loyalists who so craved stimulating entertainment that they could endure an evening program that would begin with a play, continue with an interlude and an after-piece—a shorter play or opera—and might conclude with a dance. Frequency varied. A Montreal citizen had the opportunity to hear seven opera performances in the decade after 1786; later, in the short period December 1804 to June 1805, the Quebec Gazette announced a play nearly every other week and four performances of three operas as well as one opera performance in Montreal. The operas included some of the most popular ones then in the repertoire, *The Padlock* [Charles Dibdin, 1768], *The Poor Soldier* [William Shield, 1783] and *Les deux chasseurs et la laitière* [Egidio Duni, 1763]. Shakespeare and Molière were among the more popular playwrights.

Colas et Colinette and Its First Performances

It is the year of the French Revolution [1789]; Mozart is commissioned to write *Così fan tutte*; Alexander Mackenzie follows the Mackenzie River to its mouth at the Arctic Ocean. In Montreal six prominent citizens, Quesnel among them, appear before a notary on 11 November and sign a contract with one Sieur Louis Dulongpré whom they appoint manager of the new Théâtre de Société. In his way as versatile as Quesnel, Dulongpré, the dancing master, music teacher and well-known portrait painter, undertook to set up a stage, paint the scenery, hire the musicians and write advertisements. Before November had passed this Canadian company presented its first show. A few months later, on 11 February 1790, the Montreal *Gazette* reported under the heading "Theatre":

> On Tuesday night the *Théâtre de Société* closed with the Representation of the *Légataire*[6] and the after-piece of *Colas & Colinette* for the Benefit of the Poor.

A brief review followed:

> Thus far let an English Spectator do justice to their merit and to his own Feelings and particularly to the Performance and Composition of Mr. Quesnel the Roscius[7] of this little Stage—the last verse of the *finale* Song in *Colas & Colinette* contained a Compliment to him very happily expressed and not less unexpected (we are convinced) by himself than by the audience whose satisfaction on the occasion seemed much greater than his.
>
> We have only to hope that on some future Day he will again unite his Talents with those of the other Gentlemen of the *Théâtre de Société* to please the candid and judicious and to relieve the Poor.

This first known performance of a Canadian opera took place on 9 February 1790 in Montreal, two Tuesdays after the première of *Così fan tutte* in Vienna.[8] *Colas* was revived in Quebec City in 1805 and again received exceptional newspaper coverage, pushing aside the usual foreign reports, royal proclamations and advertisements.

> Mardi le 29 présent, au Théâtre Patagon sera représenté: LE BAILLI DUPÉ; Opéra en trois Actes, par M. QUESNEL, suivi de LA SERENADE, Comédie en deux Actes, par REGNARD ...

The Quebec *Gazette* of 31 January 1805 reviewed the performance, both in French and English.

> On Tuesday evening was represented a French Opera, called the *Bailli Dupé*, or *Colas & Colinette*. The Dialogue, Songs and Music by Mr. QUESNEL, of Boucherville.

A cast list and an outline of the plot are followed by this appraisal:

> This is perhaps the first piece of this kind that has been written and performed in this province. The dialogue, the songs and the music, are, we understand the composition of M. Quesnel, and as a colonial production, it possesses considerable merit. It rarely happens that the Poetry and Music are composed by the same person.
> It was the union of these two arts that gave to the operas of Rousseau, a superiority over those of his contemporaries, and impressed his audience with the most powerful emotions of sympathy.
> With regard to the Actors in the Piece of Tuesday night, it must be confessed that they sustained their parts with ability, particularly the two who personated the *Bailli*, and the peasant servant. The character of *Lepine*[9] could not have been exhibited with more native humour, on any stage in the world, and the young man who appeared in it, possesses in that line, considerable comic powers. The *Bailli*, perhaps at times, displayed rather too much activity for a person so advanced in life.

It was Quesnel month, so to speak. A week later the Quebec *Gazette* printed Quesnel's didactic poem "Adresse aux jeunes acteurs," identifying the author only as a man well known "par ses talens (sic) pour la poësie Lyrique et Dramatique." The editor, John Neilson, thought the moment opportune to campaign for a permanent theatre. An editorial argued that acting would be a worthwhile pursuit for gifted young men in the city. It defended theatre as a positive moral influence, obviously responding to or anticipating clerical opposition. Finally the editorial proposed a campaign to raise £800 for the erection of a proper building. Response must have been heartening and "at the request of several persons" a second performance of *Colas et Colinette* was given on Saturday, 23 February.[10]

One of the most pleasant observations about all these activities is the mutual interest of the French and British elements of the population. British officers had introduced Molière to Canada in the original language; an "English Spectator" wrote the Montreal review of *Colas*; names of both nationalities are found in the Quebec performances. Scottish-born John Neilson remained a faithful supporter of Quesnel. In 1808 he published the text of *Colas* in book form at his own expense.[11]

The Revival

The largest body of Quesnel material is in the Archives du Séminaire de Québec and forms part of *Ma Saberdache*. This is a collection of historical documents assembled throughout his lifetime by Jacques Viger, a younger contemporary of Quesnel and the first mayor of Montreal. *Ma Saberdache* includes some thirty-six Quesnel poems, plays and other writings totaling 249 pages. In addition there are the unaccompanied vocal parts of *Colas et Colinette* and another opera, *Lucas et Cécile,* and the second violin part of the former. The second violin is the most fortunate part that could have been preserved: the first must have duplicated the vocal line much of the time while the second underlines it in thirds or sixths, thus providing also a clue to the harmony and bass progression. The music of *Colas* was obtained on microfilm from the Archives du Séminaire de Québec through the CBC Toronto Music Library for the Ten Centuries restoration.

The restoration of the music was undertaken with great enthusiasm by Godfrey Ridout of the Faculty of Music, University of Toronto. With a few small exceptions, where the notation or part-writing needed correction, the surviving music has been preserved faithfully. At times the fragment suggested its completion; at times Ridout has supplied his own creative ideas. One detail: the opening tune of the little whirlwind duet, No. 8 (the second between Colas and le Bailli) foreshadows Rossini and accordingly Ridout has provided a typical Rossini bass.

The surviving evidence of orchestral music in the Quebec of Quesnel's time—performed by members of military bands and "gentlemen amateurs"—justified Ridout's scoring of the accompaniment for a flexible chamber orchestra.

An oddity of the surviving manuscript is the notation of all voice parts in the treble clef, despite the fact that in the Quebec production male singers were employed for all roles, even that of Colinette (ladies did not appear on the stage in those days). The reverse is true of [our] presentation, in which the roles of both Colas and Colinette will be sung by young women.[12] The obvious discrepancy of the sex of the hero is overridden in this case by the musical considerations inherent in the voicing of some concerted numbers.

Ten Centuries Concerts will not present a complete performance of the three-act opera. Nearly all the musical numbers will be sung (in the original French) under the direction of Mr. Ridout. The spoken dialogue will be summarized and narrated in English by Professor John Walker of the French Department, University College, University of Toronto.

The Work, the Criticism and the Achievement

Apart from *Colas et Colinette*, Quesnel wrote three other works for the stage: *Lucas et Cécile*, with words and music; *Les républicains français*, a one-act prose comedy; and *L'anglomanie*, a one-act verse comedy which was printed in 1802 and reprinted in *Le Canada français* in 1932/33. The last named is the only play with a Canadian setting. It satirizes the aping of British manners by a certain sector of French Canadian society. Historians have not reported any performances besides those of *Colas*.

Colas is supposed to have been written in 1788; the date of *Lucas* is not recorded. Thus the question remains open which of the two is Quesnel's first opera. It appears certain only that *Colas* was the first performed.

Is it really accurate to call these two works operas or are they merely plays with songs? Neither one includes an overture or other purely instrumental numbers. *Colas* has fourteen and *Lucas* has seventeen vocal pieces. The published edition of 1808 calls *Colas* a Comédie en prose mêlée d'ariettes. This is the proper technical label, one applied also to the works of Rousseau, Grétry, Monsignor, Philidor and their contemporaries. In such company the works of Quesnel may claim a place in operatic as well as theatrical history.

Godfrey Ridout has gained the impression that Quesnel threw the songs together in some haste, a view supported by the occasionally mechanical second violin part: "Like Grétry he was lousy at four-part writing but I think he was a better melodist [than Grétry] when he was 'on' and despite what I've said about haste, a sophisticated and resourceful harmonist." Decidedly Quesnel was an amateur composer only in that he lacked the opportunity of a professional, not in the sense of being a dabbler. His melodies range from the folksong quality of No. 9 (Bailli) and No. 11 (Colas) to the exalted beauty of Colinette's aria (No. 5). Some of the duets breathe true comic-opera spirit although characterization is rarely attempted in detail. The form usually follows an ABA pattern, but occasionally this is restricted to key sequence while the melody presents a new idea with every new line of words. This lack of the repetition of previous phrases (Nos. 5 and 10 in *Colas* and occasionally in *Lucas*) is a weakness only from an academic point of view; an overall feeling of unity pervades even these particular ariettas.

It is surprising that French-Canadian scholars have not yet produced a complete edition of the surviving works of the man they acknowledge as their first poet and playwright.[13] The selection included in [James] Huston's *Répertoire national* (1848–50; 1893)[14] whets the appetite for more. As far as I can ascertain this fascinating man has not even been selected as the subject for a dissertation.[15] The longest discussion of Quesnel I can find, by Camille Roy in his *Nos origines littéraires* (1909)[16] measures only thirty-odd small pages, and many of these contain quotations. In the writings of other historians of French-Canadian literature one finds little evidence of original research and critical reading. The fact that the songs from *Lucas* have survived has never been noted; the newspaper excerpts quoted here have been ignored.[17]

The gist of this meagre criticism is that Quesnel shows the influence of Molière, J.-J. Rousseau and Boileau whose works he knew well. Indeed, the "back to nature" ideas of Rousseau would seem to echo in the plot, common to both *Colas* and *Lucas*, of a refined young girl selecting a simple-minded but honest peasant as her husband in preference to a well-established but crafty suitor. The critics credit Quesnel with more facility than originality: this fluency and ease of expression, both in words and music, occasionally leads to carelessness of detail. The stage works are judged to display elegance and gaiety, seasoned with a touch of biting irony. At the same time the poetry reveals a gifted nature poet and a melancholy dreamer. Camille Roy called Quesnel's work "amaible et moyenne";[18] Jean Béraud concludes that "Ni l'esprit ni le texte de Quesnel ne pouvait faire mal à une mouche."[19]

Was Quesnel appreciated in his own lifetime? The few known performances and publications in his lifetime could hardly have resulted in wide public familiarity with his works, although there may have been private readings and at least a small circle of understanding friends gave him faithful support. Quesnel himself felt unappreciated. His "Épître à M. Généreux Labadie," written to console an even less successful poet-friend, remains the classic statement of the un-appreciated Canadian artist echoed many times (and with the same element of slight exaggeration) in the century-and-a-half that has passed.[20]

As a composer Quesnel had no immediate heirs. As a promoter of the stage arts he gave practical proof that there was room for theatre in Canada, although his efforts were too premature to establish a continuous tradition. As a writer he helped to awaken interest in literature and, in spite of his negative appraisal of his success, made a modest impact upon younger writers, who paid him homage in verses and fondly nicknamed him "Le père des amours." This is also the title of an opera by the Montreal composer Eugène Lapierre, written and performed in 1942, based on the life of Quesnel but not using his music.[21] The Ten Centuries performance would seem to be the first modern revival of *Colas*, either as a play or an opera.

Will Quesnel's work "yet be known from Vaudreuil to Kamouraska?"[22] Does *Colas* "possess considerable merit" not only "as a colonial production" but as a piece in its own right that can charm and amuse twentieth-century audiences? The revival will help to answer these questions.

NOTES

1. John Adaskin, "Canadian Music Centre Eagerly Awaits More 'Native' Operas," *Opera in Canada* 9 (15 February 1962), 11. [*Ed.*]
2. John E. Hare subsequently established the date of Quesnel's birth as 15 November 1746; see his article "Quesnel, Joseph," *Dictionary of Canadian Biography*, vol. 5: *1801–1820* (Toronto: University of Toronto Press, 1983). [*Ed.*]
3. William Notman, *Portraits of British Americans*, vol. 3 (Montreal: W. Notman, 1868), 43. [*Ed.*]
4. The poem, in a translation by John Glassco, is in Michael Gnarowski, ed. *Joseph Quesnel, 1749–1809: Selected Poems and Songs after the Manuscripts in the Lande Collection* (Montreal: Lawrence M. Lande Foundation at the McLennan Library, McGill University, 1970), 57–60. [*Ed.*]

5   James Huston, ed., *Le répertoire national, ou, Recueil de littérature canadienne*, 2nd ed., 4 vols. (Montreal: J.M. Valois, 1893), vol. 1: 18–19n2. [*Ed.*]
6   Jean-François Regnard's comedy in verse *Le légataire universelle* (1706). [*Ed.*]
7   Roscius was a famous Roman actor.
8   By the time HK reworked this essay in 1968 for the liner notes of the recording of *Colas et Colinette* (RCI 234), he had established that the first performance of *Colas et Colinette* by the Théâtre de Société in Montreal took place on 14 January 1790, twelve days *before* the premiere of *Così fan tutte*, part of a double bill with *Le médecin malgré lui* by Molière. The performance on 9 February 1790 was the second presentation of the work. Documentation of the premiere of *Colas et Colinette* is reproduced in Juliette Bourassa-Trépanier and Lucien Poirier, eds., *Répertoire des données musicales de la presse québécoise; Tome I: Canada, Volume 1: 1764–1799* (Quebec: Les Presses de l'Université Laval, 1990), 36, 40–41, 100–2. The title of "first known performance of a Canadian opera" may rightly belong to John Bentley's *The Enchanters or The Triumph of Genius*, staged in Montreal on 12 May 1786, but the music of this work has been lost; see "Bentley, John" in *Encyclopedia of Music in Canada*, 2nd ed. [*Ed.*]
9   A speaking part, omitted in the Ten Centuries presentation.
10 Information on the performances of *Colas et Colinette* in Quebec City in 1805 and 1807 is in Juliette Bourassa and Lucien Poirier, eds., *Répertoire des données musicales de la presse québécoise, Tome I: Canada, Volume 2: 1800–1824, Les divertissements urbains: confrontations de deux cultures* (Quebec: Faculté de musique, Université Laval, 2003): 68–70, 83 (discussion) and on the book's website, hosted at http://www.ourroots.ca (documentation). [*Ed.*]
11 The Toronto Public Libraries own a copy. The preface reveals that the author was publicity-shy and had consented to publication only after long and persistent pressure. [Neilson's publication of the libretto of *Colas et Colinette* is available online at http://archive.org/details/cihm_41939. (*Ed.*)]
12 The singers for the Ten Centuries performance were Geneviève Perreault (Colas) and Judith Lebane (Colinette). For the LP recording of the work, the role of Colas was sung by the tenor Léopold Simoneau, with his wife, the soprano Pierrette Alarie, as Colinette. [*Ed.*]
13 Hare, "Quesnel, Joseph," reports that "Helmut Kallmann and John E. Hare are preparing a critical edition of Quesnel's works from his recently discovered workbook; this publication should include 30 poems, as well as a few titles attributed to him." Selected works by Quesnel have appeared in various modern editions, but this projected complete works edition was never published. [*Ed.*]
14 Huston, ed., *Le répertoire national*, vol. 1: 18–71. [*Ed.*]

15 A dissertation has since been written about Quesnel: Benoît Moncion, "L'humour de Joseph Quesnel (1746–1809): naissance de l'écrivain canadien" (MA thesis in Literary Studies, Université du Québec à Montréal, 2007). [*Ed.*]
16 Camille Roy, *Nos origines littéraires* (Quebec: Imprimerie de l'Action sociale, 1909), 125–57. [*Ed.*]
17 Subsequent publications on Quesnel as a musician include Lucien Poirier, "La fortune de deux oeuvres de Jean-Jacques Rousseau au Canada français entre 1790 et 1850," in *Musical Canada: Words and Music Honouring Helmut Kallmann*, ed. John Beckwith and Frederick A. Hall (Toronto: University of Toronto Press, 1988), 60–70 (on the influence of Rousseau's *Le Devin du village* on *Colas et Colinette*); John Beckwith, "*Le Lucas et Cécile* de Joseph Quesnel: quelques problèmes de restauration," *Les Cahiers de l'ARMuQ* 13 (May 1991), 10–28, and "Restoring Joseph Quesnel's Other Operetta *Lucas et Cécile*," *Notations* 3/4 (October 1991), 5, 7; Elaine Keillor, *Music in Canada: Capturing Landscape and Diversity* (Montreal and Kingston: McGill-Queen's University Press, 2006), 89–91. Jean Marmier was the first to publish Quesnel's libretto for *Lucas et Cécile* in his article "Joseph Quesnel: *Lucas et Cécile*, texte inédit," *Études canadiennes* 16 (1984): 23–30. Marmier also published some lesser-known works by Quesnel in "Joseph Quesnel: quelques vers inédits ou inaccessibles," *Études canadiennes* 6 (1979): 81–86, and gave an account of Quesnel's career as a wine merchant in "Trente barriques de vin de Bordeaux, de Montréal aux Grands Lacs. Une équipée commercial de Joseph Quesnel (1791)," *Études canadiennes* 35 (1993): 301–10. On Quesnel in the context of the Théâtre de Société, see André-Gilles Bourassa, "Feux de la rampe et feu de l'action," *L'Annuaire théâtral: revue québécoise d'études théâtrales* 35 (2004), 155–76. An excellent website which offers documents, sound excerpts, and illustrations of Quesnel's music is at http://www.unites.uqam.ca/expo/; it is derived from the exhibition Images from the Turn of a Century 1760–1840: A Portrait of Arts, Literature and Eloquence in Quebec, which was mounted at Montreal's Château Ramezay Museum in 2000; a production of *Lucas et Cécile* took place in April 2000 in the context of this exhibition. [*Ed.*]
18 Roy, *Nos origines*, 145. [*Ed.*]
19 Jean Béraud, *350 ans de théâtre au Canada français* (Montreal: Cercle du Livre de France, 1958), 22. [*Ed.*]
20 For example, Quesnel writes in this poem that "partout on fête le génie / Hormis en ce pays; car l'ingrat Canadien / Aux talents de l'esprit n'accorde jamais rien." Quoted by HK in his *A History of Music in Canada* (Toronto: University of Toronto Press, 1960), 66. English translation by John Glassco: "And wit is honoured everywhere, you'll find, / Except in Canada, whose graceless brood / Witholds from talent ev'n a livelihood." [*Ed.*]

21 Concerning the work by Lapierre, see John Beckwith, "Father of Romance, Vagabond of Glory: Two Canadian Composers as Stage Heroes," in *Music Traditions, Cultures, and Contexts*, ed. Robin Elliott and Gordon E. Smith (Waterloo, ON: Wilfrid Laurier University Press, 2010), 227–59. [*Ed.*]
22 To quote from his "Épître à M. Généreux Labadie."

6
Music Library Association Digs Up Our Musical Past

HK was an inveterate collector of old Canadian sheet music and amassed an extraordinary number of such materials by dint of many hours spent visiting used bookstores, rummage sales, flea markets, and anywhere else that old sheet music might be found. This hobby was to become a major focal point of his career. As HK relates in this article, the cataloguing of musical Canadiana was taken up as a Centennial project by the Canadian Music Library Association.[1] This initiative was continued by staff at the National Library of Canada under HK's leadership from 1970 on. From the thousand or so pieces catalogued by volunteers for the CMLA in the Centennial year, the National Library's *Union Catalogue of Canadian Music Publications to 1950* grew to number over 20,000 items. A further collaboration with the Canadian Musical Heritage Society led to the *Inventory of Notated Canadian Music to 1950*, with over 30,000 items (online at http://cliffordfordpublications .ca/). Further details about all of the pieces mentioned in this article can be found in the *Inventory*. A selection of representative sheet music from the Library and Archives Canada collection has been digitized and made available on the website "Sheet Music from Canada's Past" (http://www.collectionscanada.gc.ca/sheetmusic/). Some of these publications exist in only a very small number of copies, and it is to HK's credit that they have been preserved rather than "lost forever."

The Canadian Composer 11 (October 1966), 18, 28. *The Canadian Composer* was published by CAPAC, a predecessor of SOCAN; article republished by permission of SOCAN

Canadian copyright entry No. 9472, deposited in the Library of Parliament on 18 September 1897 reads, "*Rush to the Klondyke.* (Song.) Words and Music by W.T. Diefenbaker." One cannot help but picture Mr. Diefenbaker singing his song to the infant son on his knee. Was this John's first lesson in Canadian geography—and economics?

Many other compositions recall the excitement of pioneer days or are linked to famous persons. Begin to search and you will find music named after localities and rivers, inspired by historical incidents or associated with the sports and pastimes of nineteenth-century Canada. "Shoulder to Shoulder, on to the Border," exhorts Canadians to resist the Fenian invaders while the *Cantate pour l'arrivée du Prince de Galles en Canada* celebrates the Prince of Wales' visit in 1860. You may come across the *Snow Shoe Tramp,* and *Civil Service Galop,* a *Chanson du Métis* and the *Ontario Agricultural College Polka.* The *Splash and Dash Polka* is dedicated to the Ottawa Rowing Club and *Le Jour de l'an à la campagne* describes a snowy holiday.

It will be possible shortly to trace early Canadian music publications by subject, composer, cover illustration or dedicatee. In adopting the locating and cataloguing of music published in Canada (or outside, if it is related to Canada) up to 1921 as its Centennial project, the Canadian Music Library Association is attempting more than to fill a gap in Canadian bibliography or to indulge in a fad of collecting yet another little known type of Canadiana. Among practical benefits, the project will provide material for performers with an interest in our musical past and will furnish authentic period pieces to producers of plays and pageants relating to our history. It has already revealed a wealth of cover pictures depicting pioneer life and personalities which could enliven exhibits in museums and pioneer villages.

There are important theoretical implications as well. By documenting the beginnings of published composition the project will for the first time provide a faithful impression of musical taste and creativity in Canada's formative period, with all its weaknesses and virtues. Further, by paralleling the collecting and indexing that has already been accomplished in the folksong field, a new assessment will be possible of the relative impact and role in pioneer society of orally transmitted folk music and music spread by means of print. Having had a head start, folksong research has given the impression that a century ago the musical diet of Canadians consisted almost entirely of folksongs. The probability is that tunes from *La traviata* and *The Bohemian Girl* and current popular ballads were far more widely sung and played.

In both fields—untutored and sophisticated music—the native product formed a small fraction of the repertoire. Granted that folksong reflects life's experience more directly and spontaneously, the songs of the local piano teacher and the polkas of the bandmaster are equally valid manifestations of pioneer culture.

Reprints of foreign music apart, nineteenth-century Canadian publications range from well-intentioned but hopelessly amateurish patriotic songs and cheap sentimental ballads to ambitious choral-orchestral cantatas and learned preludes and fugues for keyboard. Between these extremes lies routine dance and march music, trivial but competently written. Today it is fashionable to sneer at Victorian taste, but the best of the Canadian output conveys a sense of fun and physical well-being that is rarely found in the modern equivalent.

Early music publications varied not only in quality but covered a wide range of genres for greatly diversified aims. This reminds us that a colonial setting, while lacking facilities for elaborate performance and professional training, exhibits a complex variety of musical activities from early times on. About the year 1800 church music ranged from plainchant to the "fugued" hymn; chamber music was cultivated; military bands and amateur players joined in the performance of orchestral music. While the rivers echoed to the sound of voyageur songs, city folk applauded performances of English ballad operas and French *opéras comiques*.

The year 1800 also marked the publication of the first music in Canada, *Le Gradual romain*, a book of over 600 pages of plainsong for use in the diocese of Quebec. *The Vocal Preceptor* or *Key to Sacred Music* of 1811 was the first instruction book. Collections of secular songs appeared in the 1830s and from 1839 literary journals featured the odd piece of music. A few years later separate pieces of quarto-size sheet music became available, culminating in the thirty-page publication of [J.P.] Clarke's charming song cycle *Lays of the Maple Leaf (Songs of Canada)* in 1853.

Towards the turn of the century, just as today, musical publications averaged roughly 150 a year. Nearly all were for piano solo, piano and voice, or chorus. Canadian musicians were luckier than today in getting long works published. *Seize mélodies* by the Comte de Premio-Real (1879), Telgmann's military opera *Leo, the Royal Cadet* (1889), Gagnon's *Accompagnement d'orgue des chants liturgiques* (1903) and Vogt's *Modern Pianoforte Technique* (1900) all have a hundred or more pages in large format. Further, commercial success was not unknown. Ambrose's "One Sweetly Solemn Thought" (1876) and Lavallée's *[Le] Papillon* étude (1875, first published in Paris), not to mention the well-known patriotic songs, were reprinted by many publishers.

A dozen volunteer workers have already catalogued nearly a thousand items for the Canadian Music Library Association in one of the few Centennial projects that so far has not required any financial grant. Rather, the help needed is to receive donations of old music (in sheet or album form) with a Canadian imprint or to receive reports about such music from anyone who can spot it in his attic, the archives of his church or at a second-hand store. Contact should be made with the Music Division of the Toronto Public Library at 559 Avenue Road or the CBC's Toronto Music Library at 354 Jarvis Street. If we do not succeed in collecting the documents of early Canadian musical life now, they may be lost forever.

NOTE

1 The Canadian Music Library Association was founded in 1956, and was reconstituted in 1971 as the Canadian Association of Music Libraries, with "Archives and Documentation Centres" added to the organization's name in 1992.

7
James Paton Clarke, Canada's First Mus.Bac.

Many of HK's findings on the Scottish-born Canadian musical pioneer James Paton Clarke had been included in his book *A History of Music in Canada 1534–1914* a decade before this essay was first published. Here he reveals how as a historian he sorted out conflicting biographical information; he also comments critically on the main items in Clarke's creative output. The result is an unusually full picture of a professional musician and his local environment in a mid-nineteenth-century Canadian city (Toronto). Examples of Clarke's music are reproduced in *The Canadian Musical Heritage/Le Patrimoine musical canadien*, volumes 1, 2, 3, 5, and 17.

James Paton Clarke was the first person in Canada to receive an academic music degree. This distinction alone should arouse our curiosity about his career. But Clarke also may be considered the first musician who had a substantial number of compositions published in Canada and the first in Toronto whose activities were sufficiently broad in scope to stamp him as the leading musician of the city, even though he enjoyed this role neither for as long a period nor as firmly as Frederick Herbert Torrington, Augustus Stephen Vogt and Sir Ernest MacMillan did in later years.

Yet another "first" has to be registered: Clarke was the first musician in Canada whose name has been entered in a large number of music

---

The Canada Music Book / Les Cahiers canadiens de musique 1 (Spring-Summer 1970), 41–51. The list of works by J.P. Clarke (pages 52–53) has been omitted here.

dictionaries, including such standard works as *Baker's*, *Grove's*, *Riemann's* and *Thompson's*.[1] And in this circumstance of Clarke's posthumous reputation lies fascination as well as mystery for the curious student. It is easy to demonstrate why by juxtaposing a few salient quotations:

> *Clarke, James Peyton, Scottish organist; b. 1808; d. Toronto, Aug. 27, 1877. In 1829, leader of psalmody in St. George's Church, Edinburgh ... emigrated to Canada, 1835, settling as a farmer in Ellora, but went to Toronto about 1841; about 1845 was elected prof. of music in Upper Canada University ...*
> (*Baker's Biographical Dictionary of Musicians*, 5th ed., 1958)[2]
>
> *He was born in 1807 ... His position as an organist and teacher was of such distinction that Toronto University gave him his doctorate in 1877 ...*
> (John D. Mahoney, "Dr. Hugh A. Clarke, Musician," *General Magazine and Historical Chronicle,* Pennsylvania University, General Alumni Society, Philadelphia, vol. 48, April 1941).
>
> *James Paton C. was an Oxford Mus. Doc., prof. of music at Upper Canada Univ.*
> (J. D. Champlin, *Cyclopedia of Music and Musicians*, New York, 1888–90).
>
> *James Peyton Clarke, a Scottish organist (1808–77) who, after an active career in Edinburgh, went to Canada to become organist of St. James's Cathedral, Toronto, and was later head of the musical faculty of the University of Toronto.*
> (Hector Charlesworth, *Grove's Dictionary of Music and Musicians*, Supplementary Volume, ed. H.C. Colles, 1940).
>
> *Mus. Dr. James Paton C. (1808–77, Musiklehrer an der Canadischen Universität) ...*
> (*Riemanns Musiklexikon*, 11th ed., 1929).

Clarke's is obviously a classic case of biographical distortion through superficial research and careless copying by one writer or editor from another. The only undisputed facts in the above excerpts are the spelling of James and Clarke and the dates of his emigration and death! Nearly all other facets of his career—his middle name, the identity of his father, the location of St. George's Church, the nature of his association with the University of Toronto, his doctoral degree—have been handed down in conflicting versions, adding an element of speculation and mystery to a man who appears to have been a rather sober and quiet kind of person, a "conscientious and earnest musician."[3] The account which follows clarifies some of the puzzles but leaves open a wide field for future investigation.[4]

Clarke's earliest reported activity was that of a music-seller's assistant in Edinburgh. Indeed, his middle name Paton (the correct spelling) points towards his roots in that city. One of the Edinburgh Patons, Mary Ann (1802–1864) became a famous singer; her father was an amateur musician. Since the middle name Archibald appears in J.P. Clarke's son and granddaughter, one might speculate whether he had any family connection with Andrew Archibald Paton (1811–1874), an author and diplomat from Edinburgh. The identity of Clarke's father is also open to speculation, but at least there is agreement that he was a musician. Mahoney, an associate of Clarke's son Hugh at the University of Pennsylvania, has claimed the Cambridge music professor John Clarke-Whitfeld as the father, a man who never lived in Scotland. A more likely person was the Edinburgh organist William Clarke (about 1780–1820), himself the son of Stephen Clarke, an organist and friend of Robert Burns.

In 1829 Clarke was leader of psalmody at St. George's Church in Glasgow (not Edinburgh) and two years later he signed the preface to the second edition of his *Parochial Psalmody*[5] as Leader of the Music of that church and "Professor of the Piano Forte and Singing." The volume included several of Clarke's own tunes, for example "St. George's, Glasgow, LMD." On Christmas Day of 1831 Clarke married Helen Fullerton. In 1834 he became organist at St. Mary's Episcopal Chapel in Glasgow. When *The Choir*, a selection of choruses, anthems and other music, co-edited with A. Thomson, appeared in 1835, Clarke was identified as the *late* organist of that church. He had already left Scotland for Canada earlier in the same year.

In Canada the Clarkes settled at Elora as farmers. Though this information is found only in two dictionaries (*Baker's* of 1899, later copied by *Thompson's*) it does sound plausible, for several parties of emigrants left Scotland for Elora in 1835.[6] At least by 1842 Clarke had established contact with Toronto, for a Mr. J. Clarke was paid for organ and piano tuning at St. James's Cathedral; his new *Te Deum* was performed there in 1843. His first position in Canada of which records have been traced, however, was that of organist at Christ Church (Church of England) in Hamilton in 1844 and 1845. In 1842 the singing in that church was supported by a French horn; the following year an organ fund was established; an organist's quarter-yearly salary is recorded for the first time in 1844. It amounted to £ 2/1/11 for the three month period but had been raised to £ 3/15/– when Clarke received his last payment in October 1845. He was paid separately for organ tuning and installation work.

Mapping Canada's Music

In Hamilton Clarke compiled his first Canadian publication, a volume called *Canadian Church Psalmody*, sanctioned by the Lord Bishop of Toronto and published by H. & W. Rowsell of Toronto. 1845, the year of its appearance, was a decisive one for Clarke. In April he attended the founding meeting of the Toronto Choral Society; in June he participated in a concert for the opening of St. George's Church in Toronto;[7] and in October he conducted one of two concerts in celebration of King's College's Triennial Commemoration. This concert at King's College Hall featured the Toronto Choral Society, an orchestra of musicians and amateurs and the band of the 82nd Regiment. It included the overtures to Beethoven's *Prometheus* and Mendelssohn's *St. Paul*, excerpts from the sacred music of Handel, Haydn and Rossini as well as music by Mozart, Pergolesi, Spohr and lesser-known composers. The reputation built up through the *Canadian Church Psalmody* and the success of his concerts may have induced his decision to move to Toronto. Above all, however, this move must have been due to the encouragement he received from Dr. John McCaul (1807–1886), then the vice-president of King's College, who recognized Clarke's talent and made him his protégé. It was McCaul, an ardent promoter of fine music, who had conceived the plan for the two October concerts. As president of the newly formed Philharmonic Society, which gave its first concert on Boxing Day that year, he chose Clarke as conductor. When the college had been renamed University of Toronto (1850) and McCaul had become its president, a similar association continued for 1851–53 in the Toronto Vocal Music Society and 1855 and 1872–73 in the Toronto Philharmonic Society.

Whether one looks at Toronto or other Canadian cities of the pioneer age, the short-livedness of musical societies was as typical as the colourful mixture of performers and selections represented by the programs. Orchestral pieces, vocal solos, choral music or instrumental virtuoso pieces would follow each other, presented by amateurs and professionals of varying degrees of competence. Regimental band musicians were rarely missing. Clarke's role was not always that of a conductor; he also appeared as piano accompanist (rarely as soloist) and, usually in ensembles, as a singer. McCaul's influence may be detected in the fact that Clarke's programs under McCaul's presidency were of a higher standard than others in which he participated. Beethoven, Mozart, or Haydn were nearly always represented. Clarke performed several symphonies by Mozart (including the *Linz*) and Beethoven (probably the first two and the funeral march from the *Eroica*), although he may not have given them in their entirety and hardly in their full instrumentation. Overtures included *Don Giovanni*, *Prometheus*, *The Barber of Seville*, *Fra Diavolo*, *Semiramide* and *St. Paul*. Highlights of his vocal programming were excerpts from Handel and Haydn oratorios, from Beethoven's *Mount of Olives*, Rossini's *Stabat Mater* and Weber's operas. Undoubtedly, many of these performances were Toronto, if not Canadian, premieres. There was also a good share of sacred, "national," or humorous songs, Italian arias and Clarke's own vocal pieces.

Although Clarke had had associations with Toronto's St. James's Cathedral previously, the Churchwardens' Register and Minute Book dates his appointment as organist—at the salary of £50 per annum, nearly four times his Hamilton income—only 1 July 1848. Belying the assertion made by Charlesworth and others that Clarke came to Toronto *because* of this position and that it was his main activity in the city, the fact is that he occupied it for less than a year. Fire damaged the church on 7 April 1849 and though Clarke promised to lead the choir without remuneration, the building had to be closed. When a new one was opened in 1853, R.G. Paige was appointed organist and Clarke never returned to the office. He is said to have become organist at St. Michael's Roman Catholic Cathedral. On 3 January 1852 "Mr. Clarke," organist at that church, was advised of his deficiencies and soon received "payment of his last quarter ending the 31st for his service as organist at church."[8] Since the first name is not indicated there is a possibility that the deficient organist was Clarke's son Hugh who is reported to have been an organist at the age of twelve, just at that time. Besides, neither Clarke may have been sufficiently familiar with the Roman Catholic liturgy.

Clarke became part of the local intellectual circle, not only as leader of musical societies but as composer. His songs appeared in *The Anglo-American Magazine* in 1852 and 1853 or as separate sheet music published by A. & S. Nordheimer, the Canadian pioneer music publishers. The songs include settings of poems by Samuel Thompson, Rev. Robert Jackson MacGeorge, James Paterson and others. Some of the texts were selected from the *Maple Leaf*, a pioneer literary annual edited by McCaul. Clarke's song-writing culminated in 1853 in the *Lays of the Maple Leaf, or Songs of Canada*, a setting of seven poems from the *Maple Leaf* dedicated to the Countess of Elgin and Kincardine, the governor general's wife. The cycle contains an opening glee, four solos and one duet with piano accompaniment and a final "Chorus of Hunters" in six unaccompanied parts. Its thirty large pages make it the longest secular composition published in Canada up to this time; it is inspired by the country's scenery, pioneers, hunters and woodsmen.[9] *The Anglo-American* in its June 1853 issue showered flattery upon its own contributor:

> It is with great pleasure that we welcome the appearance of this very creditable publication, which does much honour to Canada. Although the words and music are by children of another soil, to whom "the fair forest land," is but an adopted mother, yet the tone of feeling is thoroughly Canadian ... whilst due filial respect is shown, as it ought to be, to the rose, shamrock, and thistle, severally, as emblems of the three Kingdoms, which form the Parent-State.
>
> The duett, "Home Flowers," though pretty, is not much to our taste; but "The Chorus of Hunters," is a gem. It is a fine spirited burst of feeling, after the German model. The theme is skilfully handled, and the piece is strikingly effective.
>
> The publication, we repeat, does honour to Canada, and will, we trust, be so remunerative to the author, as to induce him ere long again to gratify the public by other strains of that harp, which he touches with so masterly a finger ...

In 1846 Clarke obtained the Bachelor of Music degree from King's College, almost certainly the first to have been granted by a Canadian university. The college had enacted statutes establishing a professorship and degrees in music, paving the way for future developments rather than aiming at immediate implementation.[10] Clarke's exercise was an eight-part setting of the anthem, *Arise, O Lord God, forget not the poor*. In his *Bibliotheca Canadensis* (1867) Henry James Morgan reported its length as forty-six pages, not specifying whether the work was printed or in manuscript. One may wonder with Sir Ernest MacMillan "whether Clarke may have acted as his own examiner for the Baccalaureate" but most likely Dr. McCaul, an amateur pianist and composer, possessed a sound enough training to judge the correctness and merit of the exercise.[11]

Clarke's further association with the College and its successor, the University of Toronto, remains the most puzzling aspect of his biography. The frequently repeated statement that he was an instructor goes hand in hand with the misnomer of the University as "Upper Canada" or "Canadian." Charlesworth's assertion that Clarke was appointed music instructor at King's College in 1845 through McCaul's instrumentality and continued in this office when the University of Toronto came into existence is not borne out by the salary records and staff lists.[12] In 1851 (3 January) the Toronto *Globe* referred to Clarke as "Music Bachelor, and Professor of Music, King's College, Toronto," but since the name of the college was then obsolete, its mention probably merely identified the source of the degree. The title professor was commonly applied to private music teachers. It is known, on the other hand, that for brief periods Clarke taught at the Toronto Normal School (about 1848) and the Toronto Academy, a school for boys (about 1850). One possible explanation of Clarke's association with the University is that he served as an honorary adviser and that he was recommended to students wishing to take private lessons who would pay him directly.

In 1848 the Hon. W.H. Draper presented three special prizes to Clarke, the results of a contest in composition (and other subjects) announced by the president of King's College. Clarke obtained £5 for a trio (possibly "Airy Spirits"), £3 for a duet ("Tell me fair maid") and £1 for a ballad ("I dreamt last night"). Was Clarke also the recipient of the first musical doctorate in Canada? The program for the Commencement on 1 July 1856 listed Clarke as one to receive the degree. On the University Archives copy of the program, however, his name is crossed out with a delete symbol marked against it. Perhaps this meant only that he was unable to attend the ceremony. The *University of Toronto Fasti, from 1850 to 1887* (1887), the Graduate's Register file and, hence, various dictionaries report the degree as a fact. On the other hand, neither the *Annual Report* of the university senate for 1856 with its lists of staff, examiners, salaries, expenses, and degrees conferred, nor its minute book for that year mention the granting of such a degree as a fact or as being contemplated. Further, in none of his newspaper advertisements after 1856 did Clarke identify himself as anything but a Mus.Bac. Towards the end of his life, however, Toronto newspapers spoke of him as "Doctor Clarke" (e.g. *The Leader*, 8 Oct. 1872 as "M.D., Mus.Bac.") and at his death the legend spread that his doctoral degree came from Oxford (death notices in *The Mail*, 30 Aug. 1877 and the *Weekly Globe*, 31 Aug. 1877).[13] Oxford University has no record of Clarke as a student or of his degree.

Whatever the circumstances of the degree, the affair signifies something of a defeat. There had been reverses to his fortune for some years. A Mr. Paige and his daughter appeared in one of Clarke's concerts in 1852 and became so popular with the public that the following year Paige was elected conductor of the Toronto Vocal Music Society in place of Clarke. *The Anglo-American Magazine*, Clarke's staunch supporter, noted in March 1853 "We are quite in the dark as to the why and wherefore the change has been made." Soon after the Society "broke up in consequence of internal dissensions ... Dr. Clarke's friends seceded, and their assistance being indispensible, Mr. Paige was unable to keep the Society in operation."[14] In the spring of that year Clarke applied for a professorship at Trinity College, but the position was given to George William Strathy, whose musical doctorate from Trinity (1858) does not appear to stand in doubt. And in contrast to the flattery and support Clarke received from his *Anglo-American* friends, an anonymous article on "Music and Composers" in *The Daily Leader* (31 May 1854) attacked his songs, calling his output "below mediocrity" and "sadly deficient in both design and originality." The writer argued that the melody of a song must be of merit even if separated from "the meretricious drapery of the accompaniment which, however pleasing, cannot be taken into consideration, or looked upon as affecting the beauty of the theme in any degree whatever ... Clarke and ten thousand others" have failed in this respect. On one hand this view is contradicted by some great songs of Schubert or Schumann, on the other it hardly applies to Clarke whose melodies are supported rather than draped by the piano part. If his melodies are weak, the accompaniment does little to hide the fact. Of his known songs, only "Away to Loch Long," from his Scottish period, gives the piano a more than subsidiary part.

These events seem to signify more than a series of unlucky incidents for they mark the waning of Clarke's star and the beginning of two decades of rarely interrupted obscurity. The man who hitherto had stood in the forefront of local musical life is not known to have published any compositions after 1853 or to have occupied any church or school position. He led only one musical society, for one season. In the 1860s John Carter, organist at St. James's and leader of the Musical Union became the dominant figure. Was Clarke pushed aside by rivals, was his health frail, was he by nature retiring, preferring private teaching to public appearance—or are the documents of his further public career merely missing? All these are possibilities. It is also known that economic recession which began in Toronto in the late 1850s had a negative effect on musical life for over a decade.

For some years Clarke must have been absent from Toronto.[15] In 1861 he advertised that he "resumes his profession in Toronto." He not only took up teaching but together with Carter and Strathy edited *A Selection of Chants and Tunes* for the Diocesan Synod of Toronto (Church of England). In September he directed a special concert at Yorkville Town Hall (followed by a grand ball) to celebrate the opening of the Toronto Street Railway. Toronto's streetcars, it may be remembered, are not only Canada's last but were also its first.

Clarke spent the last dozen or so years of his life in the village of Yorkville, long since absorbed by the city of Toronto. His last address was 5 Gwynne Street, later renamed Park Road, a "musical street" which has been the address for Leo Smith, Healey Willan, Hyman Goodman, Seiji Ozawa and Sir Ernest MacMillan. The city directories identified Clarke as a music teacher or professor of music. Once again, however, he rose to his former position of leadership. After a long lapse a new effort was made to revive the Philharmonic Society in 1872. Once again Dr. McCaul was appointed president and Clarke conductor. Rehearsals began in October for *Messiah* and continued throughout the season. A public rehearsal took place on 15 January 1873 and a Grand Sacred Concert was given at Shaftesbury Hall on 28 February with 160 singers and an orchestra of thirty players before an overflow audience. The orchestra of twenty strings, two flutes, two clarinets, bassoon, French horn, two trumpets and two drums was considered excellent,[16] but in order to get support, the Society had to accept singers without regard to proper qualifications and there were occasional lapses in shading and attack. In view of the circumstances, however, the performance was judged "exceedingly creditable" (*The Mail*, 1 March 1873).

Clarke's first known Toronto performance of an entire oratorio was to remain his last one. His health was failing and the Philharmonic Society continued its work under other conductors. F.H. Torrington in a period of over twenty years made the Philharmonic Toronto's first important and enduring musical society. Clarke's death came suddenly on 27 August 1877 from heart failure, while walking to the breakfast table. He was in his seventieth year. The newspapers brought only short notices of the event. New musical leaders and new institutions put earlier efforts into the shade and Clarke's name was soon forgotten—except by the dictionary editors outside Canada. No stone marks the site of the grave in St. James's Cemetery of Toronto's first outstanding resident musician and Canada's first Bachelor of Music.

There is no doubt that Clarke enjoyed wide respect among his contemporaries. Even as a young man, in Scotland, he "had the reputation of being an excellent musician and vocalist."[17] During the *Messiah* performance he "wielded the *baton* in his usual quiet but effective manner" (*The Mail*, 1 March 1873). The writer of "Music in Toronto" (1878) characterized Clarke as a "conscientious and earnest musician, a clever composer, and an able and successful teacher of the piano forte." Even the derogatory article in *The Daily Leader* (1854) admitted that his musical education was excellent. W.H. Pearson, who had known Clarke since his own (Pearson's) days as a choir boy called him "a musician of considerable eminence" (*Op. cit.*).

Like any other pioneer musician in a colonial country, Clarke had to be versatile. His activities ranged from church services to opera meetings, they included teaching, composing, conducting, singing and playing on keyboard and stringed instruments. He tuned and repaired organs and is said to have "invented an organ with glass tubes which, he held, afforded increased opportunity for tonal variation."[18] In later years he took second violin or viola parts in several short-lived string quartets.

As a piano teacher, at least in Scotland, Clarke had propagated the Logier system, developed by Johann Bernhard Logier (1777–1846) after his establishment in Dublin in 1809. Although the system's mechanical devices for finger training were unsound, its principle of piano group instruction was progressive. Of Clarke's pupils few appear to have made a mark on Toronto's musical life. His most famous pupil was his son Hugh Archibald (1839–1927) who made his debut as a pianist with the Philharmonic Society in 1854 and was trained entirely by his father. As the father was associated with the beginning of the academic recognition of music in Canada, so the son, in Philadelphia since 1859, was appointed a professor of music at the University of Pennsylvania in 1875. It was the earliest such appointment in the United States, coincidental however with that of J.K. Paine at Harvard.[19] Considered an excellent contrapuntist and a devout formalist, Hugh Clarke held his position for the remainder of his long life.

Clarke had at least two other sons, Alexander and James Fullerton, but it appears they left Toronto or died young.[20] When Clarke's widow died in 1881 she left her entire estate, worth $2,200, to her daughter Elizabeth Harriet Fullerton Clarke. The family's talent persisted in another generation, the fourth or fifth of musicians. Hugh's daughter Helen Archibald Clarke (1860–1926) was a composer, poetry scholar and co-editor of the magazine *Poet Lore*.

On first acquaintance Clarke's songs may appear somewhat primitive in their simplicity and faulty in harmony. Familiarity will however reveal that the simplicity is a deliberate one and that printing errors account for some oddities in the harmony. The brief piano postludes to "O could to me" with its Mozartean chromatic inner part and to "The Emigrant's Bride," patterned after the ending of Pamina's G-minor aria in *The Magic Flute,* could not have been written by an untrained backwoods musician. As a songwriter Clarke belonged to a movement anxious to cultivate a national literature and to contribute to it "songs in the popular tone," songs that were meant "for the people" but also intended to charm the educated. Haydn's and Beethoven's harmonizations of Irish, Scottish and Welsh songs were such contributions; in Germany songwriters like Silcher and Zelter pursued similar tendencies. "O cauld to me," first published in Thomas Atkinson's *Western Garland* was chosen for reprint in the music journal *Harmonicon* (December 1832) because it "possesses all the qualities that operate so powerfully in the Caledonian poetry and music of days gone by." Clarke's choice of poems from the *Maple Leaf* shows that he was eager to compose songs that had an immediate appeal and a special meaning to Canadians; in adopting this view and realizing it in so many published songs he was certainly a pioneer. The more attractive of his melodies, such as "Come to the woods" and "The Chopper's song" have a fresh outdoors quality. The sincerity and the clean harmonies of Clarke's unsophisticated songs stand in contrast to the flood of cheap sentimental and pseudo-emotional ballads that began to be produced after 1850. The same contrast between clean simplicity and pretentious poor taste was apparent in the development of Canadian architecture.

Two of Clarke's known compositions stand apart from the remainder.[21] "Away to Loch Long" (published in Atkinson's *Chameleon* in 1833) with its richly varied piano part, its considerable harmonic range and its midway change from 6/8 to 2/4 time is a close approach to a through-composed art song. The other work is the *Favorite Toronto Air, arranged as a Rondo*, dedicated to Mrs. John McCaul, Clarke's only rediscovered instrumental composition. A jolly piano piece, its main theme (probably Clarke's own despite the title) appears to be modelled on the rhythm of the opening theme of the last movement of Schubert's Piano Sonata, Op. 53 [for a musical excerpt, see page 152]. The style of the Rondo is that of the early nineteenth century, pre-Mendelssohn and pre-Chopin.

Many details of Clarke's life remain to be clarified and discovered. The author of "Music in Toronto" (1878) asserted that "During the latter portion of his career he composed a number of chamber trios and quartettes of an original and pleasing character, and constructed on the best classical models." Perhaps the term "chamber" is applied here to vocal music; yet Clarke's participation in string quartets suggests that an eager researcher of the future may discover yet another "first" for Clarke: Canada's pioneer composer of sonata-form instrumental music. Let us resurrect some of Clarke's vocal music in publication and performance; let us keep up the search for more of his music.

NOTES

1 Clarke appears only in certain editions of *Grove's* and *Riemann's*; in some works he is found under the name of his son Hugh Archibald. According to the Canadian Music Library Association's *A Bio-Bibliographical Finding List of Canadian Musicians* (Ottawa, 1961) which shows in which dictionary or reference book information about some 2,000 individuals may be found, Clarke is among the forty with the most frequent coverage. Of course, this is not an accurate yardstick for measuring fame, for obviously the earlier musicians have found their way into more books than those of the present generation. In order of frequency of entry the list is headed by Mme Albani, Sir Ernest MacMillan, Gena Branscombe, A.S. Vogt, Healey Willan, Boris Hambourg and Calixa Lavallée.
2 In fairness it must be pointed out that the 1965 supplement, edited by Nicolas Slonimsky, has corrected the errors, following the author's suggestions.
3 The quotation is from "Music in Toronto," *The Mail, Supplement,* Toronto, 21 December 1878. [*Ed.*]
4 The author owes a debt of gratitude to Mr. David John Sale and Dr. Carl Morey and their research into Toronto musical history and to University of Toronto Archivist Miss E. Harlow, Professor Humphrey Milnes of the University College Archives and Col. Crawford Grier of the Office of Statistics and Records, University of Toronto.
5 A copy of the first edition (about 1830) has not been traced. The volume includes "Lessons in the Art of Singing" and was compiled in order to have "in one book, of convenient size, all the tunes usually sung in that church."
6 Clarke's dedication of his song "A Forest Home" in 1852 to Dr. Mutch of Fergus, close to Elora, provides one clue. Another is the name Gilkison, found in early Elora, which was the name of his colleague and predecessor at St. James's Cathedral. Several Gilkisons of Elora are buried close to Clarke. Finally, the identification of Hugh Clarke's birthplace (1839) in some books as "near Toronto" suggests that Clarke lived in a small town or village during his first years in Canada.
7 David John Sale in his invaluable dissertation "Toronto's Pre-Confederation Music Societies 1845–1867" (MA, University of Toronto, 1968) could not find a conductor's name in contemporary newspapers. He discovered that a chorus and orchestra of 100 to 150 amateurs and professionals from Toronto, Hamilton, Niagara, and other nearby localities participated on 25 June. However, W.H. Pearson recalls in his *Recollections and Records of Toronto of Old* (1914) that he participated as a choir boy under J.P. Clarke.
8 St. Michael's Cathedral, *Memorandum Book for His Lordship,* entry for 30 January 1852; reported by Dr. Carl Morey.
9 The only known rival in length is Clarke's anthem to be discussed in the next paragraph.

10 See J. George Hodgins [ed.], *Documentary History of Education in Upper Canada*, vol. V, Toronto, 1897, pp. 145, 147.
11 Sir Ernest MacMillan's speech at the opening of the Edward Johnson Building, University of Toronto, 2 March 1964. Manuscript.
12 Hector Charlesworth, *More Candid Chronicles* (1928), p. 52. He had been asked by the dean of the Faculty of Music to investigate the musical history of the University of Toronto and reported his findings first in the *Conservatory Quarterly Review* of November 1924, without supplying documentation. His description of Clarke in the 1940 supplement to *Grove's Dictionary* as head of the musical faculty appears to be pure guesswork.
13 Hugh Clarke seems to have contributed to this legend, as his biographer Mahoney [John D. Mahoney, "Dr. Hugh A. Clarke, Musician," *General Magazine and Historical Chronicle,* Philadelphia, 48 (April 1941)] found it mentioned in a statement in Hugh's handwriting. A well-known musician, Hugh would also appear the logical source of the misinformation found in the early editions of *Baker's Biographical Dictionary.*
14 "Music in Toronto," *The Mail, Supplement,* Toronto, 21 Dec. 1878.
15 David John Sale, *Op. cit.*, did not find Clarke's name in connection with concerts in the years 1855 to 1860. While there are no city directories for 1857 and 1858, the ones for 1859 to 1861 do not list him. Strangely enough, Hugh Clarke did participate in musical societies in 1858 and 1859, the year of his departure for Philadelphia.
16 The instrumentation listed suggests that *Messiah* was performed in the arrangement by W.A. Mozart. [*Ed.*]
17 James Love, *Scottish Church Music, Its Composers and Sources* (Edinburgh & London, 1891), p. 320.
18 Mahoney, "Dr. Hugh A. Clarke."
19 Mary Jane Corry reported in the *Institute for Studies in American Music Newsletter* 14/2 (May 1985), 4, that the title of first professor of music at an American university should rightfully go to neither Paine nor Clarke, but rather to Edward Wiebé, who was appointed as Professor of Music at Vassar College in 1865. [*Ed.*]
20 A.H. Young, *Roll of Pupils of Upper Canada College, 1830–1916* (Kingston, 1917). Both sons enrolled at the school in 1846.
21 A number of British publications of dance music by J.P. Clarke, listed in Pazdirek's *Universal-Handbuch der Musikliteratur* [1904–1910] are most probably from the pen of James Power Clarke (1816–1889), a British bandmaster. In his dissertation D.J. Sale identifies J. Clarke as the composer and performer of the song "The Maid of Llangollen" in a Toronto concert of 20 February 1846, conducted by J.P. Clarke, but in his *Musical Biography* (1883) David Baptie ascribes this song to London-born James Clarke (1793–1859).

8
The Music Division of the National Library: The First Five Years

This article may be the most outdated item in this book. In HK's first five years as chief of the Music Division, library routine and methods had not yet been transformed by technology, as was to happen in the following couple of decades. HK here speaks of card catalogues, study and retrieval space—concepts which a generation later had either been abandoned or unrecognizably changed. The document is, however, significant as evidence of the principles which characterized the Division at its inception and the strengths of its holdings in the early stages. The number of archival collections of noted musicians expanded greatly in the 1980s and 1990s; by 2007 there were well over 300. HK had placed special emphasis on these, for example by organizing public exhibitions of the Willan, Contant, MacMillan, and Gould papers, and writing introductions to their printed catalogues. Expansion in other areas was no less remarkable (see page 86, note 3). This résumé has a downside: since 2004, when the National Library and Public Archives merged to become Library and Archives Canada, there is no longer a distinct Music Division with its own chief. A large part of the collection no longer occupies its former space in the Wellington Street building, having been dispersed in 2006 to storage several kilometres away in Gatineau. In 2012 there were disturbing suggestions that funding cutbacks would prevent future acquisitions of archival materials. HK's article remains as the "map" of what he and his colleagues thought the Division ought to be.

The Canada Music Book / Les Cahiers canadiens de musique 10 (Spring/Summer 1975), 95–100

National libraries commonly contain the largest, if not always the oldest, collections of printed materials in their respective countries. The National Library of Canada is an exception on both counts. Established as recently as 1953, and without permanent quarters until 1967, it has not attempted to surpass, or even equal, the holdings of long-established libraries in Toronto, Montreal, and other cities. Aware of its national function, it has always emphasized services—for example, the locating of books through a national union catalogue, the publishing of the current national bibliography, *Canadiana*, the exchange of surplus library stock, as well as the traditional readers' and reference services. However, it does have an excellent collection of reference books and of Canadiana. It receives current Canadian publications on legal deposit (musical scores since 1953 and sound recordings since 1969), and at the same time a retrospective Canadian collection has been built up.

The Foundations

From the beginning, the Music Division has formed part of the Library's Reference (now renamed Public Services) Branch. Opened in April 1970, it was the first division to be devoted to a special subject rather than a type of service or material. At that time, however, the Library already owned a substantial music collection or, more precisely, a number of separate collections of various origins. There were several thousand pieces of sheet music, deposited by Canadian publishers in the late nineteenth and early twentieth centuries for copyright purposes and transferred to the National Library by other government departments. There were the current materials, dating from the early 1950s. A collection of vocal scores, mostly published in nineteenth-century France, had been moved from the Library of Parliament.

By far the largest and most basic component of the music collection was the library of Percy Scholes, the British scholar, which had been purchased in 1957. An excellent basic all-round collection, it was strong in reference and biographical works but also included important sets of periodicals and complete editions. One unique feature was some 500,000 pieces of vertical file material—clippings, leaflets, pictures, correspondence, etc.—on all branches of music. With the purchase of the Scholes collection, there also began a policy of volume-by-volume selection of important new non-Canadian publications, to keep the collection up-to-date.

The Music Division of the National Library: The First Five Years

In 1967, the British Government presented a collection of books to the National Library that included many British music publications. In the same year, a collection of sound recordings of Canadian interest (containing over 3,500 discs), assembled by Edward B. Moogk with the assistance of a Centennial Commission grant, was placed in the National Library. Two years later, a French collection of nearly 20,000 sheet music covers (and, in many cases, entire publications) was acquired. And last but not least, the collection of the distinguished British-born Canadian composer Healey Willan (1880–1968) was acquired in 1969, embracing many of his manuscripts, printed works, his personal library, papers, and memorabilia. The significance of this acquisition went beyond the intrinsic value of the Willan papers: it affirmed public responsibility for the preservation of the historical documents of Canada's composed music, a principle that had been applied for many decades to folk music and to other arts. The principle has become a guiding aim for the Music Division that was to be established several months later.

Five Years of Growth

Imagine yourself facing such diverse collections, spread over five floors and more than five rooms of a large building. Only a small part of the holdings is fully catalogued. Then imagine yourself trying to organize a new division with the help of a single clerical assistant. My first impulse was to publicize the collection and tell the musical community—in articles, circular letters, or by addressing meetings—about this rich accumulation of music, virtually unknown and unsuspected, abounding in both Canadian and foreign materials that were not to be found anywhere else in Canada. Desirable though this was, it would have been unwise. While public utilization and enjoyment of the collection are the ultimate, and really the only, aims of all staff efforts, to have opened the doors too wide before setting up shop properly would have been to invite chaos. These then were the tasks for the first few years: to organize the collection, to select and train staff, to establish collecting policies, and to ensure the growth of the collection. Although publicity took a back seat, being restricted largely to word-of-mouth and the occasional newspaper or broadcast interview and lecture, the number of inquiries has tripled from 1970–71 to 1974–75.

Organizing the collection meant to unite the different components in one area of the building and to make the collection accessible through catalogues and other finding aids. A separate area was assigned to the Music Division in 1972, consisting of a combined office and reading area, a stockroom, a recorded-sound listening room and, a short distance away, a piano room. The transfer of materials was completed in 1975 with the move of all music periodicals to the Division. A duplicate card catalogue is being established, saving time-consuming trips to the Library's main catalogue. While cataloguing is done by the Library's Cataloguing Branch, the Music Division has developed a number of supplementary finding aids, including a brief listing of sound recordings (many of which have yet to be catalogued in detail) and a set of "data sheets" for Canadian music publications to 1950; these "data sheets" also serve as a sort of national union catalogue. Vertical files, containing articles and clippings, pictures of musical interest, and concert programmes, are self-indexing. Although there are considerable cataloguing backlogs, no materials are "packed away": most uncatalogued or uncataloguable items can be retrieved by the staff within minutes.

The staff of the Music Division has grown from two in the first year to six. It includes specialists in the three main areas: Edward B. Moogk, the foremost authority on the history of Canadian recorded sound, as head of the Recorded Sound Collection, Maria Calderisi, one of the very few Canadians with both music and music librarianship degrees, whose area is the printed collection and general reference service, and Dr. Stephen Willis, a musicologist, who takes care of the collections of manuscripts and papers of Canadian musicians and musical organizations.

The many separate components that made up the musical holdings in 1970 were not nearly as heterogeneous as it appeared at first glimpse. Canadian materials were represented without discrimination, there was strength in books and scores from Great Britain and France, and there was a fair sampling of the basic literature of the rest of the world. This indeed became the guiding acquisition policy. The main emphasis is on Canadian materials, the only area in which sound recordings and manuscripts are collected. The area of "selective concentration" has been enlarged to include our neighbour, the United States, and the mother countries of other large ethnic groups in Canada. In other fields, the Library depends largely on gifts. Thus, it was possible to fill certain glaring gaps in the music of Beethoven, Brahms, or Mahler through the donation, in 1974, of the library of the late conductor Heinz Unger. There are certain exceptions to this three-tier approach. Strength is sought in basic reference works: dictionaries, bibliographies, thematic catalogues, and the like, while rare or expensive items are sometimes bought to supplement the resources of other Canadian libraries. Besides, the Music Division may acquire private collections of sometimes highly specialized materials with a view to preserving them for the use of the Canadian public, especially if there is a danger that they may become scattered or sold to a buyer in another country. These and other collections (or single items) are frequently donated to the National Library as Gifts to the Crown (tax deductible).

From the beginning, the Division's acquisition policy paid special attention to materials that quickly disappear from circulation: concert programs, artists' publicity folders, conservatory and music faculty syllabi, and yearbooks, as well as second-hand Canadiana that turn up at auction and rummage sales and antiquarian stores. Above all, attention was given to collections of Canadian composers. The Willan papers were followed by those of Alexis Contant, Hector Gratton, Claude Champagne, Leo Smith, and several others. The oldest manuscripts acquired are three pieces by the French immigrant Charles Wugk Sabatier (1819–62). Parts of the papers of Murray Adaskin, S.C. Eckhardt-Gramatté, and Arnold Walter have also been deposited.

In addition to the basic tasks of organizing, policy formulating, staff training, and collecting, two major exhibitions were organized in the National Library's exhibit hall, and in conjunction with each a book was published. At the time of the exhibition "Healey Willan—the man and his music" (1972), a *Healey Willan Catalogue* by Giles Bryant appeared in print. And to coincide with the opening of the exhibition "85 years of Canadian recorded sound" (1975) a history of Canadian sound recordings to 1930, by Edward B. Moogk, entitled *Roll Back the Years (En remontant les années)* was issued.

The Collection Today

In brief, the functions of the Music Division are: 1) to provide a reference and referral service on all aspects of music to individuals and institutions across Canada (and, to some extent, abroad); 2) to aid in the preservation of Canada's cultural heritage in the special fields of art and popular music (ethnomusicology being the preserve of the National Museum of Man);[1] 3) to act as a resource centre for studies in Canadian music and its history; 4) to stimulate an awareness of Canada's musical past through publications and exhibitions; 5) to survey and, where possible, coordinate and supplement the resources of other Canadian music libraries; and 6) to maintain liaison with music library organizations and coordinate Canadian participation in certain international projects, such as RISM or RIdIM.[2] It should be emphasized that not all of these functions have been assumed to their full extent; a survey of music library resources, for example, is not slated until 1976 or 1977.

An idea of the size of the collection is best obtained by a few statistics. In December 1974, the Canadian collection included approximately:

Scores (printed volumes or sheet music): 12,000
Song and hymn books: 250
Books: 80
Pamphlets: 500
Periodicals (current): 30
Periodicals (no longer issued; complete or incomplete sets): 75
Sound recordings (discs, cylinders, tapes, master discs, piano rolls): 20,000
Programs: 13,000
Picture files: 900
Information files (biography, organizations, subjects): 5,000
Manuscripts and papers (in linear feet): 90

The international collection included:

Scores (printed and catalogued): 3,000
Scores (mostly uncatalogued sheet music): 36,000
Books: 8,000
Pamphlets: 1,000
Periodicals (current): 100
Periodicals (no longer issued or subscribed to; complete or incomplete sets): 180
Programs: 3,200
Picture files: 3,000
Information files (biography, organizations, subjects): 4,000[3]

A detailed description of the collection is beyond the scope of this sketch, but a few highlights may be pointed out. The collection of early Canadiana begins with *Extrait du processional romain* (1819) and includes the first music printed in a magazine (*Literary Garland*, 1838) and as separate sheet music (1840). Treasures of later years include the first edition of

The Music Division of the National Library: The First Five Years

"The Maple Leaf For Ever," inscribed by its author, Alexander Muir; some thirty different editions of "O Canada"; and autograph letters by Calixa Lavallée and Mme Emma Albani (as well as the first biography of the prima donna, written by Napoléon Legendre in 1874). The collections of Canadian sheet music, Canadian music periodicals, and recordings of Canadian interest are the largest of their kind. The records include a rendition of "God Save the King" made in Montreal two weeks after Queen Victoria's death, a recording made in 1925 from a radio broadcast of a Montreal church service, the first recorded sounds of the Peace Tower Carillon in Ottawa (1 July 1927), and the earliest Canadian long-playing discs. The complete or near-complete recorded repertoires of Edward Johnson, Jeanne Gordon, Christie MacDonald, the Hart House String Quartet, the Toronto Mendelssohn Choir, and other performers are represented.

The international collection of music comprises historical sets and monuments such as the *Corpus Mensurabilis Musicae, Denkmäler der Tonkunst in Österreich, Denkmäler Deutscher Tonkunst, Old English Edition, Musica Britannica, Early English Church Music* and others; collected works of individual composers such as Bach (both editions), Beethoven, Berlioz, Byrd, Chopin, Cornelius, Couperin, Gluck, Handel, Haydn, Liszt, Lully, Mahler, Mendelssohn, Monteverdi, Mozart (both editions), Palestrina, Purcell, Schoenberg, Schubert (both editions), Schütz, Schumann, Sweelinck and Vivaldi.

The following early publications, to mention only two, were among the treasures coming with the Scholes collection: *Les pseaumes de David, mis en rime françoise par Clément Marot & Théodore de Bèze* ... (Lyon, 1563) and *The whole book of Psalms with the Hymns ... newly corrected and enlarged by Tho. Ravenscroft* (London, 1633).

The Scholes collection also included original editions of dictionaries or histories by Rousseau, Burney, Hawkins, Rameau and Forkel, and volumes of such nineteenth-century periodicals as *The Quarterly Musical Magazine* (1818–29), *The Harmonicon* (1823–33), and *The Musical World* (1836–50, 1869–74). The Music Division also owns a nearly complete set of the *Revue et Gazette Musicale de Paris* (1835, 1838–48, 1851–80).

Scholes' information files with their half-million items are of unique value in documenting musical thought and musical events in the early twentieth century. They formed the basis for his compilation of the *Oxford Companion to Music* (their headings correspond closely to the entries in the *Companion*), and are still being added to, although at a slower rate.

The Future

There is a list of several dozen "projects to be undertaken" in the Music Division. These include the rerecording of early Canadian recordings and the microphotography of rare Canadian music journals; the preparation of an "O Canada" bibliography; and the acquisition, by microfilming, of rare musical Canadiana existing in other (often foreign) libraries. How many of these projects can be realized, and how soon, depends on the staff and the funds available. It also depends on the wishes expressed by the music scholars, the librarians, and the Canadian public at large. It is our sincere hope that the present sketch will encourage music lovers to make use of the national collection, through correspondence, visit, telephone, or telex, and help the staff to plan for the Music Division's second five-year period.

NOTES

1. The National Museum of Man was renamed the Canadian Museum of Civilization in 1986 and moved to new premises in Gatineau in 1989. [*Ed.*]
2. RISM = Répertoire international de sources musicales; RidIM = Répertoire international d'iconographie musicale. For the first of these two international bibliographic organizations, HK had been the Canadian contact for over twenty years. [*Ed.*]
3. For comparison, figures for 1991 and for 2007 illustrate the growth of the collection. These statistics are for the collection as a whole—that is, they are not divided into Canadian and non-Canadian items. The archival items are virtually all Canadian. 1991: 13,000 books; 11,000 printed scores; 45,000 pieces of sheet music; 1,600 periodical volumes; 62,000 concert programs; 12,600 information files; 25,000 iconographic items; 120,000 sound recordings; and nearly 300 archival collections; 2007: 22,750 books; 21,700 printed scores; 61,000 pieces of sheet music; 2,000 periodical volumes; 90,000 concert programs; 13,000 information files; 30,000 iconographic items; 310,000 sound and video recordings; and 320 archival collections. The staff complement of six in 1975 grew to eight by the time of HK's retirement, and to thirteen by 2004, the date of the Library–Archives merger; there were additional contract staff as well, and about ten cataloguers for music and sound recordings. (Sources: *Encyclopedia of Music in Canada*; *Music Directory Canada*; staff, Library and Archives Canada.) [*Ed.*]

9
The Canadian League of Composers in the 1950s: The Heroic Years

Before music can be studied or performed it must be created, which means, in the European cultures HK grew up in and knew, it must be *composed*. This principle underlies much of HK's musical effort and writing. His first book-length project was a catalogue of composers, and in the formative years of the Canadian League of Composers he acted as voluntary archivist, attended League concerts, and photographed League annual meetings. The symposium Canadian Music of the 1950s, held in October 1983 at the Faculty of Music, University of Western Ontario, featured not only analytical commentary on works by Weinzweig, Papineau-Couture, Somers, and Pentland, and historical-perspective views by George Proctor (UWO, organizer of the event) and Maryvonne Kendergi (Université de Montréal), but also HK's account of the League's foundation in 1951 and early successes. He speculates about the CLC's "mathematically" burgeoning membership: although no longer "the one organization of creative people" in music in Canada, it remains the largest; the membership in 2012 is more than double that of 1983. He ends his survey with "subjective reflections" of a sympathetic and musically educated listener. John Weinzweig, founding president of the CLC and a longtime friend, objected to these closing remarks in a letter to HK dated 24 February 1985.[1] Published in an issue of *Studies in Music from the University of Western Ontario* devoted to the symposium proceedings, HK's article was reprinted in slightly abridged form in *Célébration*, ed. Godfrey Ridout and Talivaldis Kenins (Toronto: Canadian Music Centre, 1984), 99–107.

Studies in Music from the University of Western Ontario 9 (1984), 37–54; republished by permission of the Don Wright Faculty of Music of The University of Western Ontario

In this talk I should like to examine the conditions which created the Canadian League of Composers, to review its activities and achievements during its first and most decisive decade, and finally to muse on its aspirations and ambitions from the vantage point of the 1980s. The obvious starting point for a historical account is a precise date, but here we face a curious hurdle. To be sure, Samuel Dolin, Harry Somers and John Weinzweig met at the last-named's home on 3 February 1951 and agreed to form a professional organization of composers, but the founding meeting took place, so the Minute Book tells us, on "Saturday, February 30, 1951, 2 p.m." at 101 Belgravia, Toronto, Weinzweig's address at that time. These handwritten minutes obviously were transferred from loose notepaper when a proper notebook was purchased some days after the meeting and the date recalled from memory. 1951 was not even a leap year and the closest Saturdays would have been February 24 and March 3.[2] Take your pick, for none of the seven persons present at the founding of the League (an eighth, Louis Applebaum, was invited but could not attend) has kept a diary. But the names matter more than the precise date: Murray Adaskin, Samuel Dolin, Harry Freedman, Phil Nimmons, Harry Somers, Andrew Twa, and John Weinzweig.

Whatever mystery surrounds the date, the reasons for the League's coming into existence are plain. It was the moment of intersection of three lines of development: composers' organizations on a world scale, maturing of the arts in Canada, and an organizing fever among Canadian artists. Let me examine these developments in turn.

I have not been able to find a ready-made history of composers' organizations, but their beginning may well antedate the Canadian League of Composers (hereafter referred to as CLC or League) by exactly 100 years. The *Société des auteurs, compositeurs et éditeurs de musique*, founded in France in 1851, represents one of three main types of composers' groups, the one for the protection of legal interests, such as copyright and various forms of licensing. Such organizations more often are run for than by composers, although Richard Strauss was active in setting up the German one at the turn of the century. Canada formed its Canadian Performing Rights Society in 1925 (CAPAC since 1945) and BMI Canada in 1940 (reorganized as PRO Canada in 1977), hence the CLC had no need to enter the performing rights field directly.[3]

The Canadian League of Composers in the 1950s

History offers several examples of composers drawn together by a common aesthetic outlook or sense of historical mission, often documented in manifestoes and credos. It might be farfetched to cite the Camerata Florentina of the 1580s as an example, but the Russian Five of about 1875 with their goal of a national school of composers and Les Six in France early in our own century easily spring to mind. The founders of the League agreed at the outset that they would not promote specific trends of style or technique, "Canadian" or international. They opted for a third kind of society, the one dedicated to the promotion of performance, publication, audience education and critical response. What models were there to follow? Eighty years earlier, in 1871, the *Société nationale de musique* had been formed in Paris to perform music by living composers. (Interesting to note, the *Société* provided a hearing in 1875 to an orchestral *Rêverie* by a young student from Canada, Guillaume Couture, and presumably had a hand in its publication, the first printed orchestral score by a Canadian.) The *Verein für musikalische Privataufführungen*, directed in Vienna by Schoenberg, Berg and Webern from 1918 to 1921, had a well-defined focus on avant-garde music. Probably the most important organization of its kind—because it has been international (but with national sections) from the start and because it still exists—is the International Society for Contemporary Music, which grew out of a festival held in Salzburg in the summer of 1922.[4] Of more immediate importance as potential models for the CLC, among similar organizations that had emerged in many countries by 1951, were the Composers' Guild of Great Britain (1944) and above all, the League of Composers of the United States (1923). During his studies in Rochester, NY, from 1937 to 1938, John Weinzweig had received much inspiration from the US League's magazine *Modern Music*. Throughout the following decade he closely observed the strengths and weaknesses of the League, since he and his fellow-composer and friend Applebaum often chatted about the need for a society of Canadian composers. Weinzweig concluded that the US League suffered from having too broad a base and too little internal communication. This lesson may explain in part the relatively narrow base of the CLC in its early years.

Even in Canada there had been earlier organizations for promoting composition. The Canadian Society of Musicians—essentially an Ontario organization—took composition seriously. In 1886 its members submitted compositions to a contest, using pseudonyms. Many years later, in 1936 the Vogt Society was organized in Toronto in memory of the late dean of the Faculty of Music and principal of the Toronto Conservatory. It later changed its name to Society for Contemporary Music and came to an end in 1945, but in those years it did manage to promote performances and publications of Canadian works. Its last president, Arnold Walter, was also involved in an ill-fated attempt, late in the 1940s, to establish a Canadian section of the ISCM.

But if the League had Canadian models, they were hardly the above. World War Two was over and pride in Canada's war effort spilled over into pride of Canadian achievement in the arts and sciences, and was linked with a keen social consciousness. Everyone not only dreamt of a great future but got busy building this future. In music that meant schemes for festivals, for opera, for advanced education, for an invigorated school music program, for recordings of Canadian music and a dozen other marvellous developments. One way to go about these plans was that of group-action by persons pursuing similar goals. People in all the arts became organization-conscious. Before the war it had been principally the organists (1909), the bandmasters (1931) and the registered (i.e., private) music teachers (1935) who had formed national organizations, not to forget the American Federation of Musicians, the trade union which has operated in both Canada and the USA since 1901. At the end of the war two umbrella organizations of national scope took care of musicians' broad interests: the Canadian Arts Council (1945, Canadian Conference of the Arts since 1958) for all the arts, and the Canadian Music Council (1945 but instituted in 1944 as a "music committee").[5] The associations of music publishers and competition festival organizers and the Jeunesses Musicales du Canada (all 1949) predate the League while organizations for school music educators, folk music collectors, and music librarians were among those set up later in the 1950s.

The years after the war also saw great strides in the performance and promotion of Canadian music. Dr. George Proctor in his paper "Canadian Music from 1920 to 1945: The End of the Beginning," delivered earlier this morning, has provided a historical perspective to this question, so I shall refrain from mentioning earlier instances.[6] The foremost promoter was the CBC which not only performed much of what was written at the time, but had requested it, and which led the way in selling recordings of Canadian music (beginning with a Willan and Champagne album in 1944) and cataloguing Canadian compositions (1947, 1952).[7] It also provided a forum for critical discussion. CAPAC introduced scholarships for young composers and BMI Canada a busy publishing program. "All-Canadian" concerts, not only at home but in Prague and Budapest, were occasions of patriotic pride. Publicity writers found it exciting to prove that Canada had composers writing in a contemporary style—right here in our midst! Some of these composers, Papineau-Couture, Pentland and Weinzweig among them, were engaged by music schools to teach theory and composition. All this hustle and bustle culminated in the First Symposium of Canadian Contemporary Music, a four-day event in Vancouver in May 1950 at which the music of no fewer than thirty-three composers was heard. The principal organizers of the Symposium, Jacques Singer and Alex Walton, were not composers themselves; no matter how much such people helped, there were certain things required that could be done only by composers themselves. That is why the League had to be founded.

The fact is that, despite this wave of receptiveness, most of the younger composers (the birth dates of the first group of CLC members ranged from 1906 to 1927) felt frustrated. Promoting performances and publication of one's own music was a solitary act, dependent on the degree of one's aggressiveness. Unless the composer was a performer or conductor, he or she had to knock at the door of every virtuoso and every radio producer to sell his or her work (something that will and should always remain a supplementary method of promotion). Copying parts and scores was time-consuming and expensive and few publishers wanted to risk printing a modern work by an unknown author. By contrast, countries with an established tradition of composition and larger populations had a powerful apparatus for the publishing, recording and marketing of their music (e.g., Universal Edition, B. Schott's Söhne or G. Schirmer), including a small army of touring artists who promoted their national repertoires of modern music along with the classics but took no trouble exploring the music of the countries they visited.

However, the ultimate reason for dissatisfaction among composers was not material; it had to do with a generation gap between them and the older composers as well as the concert hall audience of the day. The few universities that offered music courses taught theory and composition according to time-honoured academic rules and models and showed little interest in twentieth-century developments. Composition was discouraged except as a pastime, not only for material reasons, but because of a belief that everything worth saying in music had already been said. Conductors, even if they held more progressive views, were still busy teaching their players and audiences Bach and Brahms (though notable exceptions could be cited). Hence audiences had little exposure to contemporary idioms. And the first time Canadian composition burst upon the audience with any frequency it was music in those contemporary idioms. The equation, Canadian music is modern music (and of course modern music is dissonant!) was thus ingrained in audiences and accounts for much of the reluctance to accept our composers. (A concert of United States music might have included MacDowell, Sousa, or Gershwin along with Sessions and Carter; a Canadian concert would feature little that was written before 1940.) The Canadian situation was discouraging indeed. Weinzweig summed it up in a discussion at the Vancouver symposium when he said: "Canadian composers have the distinction of being the most unpublished, unheard and unpaid composers in the world."[8]

The new generation of its day was no longer willing to accept the restrictions that had stifled creative musicians for so long and it realized it had to fight its battle itself. That meeting on "February 30" 1951 stated the following objectives:

1 Protection of composers—clarification of collection of royalties, performance fees and rentals.
2 Promotion of Canadian music in Canada and abroad.
3 Publicity—acquainting public with Canadian composers and their music.
4 Encouragement of young Canadian composers.

The membership policy made it clear from the beginning that the League had a very specific kind of composer in mind: it wanted to put the professional musician who devotes his prime energies to creating concert music on the cultural map of Canada. The organization was not to include the many part-time composers, no matter how competent, whose entire output consisted of piano pieces for children, band marches, church anthems and the like. Instead, members were expected to have produced a modicum of substantial works that had been performed in concert (or on film). The first members were recruited by invitation. To the Weinzweig pupils present on "February 30" and the *in absentia* founder Applebaum soon were added Oskar Morawetz and Godfrey Ridout from Toronto, Alexander Brott and Jean Papineau-Couture from Montreal, Maurice Blackburn, Robert Fleming, Kenneth Peacock and Eldon Rathburn from Ottawa, Lorne Betts from Hamilton, Walter Kaufmann from Winnipeg, and Jean Coulthard from Vancouver, as well as two composers studying in Paris, John Beckwith and Clermont Pépin. Other early members were Violet Archer and Barbara Pentland. Newcomers to Canada were admitted readily, among them István Anhalt and Udo Kasemets.

That membership was heavily concentrated in Toronto and Montreal merely reflected the fact that composers were attracted by the employment opportunities of the CBC production centres and the teaching institutions in these cities. That Toronto took the lead and remained the executive seat for a long time reflects the reputation that Weinzweig had gained as a teacher of composers and the initiative he had taken. He held the term of president from 1951 until 1957 and again from 1959 until 1963. There was less contact between individual composers in Montreal and it took longer to build the membership. Jean Papineau-Couture did much to develop the League and its activities in Montreal, and served as president from 1957 until 1959 and from 1963 until 1966. Both men deserve rich credit for their work on behalf of Canadian composers in those years and ever since, and there are many others—secretaries, treasurers and the more recent presidents—who have worked hard to further the cause of their profession.

A somewhat controversial aspect of the CLC in its early years was the policy regarding age. In 1953 it was decided to set an age limit of sixty years [for members]. This was designed not only to reject applicants over that age but to change the status of existing members from voting to honorary [on reaching sixty]. When the first Montreal concert was announced to take place on 3 February 1953, Wilfrid Pelletier wrote to Weinzweig (1 February) to express his disappointment at not seeing Claude Champagne's name on the program. Pelletier had been told that Champagne's age (62) disqualified him from membership. He commented, "If the League was called the Canadian League of Young Composers I would understand." In his reply (5 March; both letters are in the CLC Collection at the National Library of Canada) Weinzweig stated that the age limit had been imposed "in an effort to prevent the league from becoming a static organization—a fate that has befallen many artistic groups. ... I hope when the time comes, the present members will retire gracefully with their creative abilities unimpaired." As a gesture of reconciliation both Champagne and Healey Willan, who had taught theory to countless students and had distinguished themselves as composers, were made honorary members in 1955. It appears also that by the time the oldest regular members reached the age of sixty, the rule had been rescinded. The truth of the whole matter, I believe, is the old one of rebellion against the father figures who as a group (and Champagne hardly was typical) were seen by many of the League's members to have been responsible for keeping contemporary music out of the classroom and concert hall. Fair or not, fighting spirit is born out of such rebellions.[9]

By the end of the 1950s membership stood at about forty. By then membership applicants had to submit a certain number of scores which were examined by a committee of composers. There had to be evidence of performances and of current activity in composition. If the committee's vote were split, the whole membership was asked to vote on the application. Fair enough, but it seems a pity that certain highly gifted composers whose productivity may not have been high at the time—men like Keith Bissell or Marvin Duchow—either did not want to join or were not admitted to the ranks.

Next in importance to building the membership was the holding of concerts. On 16 May 1951, hardly three months after the founding, Ettore Mazzoleni conducted a concert at the Royal Conservatory of Music which was broadcast by the CBC. It was an all-Weinzweig program. Did the president take undue advantage of his position? Not at all; the concert had been planned as a surprise by some of his friends before the League was formed, but the secret was lifted when it seemed opportune to make the concert the first public event under the auspices of the new organization.

Early in 1952 the League undertook a bold step: with only fifteen dollars in the bank it began to organize an orchestral concert in Massey Hall that would cost about $3,500. As expected, the CBC came to the rescue and I believe the composers broke even. But it became clear that composers were not at their best organizing concerts and so they persuaded their friends with business and organizing skills to form a concert committee which two year later, in 1954, was incorporated as the Canadian Music Associates (Ontario). This efficient organization functioned until 1958, arranging several concerts and film showings each year. It was paralleled in Montreal by *La Société de musique canadienne* (Québec) which organized an annual concert from 1954 until 1968. Altogether in the first fourteen years of its existence the League and its concert arms organized some forty concerts featuring about 200 works. There is no point analysing the contents here, but I should point out one of the highlights: a double bill of two short operas, Blackburn's *Une mesure de silence* and Somers's *The Fool*, presented in Toronto in 1956 and in Montreal in 1959. I should also mention that a few concerts took place in Hamilton and

The Canadian League of Composers in the 1950s

Ottawa. Eventually, however, the all-Canadian concert had outlived its necessity. It was criticized with some justification for feeding the listener with more new music than his ears could absorb in one evening and for combining too much heterogeneous music in order to be fair to as many different composers as possible. By the early sixties more ordinary concerts included Canadian pieces which were thus exposed to a much wider audience. I can confirm from my own memory that the League concerts were heavy with composers' friends, family and other well-wishers, with students and critics, but somewhat deficient in people who came because of a keen interest in contemporary music. But some of the well-wishers must have turned into experts on Canadian music and it would be cynical to deny that the concerts were the main achievement of the League in its early phase.

Hardly less significant was the publication of *Fourteen Piano Pieces by Canadian Composers / Quatorze pièces pour piano de compositeurs canadiens* (Frederick Harris, 1955), a volume with an attractive cover design by Jacques G. de Tonnancour, now unfortunately out of print. I played through the book recently after many years—it takes about forty-five minutes—although Morel's *Étude de sonorités No. 1* with its ten-accidentals chords defies my sight-reading ability. One observation that surprised me was that despite the different styles from neo-classicism to atonality and a sort of conservative modernism, the degree of dissonance now sounds very much the same throughout, with the exception of the first piece, by Robert Fleming, deliberately kept simple for beginners. Whether by Betts or Morawetz, Coulthard or Somers, all pieces seem to belong to their period, though thirty years ago one thought of them as decades apart.

A second League publication was the *Catalogue of Orchestral Music* which was compiled in 1957 and listed some 230 individual works by thirty-five composers (including Champagne and Willan). For each work the year of composition, duration, instrumentation, details of first performance (how often there had not been any!) and, in many cases, brief annotations were provided. The League planned one or several other catalogues of this sort but an event made that superfluous, an event for which the League bore the main responsibility. That was the opening of the Canadian Music Centre.

The League had begun to cooperate with other organizations very early. In November 1953 the chairman of the Canadian Music Council, Sir Ernest MacMillan, invited the League to become a member. And in the same month it affiliated with the International Society for Contemporary

Music. Unfortunately this link lasted only for three years and in those years only one Canadian work was performed under ISCM auspices—Pentland's *String Quartet No. 2* at the thirtieth World Music Festival in Stockholm in June 1956. Apparently the League had to struggle to gain a hearing for even that one work, and the affiliation consumed a large chunk of its finances. The majority of members felt that for the time being building a national image was more important than international exposure. The resulting separation was regrettable and it was not until the mid-70s that Canadian participation resumed.

In 1957 the Canada Council was created; the CLC and the Canadian Music Council had engaged in some effective lobbying for this action. (The League had also made a submission to the "Fowler" Royal Commission on Broadcasting in 1956.)[10] Now the time was ripe for the creation of a separate agency for the promotion and dissemination of Canadian music. Indeed the Canadian Music Centre was due largely to a blueprint drawn up by Weinzweig and Beckwith, submitted to the Canadian Music Council in January 1957 for inclusion in a package of proposals on the needs of music in Canada addressed to the Canada Council in the spring of that year. These proposals are documented in the Spring 1957 issue of the *Canadian Music Journal*; the results are history and the subject of the Centre's twenty-fifth anniversary celebrations in 1984.[11] The League, incidentally, provided more than a blueprint for the new Centre; it deposited its own collection of scores written by its members.

The last big event in the League's first decade was the International Composers' Conference in Stratford, Ontario, 7–14 August 1960. The initiative belonged to Louis Applebaum who was in charge of music at the Stratford Festival, but the CLC assumed a major role in planning the conference. After its unsatisfactory attempt to join the outside music world, it set about bringing that world to Canada. Twenty countries sent composer representatives, including such well-known figures as Luciano Berio, Karl-Birger Blomdahl, Henri Dutilleux, Ernst Krenek and Edgard Varèse. There were concerts—with a heavy emphasis on Canadian music—and there were discussions on a variety of topics, some of which have been reproduced in the book *The Modern Composer and His World* (University of Toronto Press, 1961), edited by Beckwith and Kasemets.

The foregoing pages have sketched what might justly be called the heroic phase of the League—the years of initiative, daring and sacrifice, the years that boosted composers' morale and witnessed an unprecedented growth in Canadian composition. In the years since, the organization has

The Canadian League of Composers in the 1950s

restricted its activities somewhat. Its emphasis has changed from "the promotion of Canadian music to the protection of the composers themselves, of their professional interests." That phrase was aptly coined by Marie Vachon in her 1975 Carleton University M.A. thesis, a "Survey on the Socio-Economic Status of Canadian Composers of Serious Music." For instance, the League has designed model contracts for commissions, publications and the rental of orchestral parts. It has lobbied against cutbacks in CBC serious music programming, it has spoken out on copyright and mechanical rights, and it has assured Canadian representation at international meetings. But I believe the ultimate, though unspoken, goal of an organization of composers should be a negative one—to make itself superfluous! or almost so, for there should be a core group ready to go into action when action is required. Canadian music should be programmed as a matter of course by anyone performing music; young audiences and young students should grow up in the musical idiom of their time without having to make a special effort or seeking teachers abroad.

There is little doubt, looking back in 1983: the battle waged in the 1950s has been won. There is a place in Canada for the professional composer speaking the language of our time. Weinzweig's hope, expressed in 1953, that the music get "off the shelf and where it belongs, in the hands [ears?] of the people" is much closer to fulfillment. If one could travel fast enough one could attend a live performance of Canadian music almost every day. (The choices are not always adventurous and orchestras still favour the short piece rehearsed on previous occasions, or else I would not tune in to so many radio transmissions of Morel's *Esquisse* and *Antiphonie* or Mercure's *Pantomime* and *Kaleidoscope*, competent early works not reflecting their composers' maturity.) The dissemination of Canadian music has increased tremendously, thanks primarily to the Canadian Music Centre, the CBC, many universities, and the Canadian content guidelines imposed by the CRTC and the Canada Council. In 1980 over twenty Canadian organizations specialized in the performance of contemporary music, among them the Société de musique contemporaine du Québec (SMCQ), Days Months and Years to Come of Vancouver, NOVA MUSIC of Halifax and Array of Toronto. It is also safe to estimate that if one could acquire all commercial recordings of Canadian concert music, currently available or out of print, one might come up with 200 hours of music; with the help of a radio-cassette recorder one might be able to tape, within a few years (and of course strictly for personal use!), a library of perhaps

500 hours. Music in notation is freely available from the Centre. It takes a minimum of effort to gain access to Canadian scores, recordings, or live performances.

Scholarships for students and commissions for composers are fairly plentiful (the League itself established a scholarship in 1967): patronage is provided by the Canada Council and other federal and provincial agencies and a few corporate and private foundations. Universities sponsor concerts and employ many fine composers as teachers; full or part-time careers in composition are not rare, although most composers prefer to engage in other musical occupations as well and few derive the major portion of their income from composing.

Publicity and discussion are also more plentiful, even though promotional literature is more frequent than critical analysis, and composers almost never get serious attention in the daily press. *The Music Scene, The Canadian Composer, Musicanada* and other magazines feature articles on composers or recent new works and important performances. The Canadian Music Centre issues a variety of catalogues and publicity material, and new publications and recordings are listed in the National Library's monthly *Canadiana*. Information about composers or reviews of specific genres of composition can be obtained quickly from such reference books as *Contemporary Canadian Composers* (Oxford University Press, 1975), George Proctor's *Canadian Music of the Twentieth Century* (University of Toronto Press, 1980) and the *Encyclopedia of Music in Canada* (University of Toronto Press, 1981).

In all these respects and in others the composers of the 1980s are much better off than were their elders in the 40s and 50s. However it must be recognized that composers today face a different and not altogether advantageous reality, a reality that should be faced by anyone concerned with the encouragement of young composers. I should like to point out three aspects of this reality that appear to me to work against the ideals of the League's founders: overproduction, the weight of the historical heritage, and the problem of memory retention of complex music. It is a mathematical fact that the more orchestras there are and the more of them program Canadian works with some frequency, the more Canadian music the CBC plays and records and the Canadian Music Centre disseminates—the more composers there are wishing to be heard. The League now has some 150 members instead of a few dozen and instead of a near-vacuum there is now a forty-year accumulation of Canadian works with which each new piece has to compete. No wonder that in the individual composer's perception we seem to be standing still: he or she does not seem to get more performances per year than twenty or thirty years ago. The same applies to publicity. Far more is written now, but the impact is weaker. About 1950 every news about a Somers, a Papineau-Couture or a Pentland was exciting news about the emergence at long last of gifted modern composers in our midst, about history in the making. Today we take composers for granted. Having listened to a great amount of Canadian music and having compiled or contributed to quite a few reference books that include Canadian composers, I used to know the lot by face, style and certainly name. Now I must admit that some of the younger members of the League are not even names to me. If the League has over 150 members (and some competent composers still are not members), the USA must have ten times that many, and the world between 5,000 and 10,000. Not only is it mathematically difficult for anyone to become world-famous; we do not seem to live in an age of world-famous figures. Do Boulez, Cage or Stockhausen enjoy remotely the same degree of fame and dissemination that Schoenberg or Stravinsky, Hindemith or Britten did at the same age? (For that matter, where are the Picassos or G.B. Shaws of our time? Is it harder to recognize genius? What are the reasons?)

The unlikely prospect of gaining wide recognition even within Canada should not discourage the young composer, however. On the contrary, if the world of technological unemployment and the age of leisure really are just around the corner, we should stimulate and develop more than ever the creative impulses in each individual. Have not the sages of all times told us that paradise, the world at peace, will be the world of poets, artists and musicians? Creative activity should be supported materially, but its subjective reward should lie in the doing itself and in the effect upon one's immediate environment, and should not depend on the nineteenth-century concept of "fame or failure."

I share with the founders of the League the dream of a happy society in which the music of its own time has the deepest meaning to music lovers and is performed more often than any other. There are indications that audiences have assimilated dissonance: the cry of "cacophony" is no longer rampant and I for one find much of the music of the 1970s and 80s easier to grasp and enjoy than that of the middle of the century. But the "relativity argument," as I call it, that most new music is difficult to grasp and that it becomes easy and beautiful when it has been around long enough, is and always was nothing but a half-truth, as is the argument that the classics are "pushed" by reactionary concert managers because they sell more tickets. The classics sell because they are still the most superb music in the concert repertoire. And for compelling and irreversible historical and technological reasons, the music of other centuries and civilisations is claiming an ever larger share of our attention.

If dissonance or "formlessness" no longer stand in the way of audience appreciation of contemporary music, or at least present less of an obstacle, what then prevents the building of the large audience the League's founders strove to encourage? In closing I should like to hint at a possible explanation based on my own experience, although full discussion would require a separate essay. I believe that most composers have always wished that their music not only be beheld by their audiences in performance but to some extent be absorbed and retained so that the impact would haunt the listener and at least part of the music could be "recollected in tranquillity." For this reason there exists a certain relationship between the complexity of a composition and its method of dissemination and likely frequency of performance. Folksongs and chorale tunes were written for oral transmission and rarely were long and complex. Classical chamber and piano music was written for people who could read music, absorb it through practice, and repeat it at will. Rossini or Verdi operas contained a certain number of hit-tunes so that memorization would last until the next performance a year hence, probably reinforced by the performance of medleys and fantasias. Today endless repetition through recording is possible and, though I do not think that the complexity of composition techniques and electronic sound patterns has arisen *because* of that possibility, nevertheless the composer does not have to consider memory retention. If you like a piece, just play the disc or tape over and over again. While I do not deny that extremely gifted persons can retain and recall music with sliding pitches, superimposed rhythms and other highly complex patterns, as a listener with perhaps more than average experience I still leave the concert hall or the radio broadcast without a sound echoing in my mind—though I may have enjoyed the music. This is not an argument against writing complex music or against "modern" music, because the problem does not apply to much of it and because there are passages in *The Art of Fugue* or Beethoven's late quartets that I find similarly difficult to recall mentally. Nor is it a case of lacking familiarity. It is merely an argument that may explain why audiences fail to establish an intimate relationship with a large body of music of our time, music that does not settle in the inner ear.

I may have strayed a long way from relating the story of the Canadian League of Composers in the 1950s but perhaps these subjective reflections provide some context to the League's early aspirations and their chances of fulfilment. The League continues to be one of our most important musical organizations because it is the one organization of creative people, and I certainly wish it a long and prosperous life.

NOTES

1 See *Weinzweig: Essays on His Life and Music*, ed. John Beckwith and Brian Cherney (Waterloo, ON: Wilfrid Laurier University Press, 2011), 280. Weinzweig had a more limited historical perspective than HK, and he resented the characterization of the "relativity argument" and the conservatism of concert managers as "half truths." [*Ed.*]

2 HK is uncharacteristically in error on this point. The date in the Minute Book is given as 3° Feb. (terzo, i.e. third, of February), which HK has misread as 30 Feb.; February 3rd was indeed a Saturday in 1951. [*Ed.*]

3 CAPAC = Composers, Authors, and Publishers Association of Canada; BMI = Broadcast Music Incorporated (the Canadian branch used only the initials of its US parent organization, being known as "BMI Canada"); PRO = Performing Rights Organization. PRO Canada merged with CAPAC in 1990 to form Society of Composers, Authors and Music Publishers of Canada; see Jan V. Matejcek, *History of BMI Canada Ltd. and PROCAN: Their Role in Canadian Music and in the Formation of SOCAN (1940–1990)* (Toronto: the author, 1995; rev. 2nd ed. 1996). [*Ed.*]

4 *HK's original note*: The author derives pardonable self-satisfaction from the fact that he was born on the historic day the Salzburg festival opened that resulted in the founding of the ISCM. He may thus be regarded as a living clock indicating the age of the organized promotion of contemporary music on an international scale! It adds to his pleasure that a 1924 all-Canadian concert at Hart House, Toronto and the opening of the 1960 International Composers' Conference again coincided with his birthday. [*Ed. note*: the 1924 concert to which HK refers took place on 7 August (HK's second birthday) as part of a conference of the British Association for the Advancement of Science. The works performed included Healey Willan's Piano Trio in B Minor, songs by Willan, Ernest MacMillan, and Leo Smith, a piano solo by Colin McPhee, and the last three movements of MacMillan's String Quartet in C Minor performed by the Hart House String Quartet. The 1960 International Composers' Conference opened on Sunday, 7 August 1960 in Stratford, Ontario; the proceedings were published in John Beckwith and Udo Kasemets, eds., *The Modern Composer and His World* (Toronto: University of Toronto Press, 1961).]

5 The Canadian Music Council, an umbrella organization of music societies, disbanded in 1990; see Ronald Napier, "The Canadian Music Council:

A Brief History," in *Musical Canada: Words and Music Honouring Helmut Kallmann*, ed. John Beckwith and Frederick A. Hall (Toronto: University of Toronto Press, 1988), 262–73. [*Ed.*]

6   The reference is to Proctor's keynote talk at the symposium, which was subsequently published in *Studies in Music from the University of Western Ontario* 9 (1984), 2–26. [*Ed.*]

7   The recording is RCI Canadian Album No. 1/RCA DM 1229 (four 78-rpm discs), featuring a CBC Montreal orchestra conducted by Jean-Marie Beaudet; the works recorded are Willan's Piano Concerto (with Agnes Butcher, piano) and Champagne's *Suite canadienne* (with La Cantoria choir). The catalogues of Canadian composers were compiled by J.-J. Gagnier (1947) and HK (1952) for the CBC. [*Ed.*]

8   John Weinzweig's exact remarks during this panel discussion at the First Symposium of Contemporary Canadian Music, held in Vancouver in March 1950, were that Canada's composers "have a special distinction. We are the most unpublished, unheard, unperformed and unpaid composers in the Western world." The remarks are preserved in the John Weinzweig Fonds, Mus. 154, Library and Archives Canada, 1984-3, box 11, folder 5; see *Weinzweig: Essays on His Life and Music*, ed. John Beckwith and Brian Cherney (Waterloo, ON: Wilfrid Laurier University Press, 2011), 60. [*Ed.*]

9   For a detailed discussion of the issues HK raises in this paragraph, see Benita Wolters-Fredlund, "A 'League against Willan'? The Early Years of the Canadian League of Composers, 1951–1960," *Journal of the Society for American Music* 5/4 (2011), 445–80. [*Ed.*]

10 The Royal Commission chaired by Robert Fowler was set up by the Canadian government to recommend regulatory legislation for radio, and especially television, broadcasting in Canada, and filed its report in 1957. [*Ed.*]

11 The *Canadian Music Journal* was owned and published by the Canadian Music Council. The Spring 1957 issue on "Music and the Canada Council" was a study of patronage models. The issue was written by Arnold Walter and Geoffrey Payzant; Walter contributed the articles "Music in a Technological Age" (4–13), "Problems of Patronage in a Democratic Society" (14–19), and "A Canadian Pattern" (33–39); Payzant wrote "The Actual Need" (20–32). [*Ed.*]

10
The Making of a One-Country Music Encyclopedia: An Essay after an Encyclopedia

HK was a born encyclopedist. His propensity for categorization, list making, and careful checking of facts was evident in him already as a child, and came to its fullest blossoming during his work on the two print editions of the *Encyclopedia of Music in Canada*, work which occupied him for nearly a quarter of a century. This article was intended as a guide for other national encyclopedias, and indeed *EMC* did provide a compelling model for the *Encyclopedia of Music in Ireland*, a project that itself has been a quarter of a century in the making and is due to appear in 2013.[1] HK's projected third print edition of *EMC* never came to pass. An online version of *EMC-2*, hosted on the National Library of Canada website, was mounted in 2001 and limited updates were made. In 2003 *EMC* was donated to the Historica Foundation, which had already acquired *The Canadian Encyclopedia* and had helped to digitize the *Dictionary of Canadian Biography*. The online version of *EMC* was launched on 15 October 2003 as part of Historica's *The Canadian Encyclopedia* website at http://www.thecanadianencyclopedia.com. A staff of six part-time editors is engaged in an ongoing process of gradual revisions and updates to *EMC*, but there are no plans for a third print edition. As of 2011, the online version of *EMC* was attracting ca. 100,000 unique visitors per month.[2]

After ten years of preparation, the *Encyclopedia of Music in Canada* (hereafter *EMC*) was published in November 1981; a French edition, *Encyclopédie de la musique au Canada*, followed sixteen months later. A second

---

Fontes artis musicae 41/1 (January-March 1994), 3–19

edition appeared in English in November 1992 and in French the next year, increasing the number of entries from 3,000 to 3,800, the pages (in the English edition) from just over 1,000 to 1,500. Each page had three columns, and a total of ca. 1,650 words. There were about 500 illustrations in the first edition, 585 in the second. These were large volumes indeed, for reasons which I hope to explain and justify.

This article will concentrate on the processes and techniques in compiling a one-country encyclopedia and will only incidentally reflect on its portrait of music in Canada. Since *EMC* may claim to have been the first lexicographical attempt to cover the music of one country in such detail and breadth,[3] perhaps other potential one-country lexicographers may benefit from our experiences and avoid one pitfall or another. In describing the main steps in the creation of *EMC*, oversimplification will be necessary; thus many phases in preparing each of the two editions are telescoped here into one, applying the benefit of hindsight.

The Need

The beginning of any such project is a meeting of minds in an informal exchange of ideas, opinions, and visions at an historically opportune time. For Canada, that time had come by 1970. For twenty-five years—since the end of the war—the arts had experienced a phenomenal blossoming, both in quantity and in quality. Musical performers won laurels at home and abroad; arts councils sprang up giving support and sponsorship; national organizations, formed by composers, educators, librarians, publishers, recording companies, and many other groups, defined and advanced common interests. To the intensity of musical life was added diversity as immigration from many countries brought colourful traditions and seasoned practitioners of music. Prosperity reigned; self-assurance grew.

With exciting developments in all corners of the country, it was hard to keep up documentation and dissemination of information and to find time for reflection and assessment. The national umbrella organization, the Canadian Music Council, compiled *Music in Canada* (1955), an anthology with chapters about composition, broadcasting, folk music, competition festivals, school music, and other broad areas, written by recognized or instant experts. The council's excellent *Canadian Music Journal* (1956–62) continued to supply information and discussion, but for too short a time.

The Centenary of Confederation celebrations in 1967 and the coincidental world's fair "Expo 67" in Montreal roused the world's curiosity about Canada, as for many years had Canadian choirs and orchestras, and artists the likes of Maureen Forrester, Glenn Gould, Oscar Peterson, Louis Quilico, or Jon Vickers. The lack of quick access to reliable information now became embarrassing; it is little wonder that international surveys of music often ignored Canada or at best offered hit-and-miss representation and outdated or incorrect information. A new version of the music council's anthology, *Aspects of Music in Canada* (1969) and *Aspects de la musique au Canada* (1970) only proved that the wealth of names, events, and activities had grown past the potential of the short survey essay.

Clearly, the need for alphabetically organized coverage of music was indicated; what was wanting was its intersection with ready source material, competent scholars, and generous sponsorship. Happily, that intersection occurred in 1970. John Beckwith, composer and University of Toronto professor, provided a match—an essay bemoaning our failure to publicize our own music, "About Canadian Music: The P.R. Failure";[4] Floyd Chalmers, a patron of the arts and retired editor and publisher, picked up the match—and later much of the tab; Keith MacMillan, director of the Canadian Music Centre (and for many years secretary of IAML's Music Information Centres Commission), located the kindling wood in the resources of the Centre and of the newly created Music Division at the National Library of Canada, and in the present writer's research material accumulated over twenty years. What was needed was a person to light, stoke, and control the fire. This person was found in Michael Koerner, a business executive with a long record of serving arts organizations. The project was alive.

Creating an Organization

There are different ways of creating the backup organization essential for an encyclopedia. For instance, a publisher or a university might initiate and underwrite the project, contracting an editor-in-chief. This editor might assume complete responsibility or largely delegate the choice of inclusion and exclusion of subjects and the approval of submissions to a committee of specialists. In the Canadian situation that approach would have been difficult to apply. Persons with a countrywide grasp of any particular field were rare, committee meetings in a vast country are expensive, and conflicting views about style, treatment, balance, and other aspects of dictionary-making are difficult to reconcile in any case.

EMC took a different course. It was formed as an independent corporation run by a board of directors. This board included patrons of the arts who combined business acumen with passion for music, and musicians with administrative experience. All had a strong commitment to the fostering of the arts in Canada. A clear division of business and editorial functions was made from the beginning, the board approving basic policies, establishing budgets and timeframes, raising funds,[5] and suitably exploiting individual contacts with the artistic and wider communities. Three co-editors of equal standing were to be appointed. Although ex-officio members of the board, they would have a minimal responsibility for fundraising and be free to make all editorial decisions, seeking guidance from the board only when needed.

Within a year, Michael Koerner was chosen as director-general and the editors were recruited: Gilles Potvin of Montreal, a broadcast producer and journalist with an intimate knowledge of Quebec musicians and a special interest in opera; Kenneth Winters, a seasoned music critic in Winnipeg and later Toronto, then director of the Association of Canadian Orchestras; and Helmut Kallmann of Ottawa, who had researched and written extensively on the history of music in Canada and was now building a collection of musical Canadiana at the National Library of Canada, as chief of its Music Division. The editors' different cultural backgrounds, Franco-Canadian, Anglo-Canadian and European-Canadian, assured a variety of outlook and experience.

In addition to devising proper business and editorial structures, early liaison with a publisher was invaluable for the firm's experience with marketing, pricing, production scheduling, and readers' requirements. Familiarity with house style (e.g. spellings, abbreviations, and manuscript format) saved hours of time wasted on avoidable correcting.

Basic Decisions

Once the board had given the go-ahead signal, the editors had to plan on two fronts: the intellectual concept and its practical realization. On the first, it was necessary to define scope, audience, style, degree of comprehensiveness and scale of detail. On the practical side it was necessary to enlist staff, contributors and advisers, to estimate workloads and target dates, to design workflow patterns, to equip offices and to draw up the many forms required, such as invitations to write, contracts, and reports. All this should be done before assigning the first article. The ground rules should remain firm, but their practical application flexible since after a period of experimentation and exploration, shifts of emphasis and style will be inevitable. However, the modifications that came to *EMC* related mainly to size, funding, and time for preparation. In the case of the first edition, the final amounts were roughly triple the original estimate, in the second the overrun was about 50 percent. There was, in our pioneer effort, no need to apologize for overruns.

Canadian Content Only

The "Introduction to the First Edition" (which is recommended to anyone seeking more detail) begins with the basic statement: "The *Encyclopedia of Music in Canada* is about music in Canada and Canada's musical relations with the rest of the world; it is not a Canadian version of a general reference work on music." There never was any doubt about this. While "music in Canada" excludes a sketch of Wagner's life, "musical relations" is concerned with Canadian premières of his operas and his influence on Canadian composers. Entries on general topics such as "Impressionism" or "Reed organs" usually begin with a definition and international context, but soon concentrate on Canadian aspects.

Identical English and French Editions

The majority of Canadians use English as their daily language, but some 25 to 30 percent, concentrated in the Province of Quebec, use French. Quebec has the longest documented musical history of any province, and Montreal has had more musicians than any other city. Reflecting these facts, one-third of the articles were written in French and required translation into English; two-thirds had to be translated into French (an explanation, incidentally, for the staggered dates of publication).

A Historical Dimension

Few Canadians, and fewer people elsewhere, were aware that colonial musical activity predated the births of Purcell, Rameau, Bach, and Handel and initiated the long process of cultural transplantation from Europe not just to Canada, but to North America as a whole. For example, Quebec City had the first organ on the continent (by 1657); in 1724 Jean Girard took a manuscript collection of 398 French keyboard pieces (see the entry *"Livre d'orgue de Montréal"*) along to Montreal; a later immigrant,

Joseph Quesnel, wrote the first bona fide opera (*Colas et Colinette*, 1789) in North America. We thought it important to record the work of the first Roman Catholic missionaries, the musical dabblings of colonial officials, and the singing and dancing of the habitants and voyageurs.

Global View of Musical Genres

We felt strongly about the legitimacy of all genres of music. Indeed the careers of many Canadian musicians straddle the "classical," "folk," and "popular" sides, and the genres frequently overlap or blend in composition. Military music and religious music were included, as were the traditions, cultivated or vernacular, of the aboriginals and of many ethnic communities (*if* practiced in Canada).

In line with older music encyclopedias, composition was our highest priority. In addition to entries on composers, there were to be surveys of styles and techniques such as "Aleatory," "Bluegrass," and "Electroacoustic music," of forms such as "Art songs" or "Cantata," and of functional music, such as music for "Christmas" and "Incidental music." There were to be entries about individual operas, oratorios, and other significant or popular compositions. In the treatment of dance (folk, ballroom, and ballet) only the musical part was to be discussed. Films were to be treated under two headings: "Films" (about music in Canada) and "Film scores" by Canadian composers.

Music in Society

A century ago a typical music dictionary would have limited itself to biography, terminology, organizations, and forms. A major trend in later twentieth-century musical historiography is the recognition of the connectedness of all manifestations of musical life with each other (i.e., education, composition, performance, funding, and commerce) and with society as a whole. In Canada this awareness is reinforced by the lingering memory of a pioneer society where the founding of ensembles, concert halls, and conservatories took precedence over the encouragement of composition. The present era provides its own object lessons in the interplay of art, economics, politics, and technology—our musical press offers far more discussion of policies and economics than of styles and aesthetics. Although the role of individual talent and leadership remains strong, what succeeds and what goes under so often are determined by the practical realities of life.

The Making of a One-Country Music Encyclopedia

Holding, then, that music is embedded in the cultural and social fabric of our country, we devised certain unconventional entries not traditionally found in music encyclopedias. Examples are "Medical aspects of music," "Memorials and honours," "World Soundscape Project" (sound ecology), the participation in music by "Sovereigns, statesmen, and other public figures," patterns of "Funding, patronage and volunteerism," and "Music as a social phenomenon." The music business is examined in "Broadcasting," "Music industries," the "Recorded sound industry," and "Governments and music." Relationships with sister arts are explored under "Art, visual," "Librettos," "Literature set to music," and "Literature with musical content." Local colour gets its due in entries on "Disaster songs" and music related to "Mountains," "Rivers," "Sports," and "Transportation."

Of great fascination in a country that has become a miniature United Nations is the description of various ethnic and national groups, from Inuit and other "Native North Americans in Canada" to Canadians from "Bulgaria," "Cuba," "Ireland," or, in collective entries, "Black Africa," and "South and Central America." These are counterbalanced by an entry on "Emigration" of talented Canadian-born musicians.

Practical Benefits

We wanted to enable our readers to acquire recordings and printed music, to proceed to further reading and research, and to plan their studies, competition entries, or festival attendances. Hence the many lists or statistics of archival and library holdings,[6] and of periodicals, festivals, awards, instrument collections, community orchestras, courses and degrees given at various universities, and so forth.

Fact and Evaluation

Unlike a Who's Who, an encyclopedia serves the dual functions of information and evaluation. Implicit values will show up even in the most objective exposition—future historians will readily recognize our late twentieth-century biases. Indeed, objectivity is not always a virtue; topical articles often gain interest and humanity from a subjective viewpoint. It is a different—and delicate—matter to evaluate living artists. Their career can be made or broken when an impresario, a hiring committee, a broadcast program organizer, or a journalist depends on a dictionary reference. Luckily (from the victim's point of view) or unluckily (in the editors' quest), obtaining any critical characterization—the type of assessment *Die Musik in Geschichte und Gegenwart* places in its second prose section, after the list of works—has been the most difficult part in *EMC*'s biographical entries. It was not for lack of trying. Too many times an article had to be returned to the contributor or researcher, asking about this pianist's prominent strengths or weaknesses or that composer's stylistic and aesthetic evolution. Answers did not always come, and our last resort, press quotations, rarely were adequate substitutes. If the resulting volume leans heavily towards positivistic and less towards critical treatment, the reason should be sought in the nature of a pioneer enterprise rather than the editors' philosophy.

In or Out? The List of Entries

After defining the scope and approach, the most urgent task was to decide "who and what" were "in and out." The list of entries is the very backbone of encyclopedia preparation. Its compilation is the greatest fun—and the greatest headache. It evokes a sense of power, the joy of discovery, and a foretaste of what should be said in this or that article, but above all, it instills responsibility for fairness. Having an entry or being left out can be of serious consequence for an aspiring or neglected artist.

To create order and develop yardsticks for comparison, the editors divided the field into broad areas, such as composers, performers, church music, music education, instrument making, pop music, etc. and, with suggestions from other staff, compiled a preliminary list. This was circulated among knowledgeable persons in various branches of the profession and regions of the country. Their added suggestions and their objections enabled us to compare, to balance, and to set standards. It would have been wrong, for instance, to include 200 pianists but only 20 violinists; to feature 30 choirs from British Columbia but only three from Manitoba, or to describe as many nineteenth-century concert halls as modern ones.

Some vexing problems had to be faced. If one proposed ten clarinetists for inclusion, for sure someone would assert "I know at least three who are as good or better." If one included thirteen, the same would happen again until there were twenty or thirty. Would a point system help? We felt that any rigid scale would ignore too many imponderables. In entries for individuals we postulated a minimum number of years in which an undoubted talent had been exposed before the public and we gave preference to those with a combination of activities, for example, a clarinetist

The Making of a One-Country Music Encyclopedia

who had composed, written an instruction book, or done extensive solo playing and recording. In the case of pop musicians, whose rise to stardom often is meteoric, the number of active years allowed may be shorter, and public curiosity as decisive a factor as accomplishment.

Fortunately there are devices for smoothing the transition from the tenth clarinetist who has 15 lines of text to the eleventh who has not one. A capsule biography may be given under "Woodwinds, playing and teaching," under an orchestra, university, city, or perhaps the entry of a better known relative, wife, or husband.

While an international dictionary ignores nationality or place of residence as a criterion for inclusion, its one-country cousin cannot. Who is Canadian? Obviously in a country of immigrants, birthplace is immaterial once professional activity has been established in the new home. What about those who settled here and later moved on? Some eight to ten years of major Canadian impact were expected. Moreover, musicians whose years in Canada were associated with but a single institution were dealt with only under those institutions, for example, conductors such as Seiji Ozawa or Zubin Mehta under the Toronto and Montreal symphony orchestras. And what about Canadians with a career abroad? Any hard and fast rule would have to disregard intangible factors: some emigrants continue to be claimed as "ours," while others, abroad for the same length of time, are not forgiven for having forsaken their native land (and probably for achieving stardom abroad). A more objective criterion is found in the ties maintained through touring or return after retirement. Since most emigrants went south, we devised a "mini-encyclopedia" within the "United States of America" entry. In the end, each case had to be judged on its own merits.

In borderline cases, we have erred on the generous side. While Great Britain had Brown & Stratton's *British Musical Biography* (1897) and Germany its Müller's *Deutches Musiker-Lexikon* (1929) to take care of minor figures, there had been no Who's Who of Canadian Musicians, apart from the Quebec-oriented Soeurs de Sainte-Anne's 1935 *Dictionnaire biographique des musiciens canadiens* and the CBC's *Catalogue of Canadian Composers* (1947, 1952). *EMC* was a once-or-never chance to document pioneer musicians and organizations who deserved to be remembered for their initiative, vision, and persistence in promoting standards and ideals, even if these virtues were not matched by the level of their musicianship. Without their entries, one could not trace the origins of today's topnotch orchestras, composers, and music schools. In perhaps a hundred cases when little was known about a certain person or subject, we took a risk and assigned the article, making a decision only after delivery.

One other consideration in the list of entries deserves mention. When dealing with topics rather than biographies, we had to choose between long surveys or a breakdown into many small topics. We favoured breaking down whenever a sub-topic justified treatment by itself. This saves the reader scanning pages of text. On the other hand, those looking for broad surveys are well served by the device of Reader's Guides (or Directory Entries). One such guide, "Religions and music," lists nearly 50 entries, among them "Hymns and hymn tunes," "Lutherans," or "Schola cantorum," and one under "Education" refers to 32, such as "Career counselling," "Diplomas," "Inventions and devices," "School music," or "Theory textbooks," and the names of some 40 teaching institutions.

An entry list along principles similar to the original one was compiled for the second edition but containing only new entries. The 3,000 old ones were reviewed and categorized as justifying deletion, needing no change or requiring condensing, rewriting, merging, renaming, or updating.

Staff and Contributors

Over the months and years *EMC* assembled a staff, as the need for research, record keeping, or typing arose, or as individuals with special aptitudes happened our way. At the height of production the team included twelve salaried and six part-time or occasional workers, all keenly motivated and strongly dedicated to the project. Although each had prescribed responsibilities, everyone regardless of rank was encouraged to note errors, suggest additional entries or deletions, or criticize what one of us had written—nothing mattered but to create the best possible text. This policy helped to discover and exploit special talents and to direct assignments to the most suitable person.[7] Contributors, translators, and other assistants were paid on a piece basis. Volunteers included advisers on folk and school music, and "information scouts" in various parts of Canada. The latter were invaluable in tracing the whereabouts of peripatetic artists, in checking on appointment, retirement or death dates, and in reminding contributors to complete overdue articles.

Somehow we found our contributors—and they found us—often after laborious detours of mismatching writer and subject, or misreading good intentions for ability to deliver. They were a motley crowd of academics, folk music collectors, local historians, music journalists, broadcasters, librarians, orchestra committee members, freelance music researchers (usually recent graduates), and many others. Some had thorough knowledge of a single subject—perhaps their former teacher, or the history of one orchestra—while others knew how to assemble information about people and organizations they had never heard of. Some wrote only one article, others several dozen. Some knew how to write but not how to explore and assess sources, others knew their field but were poor writers. Few articles had to be rejected, but many were rewritten by *EMC*'s staff. Even the best contributions required such adjustments as adaptation to house style, excision of material treated in related entries, or addition of current information.

It is worthwhile pointing out assignment problems special to a country where musical research and scholarship are young. In Europe editors have little trouble finding experts on the krummhorn, the musical history of Parma, or the work of Morales, Inghelbrecht, or Riisager; most incoming articles need only some pruning, polishing, and adapting to house style. By contrast, when *EMC* was begun in the early 1970s, almost the only experts were the collectors of Canadian folk music. University courses on music history and literature ignored Canada, though a very few schools began Canadian or North American courses in the late 1960s. Musicologists, often recruited from among US, British, and French scholars, focused their interest on European music. Canadian biographical studies and thesis topics were rare. Fortunately a countercurrent was stirring. Almost surreptitiously, at the 1970 Toronto conference of the American Musicological Society and the (US) College Music Society, an unofficial Canadian Studies session was called by young graduates and undergraduates determined to make the study of Canadian composition and music history a university concern and to build reputations in that field. It was among such young scholars that *EMC* found its most enthusiastic and competent contributors.

EMC's entry on "Musicology" states that "While international music encyclopedias usually are harvesters of research already done by specialists, *EMC* in its first edition was essentially a mobilizer of musicological activity." In turn this mobilization paid dividends for the second edition. Historical research had broadened during the 1980s and native, popular, jazz, and "ethnic" music had become cultivated fields. As a result, in preparing the second edition, we enlisted a greater number of academics and avoided the massive amount of rewriting that had to be done for the first edition, by assigning many of the new entries and most of the updating of old ones to our own staff to whom *EMC* style and information distribution had become second nature.

A few words should be offered about communications with contributors. For instance, we soon discovered that rigid assignment of word length simply did not work; it could lead to the suppression of essential information or to padding.[8] Another point: ideally writers should see the edited version of their assignment. Indeed, we followed this when major changes had been made or pieces were highly technical. However, under the pressure of time, routine changes could not always be submitted to the author. To protect the entity legally responsible for the project, the contract form issued to contributors should state that "in the case of significant changes and corrections, the editors will attempt to consult the contributor before publication, but no liability is assumed in this regard."

It is even more questionable whether *subjects* should see the proposed text for their entry. In cases of doubtful or missing information, it is wise to do this in a controlled situation, e.g., by telephone, quoting only essential passages ("Which of these four teachers really shaped your performance? Is it true that you were influenced by Schoenberg?"). Such checking can eradicate innocent errors. But submitting an entire article for approval might provoke entanglement with egos and cost precious time in argument. It is wiser to assemble information and self-evaluations *before* writing such articles.

Workflow and Tools

Contributors were sent basic instructions regarding style and structure along with a supply of a multicoloured snap form, so copies could be kept by the writer and distributed to all offices and editors. For some broader topics, sources and points to be covered were suggested. For instance, writers on a specific university were told to investigate the scope of music instruction, the degrees given, the main phases and names of the department's history, the current numbers of staff and students, extra-curricular activities, and recipients of honorary degrees, among other features.

EMC's administrative staff in Toronto and Montreal (for articles written in English and French, respectively) kept fastidious records of assignment and due dates, dates of submissions received and passed on to editors, and dates of final typing and payment to contributors. Statistics of assignments, completions, editions, and translations, enabled the staff and board to measure progress against previous estimates and to set new target dates.

The Making of a One-Country Music Encyclopedia

The workflow of incoming articles can be outlined here only in oversimplification. With few exceptions, all editors read every article; the associate editor for jazz and English-language pop music read all those in his realm. We would identify doubtful or duplicated information, note obvious gaps, do instant corrections, compare impressions and sometimes return the article to the author or staff for further work. If changes were substantial, a second or third reading would take place before final approval. The style editors were largely occupied with applying abbreviations, spellings, and formulas for the "banners" of biographies. They might divide long sentences, improve awkward phrasing, and eradicate inconsistencies, contradictions, and anachronisms. It is amazing how many pairs of eyes it can take to spot obvious errors.[9]

Two major procedural differences between the first and second editions must be pointed out. The first had to grope and experiment, while the second began with established rules and a group of experienced and trusted co-workers. And while the first was prepared on typewriters, the second used computers, although most contributions still were received on typewritten paper and had to be copied.

The computers were Macintoshes, and the software was Microsoft Word 4.0. Up to ten machines were in use. Communication between the various offices was by mailing floppy discs; direct communication by modem would have been prohibitively expensive. To begin with, the University of Toronto Press converted the tape from which it had produced the first English edition to text readable on the Macintosh. For the French text it was necessary to retype the entire volume into the computer. The 3,000-odd articles were then grouped into small units, commensurate with the loading capacity of hard discs and floppies. Copies of the tapes were then made. One in each language would be kept intact as a backup. Others were distributed for work at the Montreal, Ottawa, and Toronto offices.

Each article was headed by a template in "hidden text" (text not meant to be printed), onto which were entered the main stations of receiving, editing, researching, approving, indexing, etc., with dates and staff initials. For textual alterations three strict rules proved invaluable: none of the original text was deleted but, if no longer needed, merely struck through; all new text was underlined. And thirdly, all internal notes ("What did X do between 1985 and 90?"; "Listing 20 operatic roles is too much!") were placed at the end of the article as "hidden text" dated and initialed. Saving all deleted text was important because changes sometimes turned out to be miscorrections or misimprovements. One has to be able at any point to backtrack ("Where did I find that fact?" and "Is that change of spelling a mere typo?")[10] (see example 1 on page 117).

Editing

The goals of editorial work are accuracy, clarity, precision, compactness, and relevance. The enemies of encyclopedia text are vagueness, jargon, verbosity, and redundancy. It would take a separate essay to discuss each, so I shall limit myself to a few typical cases.

Accuracy

Above all, the reader expects to find correct and authoritative information. How can the editor, often ignorant of the subject, assure this? After some experience one develops a sixth sense for the reliability of sources and contributors. While sloppy writing often goes together with careless information gathering, one can be fooled by cases of good writing paired with inadequate research, and poor grammar with valid information. When years of birth or name spelling are in conflict, one soon learns to recognize which book copied from which predecessor. Ideally, all occurrences of the same facts should be checked against each other; cross-referencing and indexing are good ways to discover discrepancies. Gathering biographical information by questionnaire should be the most reliable method, and many musicians do keep meticulous records of their career, but others just vaguely remember or merely guess the date of their latest quartet—and then there are those who do not answer letters.

There are limits to checking. When someone is reported to have been born on the 9th of May and studied with teachers A, B, and C, in the end blind faith takes over. One of the most useful internal tools for achieving accuracy was an Amendment Form, devised soon after the appearance of the first edition (see example 2 on page 118). Sets with copies in different colours were distributed to each editor and office; a separate form was made up for each error or questionable fact discovered. The form was used also to hold on to the kind of newspaper or grapevine tidbit that, only a year later, might be hard to locate—foundations and dissolutions of organizations, appointments, death dates, and so on.

To assure clarity and consistency we decided to present information in complete sentences rather than in telegraphic style, except when the opening sentence provided a definition. Non-technical language was

The Making of a One-Country Music Encyclopedia

Example 1: *EMC* copy in process

Name: **Grand Theatre**
Instruction: Update

Researched: Pat Beharriell Feb 1991

Reviewed: HK 1-3-91

Copy edited: RE 2/VII/91

Approved: GP 5-7-91; HK 11-7-91

Indexed:

Grand Theatre, Kingston, Ont. Originally the Grand Opera House, built ~~in~~ 190<u>1-2</u> on the site of Martin's Opera House (1879)~~, which was destroyed by fire in 1898~~. <u>*H.M.S. Parliament and the premiere of *Leo, the Royal Cadet were given at Martin's Opera House, which also saw visits from John Philip Sousa, Oscar Wilde, and others before it was destroyed by fire 6 Dec 1898</u>. The Grand <u>opened 14 Jan 1902</u> and was bought in 1905 by Ambrose J. Small, a theatre-chain owner who had been influential in its original planning. Bernhardt, Melba, and Jolson performed there. In 1936 it was bought by Famous Players, and it reopened as a movie house ~~1920~~ May 1938<u>, but closed again in 1961</u>. The Kingston Arts Council campaigned for its restoration as a civic theatre, and as the Grand Theatre it opened 20 May 1966 with a performance of *Spring Thaw*. Its new mandate was to accommodate touring and local groups and serve as the home of the *Kingston <u>Symphony</u>. It has 832 seats, a proscenium stage, and an orchestra pit. ~~During the next 25 years the theatre went through several stages of enlargement, providing new lounges and a second theatre, The Baby Grand, opened November 1990, without a stage proper and with flexible seating. In the main theatre, the orchestra pit was levelled replaced with a removable forestage in 1991.~~ <u>An ongoing series of renovations begun in 1978 have provided new lounges, improved backstage facilities, and a second smaller theatre space, The Baby Grand, which opened in November 1990.</u>

BIBLIOGRAPHY
<u>Waldhauer, Erdmute. *Grand Theatre 1879-1979* (Kingston 1979)</u>

Patricia Beharriell

HK 1-3-91. The changes reported by PB are so small that I found it easiest to write them in myself. Send to **RE** with hard copy.
BN 19/III/91: Hard copy should already be in Tor since ML sent the article up here.
RE 2/VII/91: When I was in the Grand Theatre for a play on 28 Jun 91, I noticed that the orchestra pit renovations had not yet been done, so I altered HK's addition to this article; I also added a bit to the earlier part of the entry.

Example 2: Information Amendment Form

Entry	de Marky, Paul (already revised and approved)	E: 262c/263a	F: 268c
Reported by	HK on 21 Dec 1989	Correction New information xxx Other	

Data and source   After providing the revision on the floppy I looked at the NL of C de Marky papers, mainly to see whether the collection is substantial enough to mention. It is.
I would cross out the subtitle <u>The Trans Atlantic</u> since I cannot find that title on the ms., nor on the Vancouver program. Call it <u>Concerto pour piano en si majeur</u> instead.
The first movement of the Concerto is called <u>Ballade</u> and I strongly suspect that the Ballade he played in 1944 was just the beginning of the concerto, but we don't have to mention that.

Further research and action

---

encouraged, and Canadian (generally agreeing with British) rather than US spellings were used. An invaluable tool for staff and major contributors was *EMC's* Style Guide, growing through continuous refinement from a few pages to book size. It showed, for instance, that "London" is in England, and the Canadian city is "London, Ont.," and stipulated that "decade" should be used only to describe a span of years ending in zero.

While the personal style of a fine writer should not be disturbed, the language of a work containing the contributions of several hundred writers and detailing hundreds of careers and organizations does require a certain amount of homogenizing. For example, when describing instructors we replaced "pedagogue" with "teacher," and reserved "educator" for persons who develop curricula, invent methods, or write textbooks in addition to regular teaching. Seeming trivialities, such as the placement of "only" and "also" next to the word they qualify, or, in biographical entries, the use of the surname at the first mention in each paragraph, followed by no more than three or four repetitions of "he" or "she" before return to the surname, do make for smoother reading.

Readers also expect up-to-dateness. As work on the first edition dragged on, many entries were five or six years old and, in the case of living artists and groups, quite out-of-date. Much rewriting was then necessary. In the second edition, work began on persons who had retired or died since 1980 (or earlier, if new information was forthcoming). The most active persons were treated late, so as to avoid a second wave of information gathering. Purists to the contrary, there is no way to recount everyone's career up to the same day. Once an article had been completed, even in 1989, only important additions were made. On the other hand, while it was still possible to insert a line here or there, death dates were included up to May 1992, when the manuscript was already in the publisher's hands. A uniform cut-off date is neither possible nor desirable.

Precision

Each event should be anchored in as specific a year and place as possible rather than having taken place "recently" in "western Canada." The ambiguous term "American" was never applied to inhabitants of the USA (except in quotations); after all, Canadians, Mexicans, and Brazilians all consider themselves Americans, in a sense.

There are occasions however when vagueness is a necessity. If one does not know whether X had secured his church organist's position before his arrival in Regina or arrived and then looked for it, it is safer to say "His first position in Regina was" rather than "He came to Regina as organist at ..."

Compactness

Every word counts in encyclopedia writing; space is always at a premium. Compactness can be achieved by simplifying language, using abbreviations, and eliminating duplication by cross-referencing to other articles with related contents.

Simplifying language. The individual case may seem trivial, but three words saved here and six there soon add up to whole pages. For example, "he was the conductor of" becomes "he conducted." "From 1983 to 1985 he was assistant professor of music at" becomes "He taught 1983–5 at"; "Her works have been heard in performance" becomes "Her works have been performed"; and usually "At the age of 16" becomes "At 16."

Abbreviations and acronyms exist to save space and save reading time rather than create a guessing game and slow down comprehension. Many are well known; all used in *EMC* are explained in the preliminary pages. Possibly the most frequent abbreviations—U for university and SO for symphony orchestra—alone must have saved several pages of text. Obvious abbreviations involved names of institutions, Canadian provinces, US states, and frequently mentioned publishers. Frequently cited bibliographical sources were given in abbreviated form, the full citations being provided at the beginning of the volume.

Eliminating duplication. Basic information, such as name, launching date, and main directors in the case of an important choir, conservatory, or orchestra, necessarily must appear under the entries for the city, the directors, and the organization itself. All detail, however, should be presented only once, in its own entry. Originally our "see-also" references (by means of the asterisk) were to be given only to entries providing further information relevant to the entry in which they are placed. However, it proved impossible to examine the relevance of each of thousands of mentions of entry headings, so the asterisk was applied indiscriminately in all such cases.

In addition, *EMC*'s second edition has nearly 300 cross-reference entries, e.g., "Academies. See Conservatories and academies." Even more important as a finding aid is the Index with about 25,000 entries.

Illustrations

When an encyclopedia is to be illustrated—as ours was—planning must start early. Contributors of certain articles were asked to supply pictures or suggest sources at the time the assignment was made. Hunting for photos later on necessitates extra writing, postage, and a last-minute scramble just to get "anything." Another good reason for an early start is the need to obtain the permission for photos, new and old, from photographers whose addresses and firm name changes are often difficult to trace. Caption writing takes time too!

We were aiming at roughly one picture for every six entries. Our criteria were significance of the subject, pictorial diversity, and if possible, photographic excellence. Significance was easiest to satisfy, although pictures of even the famous are often hard to come by. Diversity was achieved through a mixture of formal portraits or action shots of individuals, group pictures, samples of manuscripts, sheet music covers, or photographs of instruments or recording sessions. Photos predominated, but visual diversity was enhanced by reproducing paintings, drawings, and sculptures.

The Making of a One-Country Music Encyclopedia

Illustrations were particularly helpful in providing local colour and historical context, e.g., pages from the first Canadian music publication of 1800 ("*Graduel romain*"), or a recording session of an Indian band in British Columbia ca. 1910 ("Recorded sound production"), in contrast to ultramodern music buildings and electronic gadgetry.

Beyond the First Edition

The first edition created something of a sensation in Canadian musical circles.[11] Reviewers and readers found a panorama of activity, the variety and intensity of which few had known or suspected. Some yielded to the tome's seduction to hours of browsing; graduate students, biographers and historians found subjects and lacunae to be researched; others greeted its practical value in their daily work as broadcasters, journalists, music dealers, or teachers. Soon we began to catch *EMC* phraseology in radio commentaries and concert program notes.

Several small disappointments in *EMC*'s reception may be noted. We had hoped that specialized Canadian magazines would review *EMC* for its coverage of their field—be it education, folk music, musicology, organ playing—but few did. We could understand that foreign reviews would find it hard to appraise *EMC*'s content, but would have appreciated comments from the viewpoint of lexicography all the more. We also had overestimated the direct response we would get from readers. There were hardly more than two dozen letters in ten years, although some offered valuable information, corrections, and even collaboration.

The need for a second edition was indicated by the continuing rapid development and changes in musical life. Musical research had expanded in such areas as biography, popular culture, music of the North American natives, the psychology and sociology of music, and many others.[12] The music of immigrant groups had assumed a larger profile. A new crop of artists and organizations had entered the scene; over a hundred young composers alone were considered worthy of inclusion.[13] Sound recording had increased exponentially. Obviously, a new edition also provided a chance to correct errors and present the fruits of new historical research.

When the time for a third edition comes, what should be done differently? I suspect that edition will be more selective and eliminate minor figures that are well covered in the earlier two; it will be able to draw on a generation of writers to whom characterizations of style and evaluations of achievements come more easily. Among new contributions, I should like to see a survey of the ideas or systems of prominent musical thinkers, an overall historical outline, entries on each province (to take care of smaller cities and give portraits of regional traditions), a discussion of computers and music, notes on the musically most important churches, and a collective entry for radio hosts of recorded or live music programs. Other prospects are a chronological chart as endpaper; the music of "O Canada," and a few other well-known songs.

Anyone planning to compile a similar reference work should have a good physical constitution and a thick skin. Dictionary making means organizing, remembering, anticipating, supervising, writing, rewriting, double-checking, cajoling, soothing, encouraging, justifying, and a host of other "-ings." A miracle perhaps, but during either term of preparation, none of our core staff lost time due to illness, not even nervous breakdowns. Pressures were strong when the board simply could not find more money, the publisher imposed a "final final" deadline, contributors let us down despite promises and constant reminders, the earliest articles received needed updating, and another 200 needed revising within four weeks—the nightmares never ended. And yet, somehow, the funds were forthcoming, the articles fell into place, the rewriting was done, the publisher was appeased, and the book rolled off the presses.

It is clear now that our editorial work was a journey of discovery and learning. Paradoxically, I found it an exercise also in forgetting: hundreds of details that I had researched over the years and jotted down on private notes, insights that I carried in my head were at last committed to print. But the greatest discovery for me was the realization how much lexicography and creative art have in common. True, the one results from observation, the other from imagination. One deals with facts, the other with inventions. One provides knowledge, the other beauty. And yet, lexicographical architecture surely is as much an exercise in creativity as is composition, painting, or play-writing. The process of translating a vision inside the mind into an artifact outside that mind, available to other minds, very closely parallels the work of a composer, the painter, the playwright, forever balancing, shaping, leaning back to view detail against overall structure, pausing to criticize what has been done against the original vision, hoping that in the end all parts will blend into a harmonious whole. And it is this emphasis on wholeness and unity in an age of growing fragmentation of musical audiences and the musical press that may prove the strongest virtue of the *Encyclopedia of Music in Canada*.

The Making of a One-Country Music Encyclopedia

NOTES

1 Harry White, "Musicology, Positivism and the Case for an Encyclopedia of Music in Ireland: Some Brief Considerations," in *Irish Musical Studies 1: Musicology in Ireland*, ed. Gerard Gillen and Harry White (Dublin: Irish Academic Press, 1990), 297, notes that "The scope and structure of *EMC* provide models for the form and content of an encyclopaedia of music in Ireland." White is the co-editor of the forthcoming *Encyclopedia of Music in Ireland*. [*Ed.*]
2 See Desmond Maley, "The *Encyclopedia of Music in Canada* at 30," *CAML Review* 39/3 (2011), 16–18. [*Ed.*]
3 *Neue Zeitschrift für Musik* 144/3 (March 1983), 40–41: "Wohl gab es zuvor auch schon Lexika speziell für die Musik eines Landes, schwerlich jedoch eines, das seinen Gegenstand in einem so umfassenden Sinn begreift." ["Indeed there have been earlier encyclopedias specifically for the music of one country, but hardly one which comprehends its subject matter in such an all-embracing sense." Transl. HK.]
4 *Musicanada* 21 (July-August, 1969), 4–7, 10–13.
5 Those interested in the analysis of *EMC*'s funding are referred to the Foreword of each edition which lists both public and private sources, the latter headed by the Chalmers family.
6 It is surprising how few music dictionaries identify the repositories of musicians' papers.
7 Next to the positions of editor, that of administrator was the most essential one; Mabel Laine filled, and largely created, its functions. Taking most administrative work off the shoulders of the editors, her duties included preparing applications for funding, bookkeeping, banking, payroll control, issuing invitations and contracts (and often, reminders) to contributors, watching deadlines, checking in incoming articles, and acting as secretary to the board. An associate editor, Mark Miller, critic and author of books on jazz, took responsibility for pop music (English language) and jazz, areas in which the editors were not at home. In the second edition, style editing of English text was assigned to the musicologist Robin Elliott, and of the French to Claire Versailles, allround office manager, computer wizard, assignment officer, and researcher in the Montreal office. Patricia Wardrop, trained as a librarian, developed into an expert bibliographer, style guide editor, and indexer. All the above, except Claire Versailles, worked in Toronto.

The foot soldiers of the team, mostly in Ottawa, were the researcher/writers who painstakingly checked our articles written by outsiders, produced many themselves, compiled lists of works and recordings, and performed dozens of incidental jobs.

8   Later, within general indications of length, we let the contributor write as much as the material justified, paying according to the length of *edited* text.
9   Nobody, not even our own staff, noticed until near the very end of preparing *EMC-2* that in the entry on Edward Moogk, a radio host playing historical recordings, a program title had been given as Den of Iniquity, although the true title, Den of Antiquity, should have been so obvious!
10 The computer took over not only the text and its editing, but most of the housekeeping records.
11 Sales of the first edition over the years amounted to nearly 7,000 copies in English and nearly 2,000 in French.
12 By 1990, according to Beverley Diamond Cavanagh, at least twenty-four universities offered courses in Canadian music.
13 Several hundred earlier entries had to be deleted to make room for these and other newcomers.

11
Music in the Internment Camps and after World War II: John Newmark's Start on a Brilliant Canadian Career

HK's memoir of his life as a so-called "enemy alien" in Canadian internment camps from 1940 to 1943 centres on an older internee, the already well-known pianist Hans Neumark (John Newmark). Newmark's full story is told in Renée Maheu's *Un piano sur la mer: John Newmark et son temps* (Montréal: Les Intouchables, ca. 1997). Life in the camps is recorded in two major studies: Ted Jones's *Both Sides of the Wire: The Fredericton Internment Camp* (Fredericton, NB: New Ireland Press, 1988) and Eric Koch's *Deemed Suspect: A Wartime Blunder* (Toronto: Methuen, 1980). Koch was an internee along with Newmark and HK. Both books quote HK extensively, from personal diaries and interviews. HK's narrative here emphasizes the members who on release from the camps settled in Canada and contributed outstandingly to the country's postwar musical life. He also cites the contributions of refugees from Nazi Germany and Austria who were not among the internees—a topic which is explored more fully in Paul Helmer's *Growing with Canada: The Émigré Tradition in Canadian Music* (Montreal: McGill-Queen's University Press, 2009). Not mentioned here by HK are the many non-musicians in the camp populations who likewise went on to important careers in Canada; many also became lifelong friends of his. Among them were the theologian Gregory (originally Gerhard) Baum, the philosopher Emil Fackenheim, the novelist Henry (Heinrich) Kreisel, the French scholar David Hoeniger, the painter Oscar Cahén, and the television journalist Joe Schlesinger. This essay gives a detailed account not only of the beginnings of Newmark's Canadian career but also of HK's own activities between the ages of seventeen and twenty-one in what Koch calls "a highly-structured miniature society."

German-Canadian Yearbook 14 (1995), 181–91; republished by permission of the Historical Society of Mecklenburg Upper Canada

Introduction

In July of 1940 some 2,300 German and Austrian male civilians in Great Britain who had been interned a couple of months earlier were sent to Canada on two ships. The largest single component (85%) was that of "non-Aryan" refugees from Nazi Germany, but there was also an incongruous assortment of Roman-Catholic priests, merchant marine sailors, trade unionists and other political refugees. The internees were housed in three or four different camps, often reshuffled, and from the end of 1940, when the first releases were granted, numbers declined and camps were amalgamated. Eventually nearly half the prisoners volunteered to return to England and join their family or to fight under the British flag. About 950 internees were released in Canada, the last in the summer of 1943. Of these, perhaps two hundred eventually went on to settle in the USA.

It was behind barbed wire, deep in New Brunswick's forests, that the Canadian career of one of this country's most distinguished musicians began. His name, John Newmark, is known best as the pianist partner of Maureen Forrester, the world-famous contralto, but he has also performed and, often, recorded with Kathleen Ferrier, Janet Baker, Donald Bell, John Boyden, Paul Tortelier and many others. Indeed, even before internment, Newmark—born as Hans Neumark in Bremen in 1904—had concertized with such celebrities as Szymon Goldberg, Max Rostal and Emmy Heim.

But first, back to the Canada of 1940. With the help of my pocket diaries and letters to a friend in New York that were returned to me after his death, I have been able to restore the beginnings of Newmark's Canadian career and at the same time document the vitality of musical life in the refugee internment camps, a vitality inhibited but not suppressed by the dearth of good instruments and of printed music.

Concerts behind Barbed Wire

The 715 prisoners-of-war "second class" who landed at Quebec on 15 July 1940 were put on a train to Trois-Rivières and marched to the local sports centre. Beside the gymnasium where we were quartered there was a smallish room and there, twelve days later, a piano was placed. On 3 August a "musical evening" took place. I remember a rehearsal of Rilke's *Die Weise von Liebe und Tod des Cornets Christoph Rilke* with Otto

John Newmark's Start on a Brilliant Canadian Career

Diamant-Admandt, a professional actor, reciting the text and Newmark playing the musical accompaniment. The music seemed incomprehensible to my ears, untrained in modern music. When I wrote Newmark on his eightieth birthday in 1984 and reminded him about what I remembered as a Dohnányi composition, he promptly replied, pointing out that the composer really was one Casimir [von] Pászthory (1914), adding "The devil knows how I had come into possession of this melodramatic rarity!"

After three weeks at Trois-Rivières, the internees (minus the piano) arrived at a proper camp, Camp B, near Fredericton, NB, on Tuesday, 13 August. In mid-October, the authorities removed the non-Jewish internees to Camp A in Farnham, Quebec, much to the chagrin of campmates who had left Germany precisely because they were victims of religious separation and who had formed friendships across such affiliations in the previous three months. Newmark stayed in Camp B.

About half the internees in Camp B were youngsters between 16 and 20 years of age. Among the older men academics, artists and other professionals were well represented and thus cultural and artistic entertainment, from lectures to theatre, flourished. But music could not flourish without a piano. Even in the absence of the instrument, Newmark made a public appearance. On 31 October 1940 a debate was held on the topic "Resolved that art is of greater value for mankind than science." Newmark and Hans (later Harry) Weihs spoke for the affirmative, Dr. Ernst Knobloch and Tola Theilhaber for the negative. (The result was that 19 voted for, 26 against, and 9 abstained.)

On 14 November an upright piano arrived at last and only one week later the first recital took place. Newmark had the choice of two artists [fellow internees] to perform with, a professional violinist, Willy Amtmann, and Gerhard Kander, a violin prodigy who had given concerts in many German Jewish *Kulturbünde* and was still only eighteen years old. But Amtmann had just arrived from Camp Q and had not yet become acquainted with Newmark. So the first recital featured Newmark and Kander. The works presented were Mozart's Sonatas in E minor, K.304 and B-flat major, K.454. The recital was repeated on 23 November. Five days later the Sonatas in F major, K.377 and C major, K.296 were performed.

Very soon, a schedule was drawn up for the use of the piano. The instrument was housed in the Recreation Hut which also served for meetings, lectures, library service, exhibitions, practise by our acrobats, the Newman Twins, and other events. Undoubtedly Newmark was assigned the lion's share of piano time, but claims were made by another professional pianist, Fritz Lewin, and three eager students, Lutz Berger (later Len Bergé), Hans Kohlmann (Harry Coleman) and myself. Did Newmark teach anyone? I remember him telling Kohlmann that he was going to work with him on the Third Beethoven Concerto, and my telling him that I had trouble with a passage in Beethoven's *Pathétique* Sonata. Why, he said, you just do it twenty times in a row and there is really nothing to it!

Our supply of printed music was small, but gradually packages from friends, donations from the YMCA or orders through our canteen added to it. In one of these packages there was what librarians call a "binder's album" in which a pianist's or singer's sheet music crop of a certain year is bound together. The National Library of Canada has collected over 100 such volumes, most dating from the late nineteenth century and containing parlour songs and salon music for piano. To somebody brought up on Bach and Beethoven, Schubert and Schumann, this album was a shock indeed. But Johnny had a sense of humour and before long he presented a "Concert of Bad Music." I doubt that it filled an evening, but it was hilarious while it lasted.

Whenever Newmark practised he had to have an audience of at least one. He had to play *to* someone. This was considered a privilege by the many youngsters who were interested in classical music. For the longest time the page-turner and listener was Walter Homburger, "Hombie" for short, who two decades later was to become managing director of the Toronto Symphony Orchestra.

Here follow notes on further recitals at Camp B:

5 December 1940. Mozart, Sonata F major, K.376, Newmark and Kander

2 January 1941. Handel, Sonata No. 1 in A; Beethoven, Sonata Op. 24; Brahms, Sonata Op. 108, Newmark and Kander

5 January 1941. Kander recital. With Newmark? program?

9 January 1941. Handel, Sonata No. 4 in D; Bach, Chaconne; Mendelssohn, Concerto; Newmark and Kander

January 1941. Newmark participated in Shaw's play *Androcles and the Lion* for performance this month

3 April 1941. Franck, Sonata, Newmark and Amtmann. Kohlmann plays piano solo.

10 April 1941. Beethoven, Sonata C minor, Op. 30, no. 2; Mozart, Sonata G major, K.379; Brahms, Sonata Op. 100, A major, Newmark and Kander

John Newmark's Start on a Brilliant Canadian Career

Early or mid-April 1941. Mozart, Sonatas in A major, K.526 and F major, K.547, Newmark and Kander

29 May 1941. Mozart, Sonata in E-flat major, K.481, Newmark and Amtmann; piano solo: Mozart, Fantasy in C (K.394 or 396), and Bach, Inventions; Franck, Sonata, Newmark and Amtmann. (It is possible that the Mozart and Bach solos were played by Fritz Lewin.)

11 June 1941. This concert featured both Amtmann and Kander, though not together. Handel, Sonata in G minor; Beethoven, Sonata in A-flat major, Op. 26 (piano solo); Mozart, Sonata in A major, K.526 (presumably the Handel was played by Amtmann, the Mozart by Kander).

I remember distinctly how Kander and Newmark were rehearsing the tricky opening of Mozart's *Presto* last movement where the violin enters one quarter beat after the piano, a mere split second. Newmark rarely played solo, but he did play the Beethoven Op. 26. I remember hearing him practise the runs in thirds in the right hand in the *Scherzo* movement which obviously needed work.

Newmark quickly became a camp celebrity. Here was a real-life artist in our midst, a person who was at the same time a good mixer, a very approachable fellow. Although he already used the name John Newmark, for most of us he remained Johnny Neumark—though never Hans—throughout the years in camp. He addressed everyone with the familiar German "du," at least everyone his age or younger.

We admired and took pride in Johnny. His performances provided eagerly craved spiritual nourishment; furthermore, since camp commanders were invited to concerts and plays, his artistry might convince the authorities that the refugees had a contribution to make to Canada and should be treated as desirable immigrants. Johnny would show them!

We all left Camp B on 21 June 1941, some, including myself, for Camp A (Farnham, Quebec), the orthodox Jews for Camp I (Île aux Noix), others, including Newmark, for Camp N (Sherbrooke). The Farnham camp, where the amateur piano duo of Wolfgang Gerson (later an architect in Vancouver) and Schneider was the main provider of music, in its turn was dissolved on 23 January 1942 and its occupants taken to Camp N where we met Newmark again. By February 1942, however, Kander had been released to study at the Toronto Conservatory. Although I remember theatre performances at Camp N, I have a record of only three Newmark recitals in Sherbrooke.

27 February 1942. Violin Sonatas, Bach, E major; Mozart, E-flat major, K.481; Brahms, G major, Op. 78, Newmark and Amtmann.

The second recital requires a short digression. As time went on, more instruments and more sheet music became available. Dr. Manfred Saalheimer, a lawyer from Würzburg, later on the staff of the Canadian Jewish Congress, played the viola, one Bretschneider, Georg Liebel and Carl Amberg (both chemists) and Kurt Levy (later chair of Latin-American studies at the University of Toronto) the cello. The astronomer Dr. Günter Archenhold, one Dr. Schnetzler, young Eribert Reckmann and Kaspar Naegele (later a sociologist at the University of British Columbia) all played the flute. I am not sure which of them participated in the following concert, apart from Dr. Saalheimer. In letters of 1 and 4 April, I reported to a friend in New York: "There was one concert in this camp recently which has surpassed all previous camp concerts in respect of its means: besides a pianist there were 2 violins, one viola, a cello, and two flutes. This was a grand orchestra indeed! They played Mozart's D-minor piano concerto [K.466] and everything but the last movement went quite well. The concert opened with a late piano trio in G major by Mozart [K.564], one of the few works of Mozart that are entirely happy." (I like to call it the "Papageno Trio" because of its childlike tunes.)

Of the third concert, I never recorded the date. It included a performance of Schubert's Fantasy in F minor, Op. 103 for piano duet, Newmark took the upper part, Helmut Blume the lower. I still hear Newmark's understated, almost drowsy, announcement of the opening theme ringing in my ears.

In May 1942 I reported to my friend that the Brahms Trio in B major, Op. 8 was being rehearsed. On one occasion when I had my assigned piano time, Newmark happened to be there with some four-hand music and we played the Scherzo of Schumann's C-major symphony. Or rather, we began to—I wasn't used to strict time counting and couldn't keep up with his fast moving upper part.

At Last, Free in Canada

Newmark was released from camp N, Sherbrooke, on 13 October 1942. His introduction to Canadian audiences came in a series of recitals in the winter of 1942/43 in Ottawa, Kingston, and other cities together with Helmut Blume and Gerhard Kander. My own release did not take place until early August 1943 when I went to Toronto to work as an audit clerk. As I looked for a place to live I ran into Johnny who lived in a rooming house at 63 Lowther Avenue run by refugees from Hungary. "Come over and speak to the landlady, she has an empty room," he advised me. And so I moved in, in the company of several other ex-internees. As far as I know, Newmark studied conducting with Ettore Mazzoleni at this time—although past piano lessons at the age of thirty-nine, he had to justify being released from camp as a "student." One day when he had spare time on his hands, he volunteered to play something for me. I asked for Schubert's A-minor Sonata Op. 143. He fetched his Schubert volume and without rehearsing gave a perfect rendition of the work. Only the last ten bars in the third movement with their staggered octave patterns made him comment on their difficulty.

Soon after—on 27 August 1943—we were both invited for dinner to a Toronto doctor's family. Of course Johnny was asked to perform but, notoriously unable to play anything from memory, he depended on whatever music happened to be on the piano. It was Variation 18 from Rachmaninoff's *Rhapsody on a Theme by Paganini*. The family's son-in-law, a gifted amateur pianist himself, asked Newmark who his favorite composer was, fully expecting to hear a confirmation of his own choice, Beethoven. His jaw dropped when he heard Newmark say: Mozart and Schubert.

A few weeks later the rooming house was sold and the new owner upped the rent so steeply that most of us had to move. Again Newmark came to my rescue. He had heard of a lady who was looking for a roomer who could play the family piano. The following year, Newmark settled in Montreal and I lost contact with him.

It was not until 1951 that I met Johnny again, although I must have heard him in one duo recital or another in Toronto. While in Montreal for research on the revised edition of the CBC's *Catalogue of Canadian Composers* I visited him on 29 January 1951 at his Crescent Street residence. I remember that he demonstrated his recently acquired Clementi piano (1810),[1] also that he gave an athletic workout to his Siamese cat.

Later we would exchange greetings at music conferences and festivals. As chief of the collection of musical Canadiana at the National Library of Canada I asked him at one time or another what would happen to his library and his papers. He was going to leave his music to his pupils but seemed inclined to deposit his career documents in Ottawa.

On 4 January 1987 Johnny called me at my home and asked me to visit him as soon as possible. He had suffered several strokes recently and wanted the National Library to have his scrapbooks of programs and reviews, his broadcast tapes and other memorabilia. I went to his apartment at 3261 Forest Hill in Montreal on 20 January to pick up the material and was pleased to find that Johnny could walk, talk and eat without help. Sadly, he no longer played the piano. Happily, he lived another four years. His death occurred on 14 October 1991.

Notes on Newmark's Canadian and international career will be found in the *Encyclopedia of Music in Canada*, and greater details and an appreciation of his artistry in a forthcoming biography of Renée Maheu. Over the years the CBC featured many ensemble broadcasts with Newmark, beginning in 1944 with the first broadcast series of the Beethoven Trios, with Alexander Brott and Roland Leduc. Always his playing had a certain flavour that made it uniquely his own. (Only in later years did I find something to criticize, a tendency to excessive use of staccato in Mozart and his contemporaries, almost a mannerism.) As piano partner—the term "accompanist" does not do justice to his work—of some eighty foreign and over 160 Canadian artists, as concerto soloist, adjudicator and music adviser, Newmark became a central figure in Canada's musical life. Nearly seventy recordings testify to his rare artistry.

A Major Contribution to Music in Canada

The extraordinary blossoming of musical activity in Canada after the Second World War undoubtedly owed much to favourable economic, technological, patriotic and other historical forces. However, it was due also to a conscious self-mobilization, a collective will to create better institutions for training and employing musicians. In this process the refugees from Hitler's Germany played a major role. As in other spheres of life, Germany's loss was Canada's gain. The areas of activity ranged from St. John's, NL, where Leipzig-born Andreas Barban (1914–1993) taught and played piano, to British Columbia, where Ida Halpern (1910–1987), a Viennese, researched and recorded Indian music and promoted concerts. Of national importance, but resident in Toronto, were Arnold Walter (1902–1973), master reformer and organizer, Nicholas Goldschmidt (b. 1908),[2] grand organizer of festivals (both Moravian-born), Herman Geiger-Torel (1907–1976) from Frankfurt/Main, genius of opera production, and the Berlin-born conductor and apostle of Bruckner and Mahler, Heinz Unger (1895–1965). Hardly less impressive were the contributions of such singers-voice teachers as Ernesto Vinci (Berlin-born), Emmy Heim and

Irene Jessner (both from Vienna), the harpsichordist Greta Kraus (from Vienna), the brothers Otto (composer and violist) and Walter (cellist) Joachim (from Düsseldorf), the conductor Mario Duschenes (from Altona), the singer Jan Simons (from Düsseldorf), the all-round musician Alfred Rosé (from Vienna) and many others.

None of the above musicians had been in Canadian refugee internment camps. To conclude I will provide a brief survey of other ex-internees who left a mark on Canadian music. Apart from Newmark's, the greatest reputations were enjoyed by Helmut Blume, Walter Homburger and Franz Kraemer. Blume (b. Berlin 1914) [d. Montreal 1998], a student of Hindemith's, and a virtuoso pianist of whose brilliant recitals in Sherbrooke's Camp N I heard only a few, spent a few years with the CBC International Service, broadcasting to Germany by shortwave. Subsequently he became well known as a music broadcaster on the CBC's domestic radio and TV services, introducing much contemporary music to Canadian listeners. At McGill University he served as professor of piano and for many years as dean of the Faculty of Music. During those years the Faculty established an electronic music studio, planned the move to a larger building and greatly expanded its music program.

Newmark's erstwhile page-turner Walter Homburger (b. Karlsruhe 1924), not a musician by training, became a concert agent whose International Artists Concert Agency introduced many great artists to Toronto and other cities. He was for some years also the manager of Glenn Gould and others. In 1962 Homburger was appointed manager of the Toronto Symphony Orchestra and was spectacularly helpful in the orchestra's rise to fame and financial health.

Franz Kraemer (b. Vienna 1914) [d. Toronto 1999], like Blume, worked in the CBC International Service for some years. When CBC television was started his Austrian background, including studies with Alban Berg, made him a natural choice for opera production, including *Peter Grimes, Elektra, The Magic Flute, Otello,* and *Louis Riel.* He also produced TV programs about Stravinsky, Gould and Rostropovich. Later, Kraemer became director of music programs for Toronto's St. Lawrence Centre and [still later] head of the Music Section of the Canada Council.

It is hardly a coincidence that the refugee internment camps produced the first two historians of Canadian music. The curious newcomer had a need for orientation but found it hard to read up on Canadian music and its roots. Willy Amtmann (b. Vienna 1910) [d. Ottawa 1996], established himself in Ottawa where he became concertmaster of the Ottawa

Philharmonic Orchestra and taught string playing in public schools. In 1968, at Carleton University, he was the first to teach Canadian music history, having written his doctoral dissertation on Music in New France. He expanded his research in a book *Music in Canada 1600–1800* and its French edition, *La Musique au Québec 1600–1875*.[3]

A self-made historian of Canadian music, the author (b. Berlin 1922) [d. Ottawa 2012] has written the pioneer text *A History of Music in Canada 1534–1914*, served as CBC music librarian for twenty years in Toronto and in 1970 organized and until 1987 headed the Music Division of the National Library in Ottawa. He was also co-editor of the two editions of the *Encyclopedia of Music in Canada / Encyclopédie de la musique au Canada* and chair of the historical anthology, *The Canadian Musical Heritage/Le Patrimoine musical canadien*. A few other musician "camp boys" should be mentioned: Hans Kaufmann, a violinist in Toronto, for many years associated with the St. Regis Hotel, and Freddie Grant (originally Fritz Grundland), a pianist associated with the city's Lichee Gardens restaurant, and composer of the song "You'll Get Used to It" which became one of the hit songs of the Second World War. (The "it" to which one should get used was one's internment, but the text was easily adapted to one's being in the armed forces.)[4]

And what became of Gerhard Kander (b. Mannheim ca. 1921) [d. Toronto 2008], who had given so many recitals with John Newmark? After camp he had lessons with the famous Kathleen Parlow and performed in public, a highlight being Brahms' Violin Concerto with the Toronto Symphony Orchestra under Sir Ernest MacMillan on 13 November 1945. Not long after, Kander gave up his musical career, continuing to play for pleasure only.

Through a combination of circumstances, such as the great opportunities for cultural pioneering in postwar Canada and their high educational average, the 950-odd German and Austrian internees released in Canada have given proof to the trust inspired by their spearheader, John Newmark. Nine have been appointed to the Order of Canada, an unusually high proportion for any group, and four of these for contributions to music. The first was our Johnny, appointed an Officer in 1973.

NOTES

1   Newmark acquired the early nineteenth-century piano, made by the London firm of Clementi, in 1950, and played many concerts, broadcasts, and recordings on it. [*Ed.*]

2 Goldschmidt died in 2004; for further information on his life see Gwenlyn Setterfield, *Nicholas Goldschmidt: A Life in Canadian Music* (Toronto: University of Toronto Press, 2003). [*Ed.*]
3 Willy Amtmann, *Music in Canada 1600–1800* (Cambridge, ON: Habitex, ca. 1975) and *La Musique au Québec 1600–1875* (Montreal: Éditions de l'homme, 1976). [*Ed.*]
4 The song "You'll Get Used to It," with words and music by the internee Fritz Grundland (later Freddie Grant), became a sensational hit towards the end of the war, when it was featured both at home and overseas in *The Navy Show*, sung by John Pratt as a long-suffering enlisted sailor. The song is a Canadian equivalent to Irving Berlin's "This Is the Army, Mr. Jones." It was the first of several notable pop tune successes by Grant. [*Ed.*]

1 The Kallmann family, Berlin, 22 August 1936. Left to right: Helmut, Fanny, Arthur, Eva. *Photographer unknown; from the collection of Dawn Keer.*

2 The 1933–34 "Quinta" class of the Hohenzollern Gymnasium, Berlin. HK is second from the left in the second row. He studied at this school from 1932 to 1938 but was forced to transfer to a school run by the Jewish Community for his final year of secondary school. *Photographer unknown; from Helmut Kallmann's archival papers.*

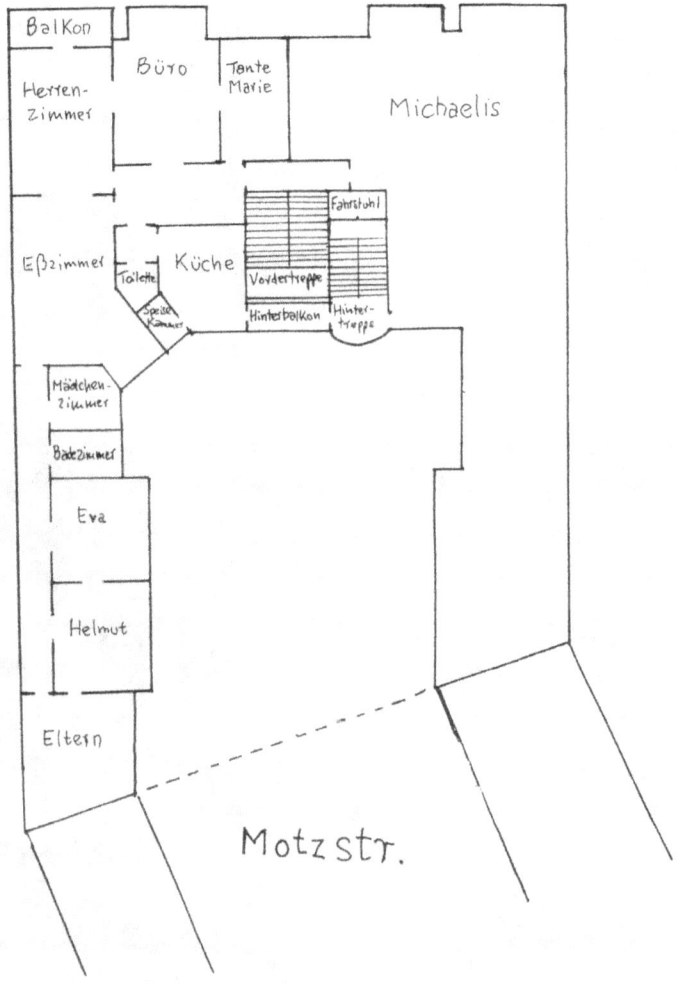

3 HK's floor plan, drawn from memory, of the family's flat, Geisbergstrasse 41, Berlin. *Pen and ink drawing; from Helmut Kallmann's archival papers.*

4 HK's *Abgangszeugnis* (Leaving Report) from the Private School of the Jewish Community is dated 7 June 1939. He departed for England five days later. *Paper document; from Helmut Kallmann's archival papers.*

5 Sketches by HK of Internment Camp I, Île aux Noix, QC, 1943. He indicates his quarters with arrows (top drawing, far left). *Pencil and paper sketch; from Helmut Kallmann's archival papers.*

6 At the piano, 10 May 1997, with a heavily censored letter he sent from internment camp in the early 1940s to his childhood friend Peter Ball, who had emigrated to New York in 1938. *Photograph by Dave Chan for the* Ottawa Citizen. *Reprinted by permission.*

7 Gordon Jocelyn and HK on their graduation day, Toronto, 1949. *Photographer unknown; from Helmut Kallmann's archival papers.*

8 HK at the files in the CBC Music Library, Toronto; the photo was taken by the Dutch conductor Henry Plukker in March 1955. *Photograph by Henry Plukker; from the collection of Dawn Keer.*

9 This posed portrait was taken on 10 December 1960, the year HK's *A History of Music in Canada 1534–1914* was published. *Photographer unknown; from Helmut Kallmann's archival papers.*

10a Berlin 1962, during HK's first return visit to Germany after the war. HK and his wife, Ruth, centre, with his friend from school days and fellow internee Guenter Bardeleben and his wife, Margaret. *Photographer unknown; from Helmut Kallmann's archival papers.*

10b Ruth Singer Kallmann, Berlin, 1962. *Photographer unknown; from Helmut Kallmann's archival papers.*

11 Press conference for the launch of the *Encyclopedia of Music in Canada* in Hart House, University of Toronto, 12 November 1981. Left to right: the editors HK, Kenneth Winters, and Gilles Potvin (unknown bystander to HK's left); the patron Floyd S. Chalmers; the director-general of the board of directors Michael Koerner. *Photograph, probably by Mark Miller, from the collection of Dawn Keer.*

12 National Library of Canada Music Division staff, 22 January 1987, at a reception in honour of HK's appointment to the Order of Canada. Left to right: Gilles Saint-Laurent, Florence Hayes, Stephen Willis, Maria Calderisi Bryce, HK, Joan Colquhoun, Gregory Renaud. *Photographer unknown, from the collection of Dawn Keer.*

13 On his sixty-seventh birthday, 7 August 1989. *Photographer unknown; from Helmut Kallmann's archival papers.*

14 A meeting of the editorial committee of the Canadian Musical Heritage Society at Carleton University, 11 December 1989. Standing, left to right: Lucien Poirier, Elaine Keillor, John Beckwith, Frederick A. Hall, Clifford Ford; at the piano, HK. *Photographer unknown; from the collection of Dawn Keer.*

15   Addressing the Ottawa meeting of the International Association of Music Libraries, 17 July 1994. *Photographer unknown; from Helmut Kallmann's archival papers.*

16   Reunion of ex-internees on the sixtieth anniversary of their deportation, 13 May 2000. Left to right: Walter Homburger, Gregory Baum, HK. *Photographer unknown; from Helmut Kallmann's archival papers.*

17 With Traute Weinberg, December 2004. *Photographer unknown; from Helmut Kallmann's archival papers.*

12
Franz Schubert in Canada: A Historical Survey of Performance, Appreciation, and Research

The conference "Austria 996–1996: Music in a Changing Society," organized by Walter Kreyszig of the University of Saskatchewan, sponsored by the Austrian government, and held in Ottawa in January 1996, comprised an unusually large number of panel discussions, lectures, and performances. HK delivered this paper, and later edited it for the published proceedings, projected but never issued. Tracing the reception history of a classical repertoire in a North American setting was the sort of research exercise HK enjoyed, and he produced some of the few Canadian examples. His previous entry in this genre was devoted to Beethoven.[1] Choosing Schubert for the present article, a composer whose work he knew well and cherished especially, he broadens the topic to include speculations, recent evidence, text criticism, and even aesthetic judgments on particular pieces. In a later article, HK compared the music of three European masters—Schubert, Mendelssohn, and Brahms—in their shared anniversary year, and concluded that Schubert's had the deepest and most universal appeal. Schubert, he argued, "was far more learned, high-aiming and self-critical than he has been given credit for."[2]

Let me begin with some statistics. Donizetti 206, Bellini 186, Verdi 144, Rossini 135, Handel 81, Balfe 76, Auber 54, Mendelssohn 50, Beethoven 48, Mozart 40, Weber 36—I'll skip a few names—Schubert 13, and for good measure Chopin 4 and Schumann 0.

Previously unpublished article, 1996

These figures are taken from David Sale's quite exhaustive index of Toronto performances between 1845 and 1867.[3] How was it possible, one may well ask, that a composer infinitely greater than Donizetti or Balfe and whose music presented no unusual technical difficulties was so little performed some thirty years after his death?

Reception in Europe

To explain the protracted introduction of Schubert's music to Canada, one has to keep in mind the uneven and slow dissemination of his music on his Central European home ground itself. Whereas many composers were famous in their time, then forgotten and later rediscovered, such as Bach, or never lost their popularity, such as Haydn, Mozart, and Beethoven, Schubert exemplifies both kinds at once. His music quickly achieved wide popularity but only by a mere fraction of his songs and piano pieces and a few chamber works, whereas the bulk of his works was only gradually discovered and printed, long after his death. The Octet came out twenty-five years after his death;[4] the *Unfinished Symphony* was discovered and first performed after thirty-seven years. The reasons for Schubert's delayed recognition are many, apart from the composer's ineptness as a businessman. Most of his contemporaries became famous first of all as virtuosi and/or opera composers. Schubert did not have those attributes nor the benefit of promotional societies, biographers, or advocating critics (although eventually Mendelssohn, Schumann, and Liszt did a great deal for his music).[5] In consequence, the literary and philosophical discussion of art and music during the nineteenth century paid little attention to the obscure songwriter and all the more to Beethoven, Berlioz, Liszt, or Wagner. Schubert's music had to make its way into the ears and hearts of listeners mainly on its own merits. It is all the more astonishing that Schubert, who had little immediate influence on nineteenth-century composers outside song, anticipated or influenced so much of the future—the short lyrical piano piece, some of Schumann, much of Brahms's chamber music, Bruckner's nearly everything (in the view of Alfred Einstein), Dvořák's almost everything, Mahler's song-symphonies, Wagner's declamatory style, and late-nineteenth-century modulations and harmonies in general. Unmistakable are the threads from Schubert to later salon music, Viennese waltzes, Sullivan's operettas, and much more. I have always wanted to assign an essay contest with the topic, "The nineteenth century put Beethoven's name on its banner, but in its bones it had Schubert."

The Dissemination in a Peripheral Country: Early Canadian Contacts

Let me now turn to Canada, but first to the realm of speculation. Were there any Canadians who met and knew Schubert? The answer is a cautionary Yes. The German-born musician Theodore Frederick Molt, who had come to Quebec City in 1822, decided three years later to revisit Europe. Upon his return to Quebec he advertised in June 1826 that he had met Beethoven, Czerny, and Moscheles. The Beethoven visit is well documented.[6] In his letter to Beethoven, written in Vienna, Molt mentions that he has already visited "several (*mehrere*) famous European composers." There is yet another source concerning Molt's journey, a biographical sketch written twelve years after his death by John K. Converse,[7] a founder and later principal of the Burlington (Vermont) Female Seminary. Converse states that Molt "also had the acquaintance and assistance of Beethoven, Franz Schubert and other distinguished pianists and composers."

If Molt had the gumption to visit the intimidating, if not choleric, Beethoven and extract a manuscript from him, surely he would not have hesitated to approach the gentler Schubert, Molt's almost exact contemporary in age. Alas, no account of Molt's visit to Europe has been traced in a Canadian newspaper. It remains instructive that Schubert's reputation was large enough in 1825 to have made personal acquaintance desirable and yet not large enough to mention him in an advertisement in the Quebec newspaper. Nor is there any evidence that Molt brought examples of printed music by Schubert back to Canada for use in his teaching.

The second early connection between Schubert and Canada is a purely musical one. It relates to a similarity between the opening theme of the Rondo of Schubert's D major Sonata Op. 53 (D.850) and the Rondo on a "Favorite Toronto Air" written in the late 1840s by the Scottish-born Canadian organist James Paton Clarke (1807 or 1808–1877), one of the first published Canadian compositions longer than a song or a waltz (see examples 1a and 1b). The similarity lies in the rhythm and the accompaniment, not in the melody. Furthermore, both are in the key of D major. It suggests one of two possibilities, either that Clarke knew Op. 53, or that the kind of theme and layout had meanwhile (and even before Schubert) been used by a variety of composers whose music is now forgotten. Probably this similarity is merely a curious coincidence; at most it shows that Clarke was familiar with Schubert's piano music. I let the reader be the judge.

Example 1a: Schubert Piano Sonata in D Major, Op. 53 (D.850): IV Rondo, bars 1–10

Example 1b: J.P. Clarke, *Favourite Toronto Air*, bars 1–8

The First Concert Performances (1845–1867)

Enough of conjecture! After a premature late-eighteenth-century blossoming in Quebec and Halifax, Canadian concert life in the sense of fairly regular seasons with local or visiting performers gained momentum in larger cities only in the 1840s. Chroniclers are only at early stages of combing through contemporary newspapers for announcements and reviews to supplement the small number of surviving program sheets. Good searching has been done for certain stretches of time in Quebec, Montreal, Kingston, Toronto, and Victoria, but the following analysis is based on fewer than half the estimated concerts. Typical for programming was the mixture of amateurs and professionals, soloists, and ensembles, each making one or two appearances. Hence a couple of Schubert songs or piano pieces are the most one may expect to find in any one concert.

Toronto

I will begin with Toronto, because its mid-nineteenth-century concerts are extremely well-documented, thanks to Sale's work. The main influences were Handel and Haydn, some Mozart and Beethoven, and much Mendelssohn, Rossini, Verdi, and Gounod. The statistics already quoted show that, typically, there were 11 Verdi offerings for one Schubert. Most frequent were "Ave Maria" and "The Wanderer," whereas an instrumental piece appeared only once.

1845	Oct 24	"Impatience" (singer not identified)
1855	May 15	Prayer "Ave Maria" Mme [Rosa] Devries
1856	Mar 3	"Ave Maria" Mme [Rosa] Devries (always a female voice!)
1856	Jul 18	"The Wanderer" Mr. Stretton (always a male voice!)
1857	Apr 24	"Ave Maria" Mme Strakosch
1860	May 4	"The Wanderer" Mr. Cook
1861	Apr 3	Serenade "Thro' the woods" J.D. Humphreys (cancelled)
1862	Nov 26	"The Wanderer" Mr. Roche
1863	Feb 16	"The Adieu" Miss Ridout
1864	Mar 17	"Ave Maria" Miss Kate McDonald
	Apr 11	Aria "Ave Maria" Miss Kate McDonald
1866	Jan 17	Impromptu in B flat "Luxembourg" (presumably by John Carter)
1867	Feb 26	"The Wanderer" Mr. Egan

Quebec City

I can report only negatively. One of the main sources in this city is the collection of music from various ensembles and amateurs of the early nineteenth century that is preserved at Laval University and the Séminaire de Québec. It does have orchestral music by such contemporaries of Schubert's as Johann Wenzel Kalliwoda or Ferdinand Ries, piano or chamber music by Haydn, Pleyel, Clementi, but I found no Schubert; of course, most of Schubert's instrumental music wasn't published yet.

Montreal

The Montreal harvest is slim. In Peter Slemon's MMA thesis on concerts in Montreal 1841–1867 (McGill University, 1976) program listings of songs are usually operatic or "national" rather than of the art variety. Schubert performances average perhaps one a year.

1855	May 25	"Ave Maria" Mme Rosa Devries
1867	May 22	Grand Concert of Classical Music (with Hone, Torrington and Jehin-Prume); the program included Beethoven, Haydn and Schubert.

Exceptional was a performance of the *Rosamunde* Overture on 12 June 1867 along with Bach, Mozart, and Beethoven at the inauguration of a new organ at St. Andrew's Church. The Germanians (Musik-Gesellschaft Germania) who visited both Montreal and Toronto as well as Quebec and Kingston, did not feature Schubert, as the limited sampling in H. Earle Johnson's *Musical Quarterly* article suggests, although they featured such modern composers as Schumann (Op. 52), Gade, and Kalliwoda.[8]

1867–1900

The period from Confederation—the founding of modern Canada in 1867—to the turn of the century saw modest progress in Schubert performances in Europe and in Canada. In the 1860s Kreissle von Hellborn wrote the first biography of Schubert, the *Unfinished* Symphony was discovered and first performed, and thirty years later the *Gesamtausgabe* was completed and the one-hundredth birthday of Schubert celebrated.

Montreal

For the period from 1867 to 1898 I found only twenty-four programs in the National Library's retrospective collection (disregarding scrapbooks). Schubert, Mozart, and Bach are nowhere to be found. Who then was performed? Chopin, Weber, Schumann, Mendelssohn, Saint-Saëns, Grieg, and Gounod were typical. However, other sources indicate at least one larger work by Schubert: *Miriams Siegesgesang* (1882). From that year also date the first Canadian Schubert publications. "Le Désir" and "Éloge des Larmes" appeared in a Montreal music periodical in 1882 and "Sérénade" was published in Quebec City.

Victoria

Dale McIntosh's thorough analysis of Victoria newspapers[9] has twenty references to Schubert. Since the earliest, a duet called "Les Dames de Seville, Op. 43" (a spurious opus number) dates from 1861 only, this means an average of a Schubert number every second year. Sometimes songs were arranged for instruments; thus the "Serenade" was played by the violinist Ede Reményi (Brahms's one-time travel companion) in 1879 and repeated the following year by a cornetist. The piano solo offerings usually were a Liszt transcription of one of the songs, e.g., "Der Erlkönig."

The 1890s to World War One—The Era of Touring Stars and Budding Canadian Orchestras

With the 1890s we enter the era of permanent orchestras in the major cities of Canada, the building of substantial concert halls or "opera houses" as they used to be called. In Europe Schubert had become one of the classics, an acknowledged master of instrumental as well as vocal music. However, we must remember that Montreal and Quebec City were fond of opera above all other kinds of art music, Ontario of oratorio, and Schubert had little vocal music to offer except songs in German. Nonetheless there was a burst of Schubert performances as his piano and chamber music gained rapidly in popularity.

Here are a few examples from Montreal.[10] In 1896 Paderewski played the Impromptu Op. 142, no. 3, D.935 (the *Rosamunde* Variations) and a Liszt transcription ("Hark! Hark!"). The same pattern held for Carreño's recital the next year: Op. 142, no. 2 and Liszt's *Soirée de Vienne*. Two years later Emil von Sauer played Liszt's "Erlkönig" transcription and Moriz Rosenthal the "Lindenbaum," presumably also in a Liszt transcription. After 1899, concerts became more numerous, and at the beginning of that year there was a veritable Schubert feast in Montreal, at least one composition per *week*. Emil von Sauer on 30 January played Liszt's "Erlkönig," a week later the Kneisel Quartet performed the *Andante con moto* and *Presto* from the D-minor Quartet, D.810, in another week "Der

Neugierige" was sung by Mme S. Cornu. On 20 February Max Heinrich sang four Schubert songs, on the 24th J.J. Goulet's Symphony Orchestra played the *Rosamunde* Overture, and on 20 March Moriz Rosenthal offered three Schubert pieces. In 1902 at last sonata movements were heard. Fanny Bloomfield-Zeisler played the Minuet from Op. 78 (D.894), Ossip Gabrilowitsch the Sonata in A (I would guess this was the shorter one, Op. 120/D.664), and Eugen d'Albert chose two Impromptus in 1905; and so it went on.

A date to remember is 23 November 1894: the Montreal SO gives the *Unfinished* Symphony under the baton of Guillaume Couture. His orchestra lasted only two seasons but also managed to present symphonies by Beethoven, Mendelssohn, Mozart, and Schumann. The *Unfinished* conquered Montreal by storm. It was given again in 1896 under Horace W. Reyner and again under Couture in 1897 in a matinee before an evening performance of Beethoven's Ninth (!) by the Montreal Philharmonic Society. J.J. Goulet performed it in 1898 and again in 1901, 1903, 1904, 1905, and 1907. On 30 March 1900 Goulet introduced the "Seventh" Symphony, undoubtedly the Great C major, repeating the *Andante con moto* and *Scherzo* a month later, and adding the *Rosamunde* Overture to his orchestra's repertoire. The first two movements of the *Tragic* Symphony, D.417 were given in 1902, the last two a year later. In that year the *Overture in Italian Style*, D. 591 in C major was presented; the Great C major, D.944 again in 1905. Thus Montreal, for another half-century Canada's largest city, was well ahead of Toronto, which had a regular orchestra only starting in 1906.[11]

The Toronto Conservatory Symphony Orchestra in its inaugural concert in April 1907 included entr'acte music from *Rosamunde*, along with three movements from Beethoven's First. The *Unfinished* followed soon after. The Toronto Symphony Orchestra, before it folded during World War One, had given the work four times (1908–1912). When the orchestra was revived in 1923 it played this work almost every year. However, the orchestra was more remarkable for its cultivation of Richard Strauss and Elgar than of Schubert. The Great C major was given its first performance only in 1924 under the Vienna-born Luigi von Kunits, twenty-four years after the Montreal premiere, and then not played for another ten years. The *Rosamunde* Overture however was played nearly every year, beginning in 1931.

Toronto and Montreal, of course, were not the only Canadian cities with orchestras early in this century. The Halifax Symphony Orchestra had presented the *Unfinished* in April 1897 under its resident conductor Max Weil in a Schubert Memorial concert. In Victoria an amateur orchestra called the Philharmonic Society introduced the entr'acte music from *Rosamunde* in 1898, and repeated it in 1899; a later orchestra presented the *Unfinished* in 1931 and, still relatively early, the Symphony No. 5, D.485 in 1949.

A word now about chamber music. In Montreal the D-minor Quartet was heard in 1903 (Kneisel Quartet), followed by the Trio in B-flat Major, Op. 99 (D.898) in 1906 (performed by the Mendelssohn Trio). In Toronto the Hambourg Concert Society in 1912 presented "first in Toronto" the String Quintet, D.956, but only the first and third movements. The Scherzo of this work was played also in 1918 in Quebec City, by an ensemble of local musicians called Le Quintette à cordes Schubert. On 7 May 1902 the Kneisel Quartet played the second movement of the D-minor Quartet in Toronto, "an excerpt very popular in this city."[12] The *Trout* Quintet (D.667) was billed in 1913 as a Toronto premiere.[13]

There is no need to detail song performances except to say that rarely more than two Schubert songs were heard in one recital and that the singers included such stars as Max Heinrich, Ernestine Schumann-Heink, and Johanna Gadski.

Women's Musical Clubs

In Canada women's musical clubs, most of them organized in the twenty-five years before World War One, were of immense importance in organizing concerts, introducing artists, and spreading musical knowledge. Often they would devote a recital to just one or two composers, in combination with a lecture. For example, the Ladies' Morning Musical Club of Montreal in 1906 presented a Schumann/Schubert recital, and the Women's Musical Club of Toronto, on 19 November 1908, a recital of Schubert and Tchaikovsky. In the latter organization, Schubert was a staple from the beginning. On 17 January 1901, an Impromptu was played by Katherine Birnie and two songs, "Lied der Mignon" and "Heidenröslein," were sung by Dora L. McMurtry, followed immediately by "Hedge-roses" sung by Violet Gooderham! In February of that year, the *Litany for All Souls' Day* (*Litanei auf das Fest aller Seelen*, D.343) was performed by Edwin B. Jackson; on 14 March "Trockene Blumen" (Mrs. Ross Hayter) and "Slumber Song" (Amy Robsart Jaffray); and in a Schubert/Brahms program in November an Impromptu from Op. 142 (D.935) (Mrs. Percival Parker), the

"Cradle Song" and "Hark, Hark the Lark" (Amy Robsart Jaffray), and the "Serenade" as a cello solo by Hilda Richardson, followed by the "Erlkönig" sung by one Mr. Drummond.

Schubert Choirs (and Other Ensembles)

The naming of choirs is a revealing barometer of musical taste. Schubert has done rather well in this respect, but the Schubert choirs rarely specialized in performances of their patron saint's music. The Schubert Choir of Brantford, Ontario, under the direction of Henri K. Jordan, 1906–1941, was the most famous of the lot, considered second only to the Toronto Mendelssohn among Canadian choirs. It won rave reviews at the New York's World Fair in 1939. Other Schubert choirs of the twentieth century were those of Ottawa, Toronto, and Windsor. Sherbrooke, Quebec, had a Schubert Music Club (1925–ca. 1950) made up of some thirty local musicians and invited soloists, and Quebec City had a Quatuor à cordes Schubert, founded by Robert Talbot in 1921. Schubert's name was thus chosen for four Canadian choirs, one string quartet, and one concert organization. How does that compare with other composers? The Index of the *Encyclopedia of Music in Canada* lists six Bach ensembles (all vocal), six Haydn (instrumental), six Mendelssohn (either vocal or instrumental), four Elgar choirs or societies, three Handel societies, one Handel-Haydn Society, three Mozart (vocal and instrumental), two Beethoven (instrumental), and single choral entries for Berlioz, Massenet, Palestrina and others. I should mention that the Toronto Mendelssohn Choir up to 1969 had sung only three Schubert works: "The Lord is my Shepherd" in 1918; "Night in the Forest" in 1926; and the ballet music from *Rosamunde* in 1936, 1937, and 1938.[14]

In passing I should mention that piano manufacturers liked to adorn their different brands or models with names of famous pianist-composers such as Beethoven, Liszt, and Mendelssohn. The Schubert Piano was a brand name of R.S. Williams and Sons of Toronto, who built pianos from 1873 till the 1930s.

Canadian Reception

In Canadian music periodicals of the nineteenth century, tables of contents, if supplied at all, are very unsystematic. Spot checks revealed only one Schubert reference, a "Souvenir de Schubert," reprinted in the

December 1882 *Album musical* of Montreal from the *Moniteur Universal*—anecdotal material without any significance. My comments on Schubert's critical reception in Canada will focus on a single article, but one written by a pre-eminent musician. In 1927 Ernest MacMillan, then principal of the Toronto (now Royal) Conservatory of Music and Dean of the Faculty of Music at the University of Toronto and soon to be appointed conductor of the Toronto Symphony Orchestra, wrote "Some Notes on Schubert"[15] to assist high-school students with their matriculation examination on the first ten songs from *Die schöne Müllerin* the following year, the centenary of Schubert's death. MacMillan's opinions of Schubert, though hardly uniquely Canadian, are of significance since they obviously shaped the views of many youngsters and since MacMillan would have repeated them in lectures and conversations. Central to MacMillan's view is that Schubert's music is "easy-going"—he uses that phrase three times—and that the music of this "simple-minded musician" "frequently displayed itself in a carelessness with regard to his works" (in fairness to MacMillan, he probably thought of careless *preservation* rather than careless *composition*). He believes that Schubert's most important contributions were his songs (by implication *not* his chamber music, his piano and symphonic music!), that he lacked self-discipline and self-criticism, that his longer movements indulge in "vain repetitions" and "have rarely, if ever, that closely-knit, logical style of development which Beethoven exhibits in so marked a degree." Beethoven is held up as the standard of judgment, a master apparently above any criticism. At least I cannot imagine MacMillan admitting that Beethoven sometimes has excessive lengths or pedestrian harmonizations!

Has anyone whose task was to foster appreciation ever inculcated such a negative view of his subject matter? And by praising Schubert's complete spontaneity, his supreme melodic gift, and extraordinary originality on the harmonic side, his seemingly unlimited range of emotional expression, MacMillan lowers his own credibility, for how can someone who obviously adores Schubert have such uninformed views of his creative process, of his handling of thematic content, and of the reasons for occasional lengths?

I am not criticizing MacMillan the individual so much as the representative of his period. His was the common attitude towards Schubert, reinforced by the Puritan tradition of North America which stood in contrast to the Viennese enjoyment of pleasure, of luxuriant sound and sheer beauty. Schubert indeed needs to be played with indulgence in ringing sound and without fear of a bit of sentimentality. In the days when I was a Toronto Symphony Orchestra subscriber, about 1950, it often struck me that MacMillan, in inherited late-nineteenth-century fashion, considered Haydn, Mozart, and Schubert as lightweight. The period's tendency to equate important music with ponderosity fortunately has been overcome meanwhile.

After the Mid-Twentieth Century—A New Schubert Picture

The second half of the twentieth century finally saw the opening up of the entire output of Schubert in performance. (To the best of my investigation, no opera has yet been staged. However, on St. Cecilia's Day 1934, the Vienna Choir Boys sang *Der häusliche Krieg* before a capacity Toronto audience. *Fierrabras* was aired in 1996 but in a European performance.)[16] The change in our Schubert image owed much to O.E. Deutsch's *Schubert, A Documentary Biography* (the 1946 expanded version of his German publication of 1914) and his *Thematic Catalogue*.[17] These publications as well as the new complete edition, begun in 1964, had a tremendous impact on performance, appreciation, and research on an international scale. The LP recording technology and the postwar flourishing of concert life were the main channels for the increased exposure of the music.

What then is the new Schubert picture? To start with, romanticized anecdotes and fables were swept aside by Maurice Brown and other scholars. Discovery of sketches and examination of manuscript scores show the composer setting himself well-defined compositional tasks—such as the path to the Great C-major Symphony. Rather than "dash[ing] them off in the white heat of his genius,"[18] Schubert shows in his works many signs of preliminary sketching and of corrections, in short, of method and self-criticism. Indeed, a textbook of sonata form could easily be limited to Schubert examples. For economy of thematic material, see the Scherzo of the B-major Sonata Op. 147 (D.575), which, including inner and bass voices, virtually lives on the first two unison bars. For unity of structure and emotion, see the "awakening" which opens the A-minor Sonata Op. 42 (D.845). For development of thematic material see the last movement of the Grand Duo Op. 140 (D.812). But the question behind the attitude of MacMillan's generation is not the tabulation of virtues and weaknesses. Rather it is, why, in musical editorializing, were (and often still are) Bach, Haydn, or Beethoven (and even Brahms) commonly held up as law-giving masters but rarely Schubert. On the contrary, discussions of Schubert used to turn quickly to the question of weaknesses. Was that because his physical appearance lacks the middle-aged aura of authority? Because his modesty makes him an easy mark for fault-finding? Or just because his name does not start with a "B"? Schubert, in summary, is one of the few composers whose music ranges from the very lightest to the heaviest weight.

In the Canadian promotion of Schubert much is owed to central Europeans, often with a Viennese background, who settled in Canada just before, during, or after the war. The pianist Lubka Kolessa broadcast a sonata series in the late 1940s on CBC. Prominent voice teachers and vocal coaches included Emmy Heim, Ernesto Vinci, Aksel Schiøtz, Bernard Diamant, Nicholas Goldschmidt (who accompanied himself in *Winterreise*), Greta Kraus, and John Newmark. Emil Gartner conducted the Toronto Jewish Folk Choir in *Miriams Siegesgesang* (D.942) in 1948. Also of major importance in the dissemination of Schubert's music was a weekly CBC program of all available recordings, presented by Allan Sangster in the 1950s or early 1960s. (Those old enough may remember the program's theme, the second of the three *Klavierstücke*, D.946.) Speaking about recordings, in 1995 the National Library of Canada's collection of Canadian performances of Schubert included fifty-four CD entries, some seventy LPs, and twenty-five cassettes—but many feature a combination of composers. A selected list follows:

> *Pianists*: Paul Berkovitz (3 last sonatas and other works); Stéphane Lemelin; Anton Kuerti (Sonata cycle, CD, with his own notes; earlier LPs)
> *Singers*: Donald Bell with J. Wustman; Maureen Forrester with John Newmark; Lois Marshall with Greta Kraus in *Die schöne Müllerin*; Lois Marshall with Anton Kuerti in *Winterreise*; Jon Vickers with Geoffrey Parsons in *Winterreise*
> *Chamber music*: Orford String Quartet (String Quintet, *Quartettsatz*)

Research in Canada

Schubert research has blossomed in many countries during recent decades. An unscientific analysis of the preliminary program for the present conference—unscientific because I could not always determine the exact contents from the title—shows that Mozart and Schoenberg were tied for first place with over twenty papers, followed by fourteen for Beethoven and Schubert—another tie.

The honour of being the first Schubert scholar in Canada belongs to Ida Halpern, a Viennese who settled in Vancouver in 1939, a year after completing her doctoral thesis in Vienna on "Franz Schubert in der zeitgenössischen Kritik" ("Franz Schubert in Contemporary Criticism"). She was co-founder and first president in 1948 of the Vancouver Friends of Chamber Music and deserves credit for the society's rich Schubert fare. The twenty-fifth anniversary brochure of the Friends lists eleven Schubert works in thirty-two performances, averaging more than one work per season.

Schubert specialists active in 1996 include William Kinderman and Harald Krebs at the University of Victoria; Rita Steblin, most recently in Vienna; Mario Leblanc at the Université de Montréal; David Schroeder at Dalhousie University in Halifax; and John Glofcheskie at Douglas College, New Westminster, British Columbia. To summarize their articles and their research projects would take another paper. Suffice it to say that the predominant subject matter has to do with tonality, harmony, and modulation, as the appended list will show. Dissertations have been written on Schubert, and according to *Schubert durch die Brille* (June 1994), there are at least three since 1990, though I cannot vouch that they have been completed:[19]

Marion, John Gregory, on motivic unity and form in the C-major Symphony, first movement (Alberta), 1991
Quantz, Donald E., on part-songs (Manitoba), 1992
Reintjes, Mikki, on cyclical structure in *Schwanengesang* (Victoria), 1990

A Schubert Symposium was held in 1984 at Brock University in St. Catharines, Ontario; a conference and festival "Schubert and the Wanderer" at the University of Victoria in 1993. There exists also in Canada a branch of the International Franz Schubert Institute of Vienna. Its members receive the periodical *Schubert durch die Brille*, but no Canadian research program or other activity has been set up so far.

Articles and Theses by Canadians

Clarke, F.R.C., "Schubert's use of tonality: some unique features." *CAUSM/ACEUM Journal* 1/2 (Fall 1971), 25–38.

Down, Philip, "On an aspect of Schubert's expressive ideas." *Studies in Music from the University of Western Ontario* 2 (1977), 41–51.

Krebs, Harald, University of Victoria. Has concentrated mainly on tonality; several articles in international musicological journals.

Leblanc, Mario, "Franz Schubert: Un pas vers atonalité." *Canadian University Music Review / Revue de musique des universités canadiennes* 9/2 (1989), 84–115.

Leblanc, Mario. "Un trait fondamental de l'écriture harmonique de Franz Schubert: la division symétrique de l'octave en trois parties." Master's thesis, McGill University, 1985.

Schroeder, David P., "Polarity in Schubert's Unfinished Symphony." *Canadian University Music Review / Revue de musique des universités canadiennes* 1 (1980), 22–34. Schroeder has also written on Schubert for *The Music Review* (1988) and *Music and Letters* (1990), and has reviewed books.

Conclusion

The reader who expected to find startling Schubert discoveries or raging controversies in Canada will be disappointed. What I have found essentially parallels and confirms the European pattern. It demonstrates that the introduction of Schubert passed through several stages, from a very narrow range of popular items to universal but limited appreciation, until (after 1950) exposure of almost the full range of compositions was achieved. Schubert has become one of the most admired masters, indeed one of the few enjoyed equally by the sophisticated and the unsophisticated.

NOTES

1 "Beethoven and Canada: A Miscellany," *The Canada Music Book* 2 (Spring/Summer 1971), 107–17; reprinted with slight revisions in *German-Canadian Yearbook* 4 (Toronto, 1978), 286–94. [*Ed.*]

2 "Brahms, Mendelssohn and Schubert: Shaking Loose the Stereotypes," *Classical Music Magazine* 20/3 (September 1997), 20–22; quoted passage is on p. 22. In the 1980s, Maynard Solomon controversially argued that Schubert may have been a pederast in "Franz Schubert and the Peacocks of Benvenuto Cellini," *Nineteenth-Century Music* 12/3 (Spring 1989), 193–206. HK was skeptical, and found more interest in the study of Schubert's musical legacy than in speculations about his sex life. [*Ed.*]

3 Part of his University of Toronto master's thesis "Toronto's Pre-Confederation Music Societies 1845–1867" (1968).
4 In 1853, the year of Verdi's *La Traviata*, the Brindisi theme of which seems a direct offshoot of the second subject in the first movement of the Octet.
5 See John H. Mueller, *The American Symphony Orchestra: A Social History of Musical Taste* (Bloomington: Indiana University Press, 1951) and Maurice J.E. Brown, *Schubert: A Critical Biography* (London: Macmillan, 1958).
6 During the conference "Austria 996–1996, Music in a Changing Society" the National Library of Canada displayed the holograph of the canon (WoO 195) Beethoven presented to Molt.
7 Rev. John K. Converse, "Burlington Female Seminary," *The Vermont Historical Gazetteer*, vol. 1, 1868. I have been able to confirm many details mentioned by Converse.
8 H. Earle Johnson, "Germania Musical Society," *Musical Quarterly* 53/1 (January 1953), 75–93.
9 Robert Dale McIntosh, *A Documentary History of Music in Victoria, British Columbia*, vol. 1: 1850–1899 (Victoria: University of Victoria, 1981).
10 Bernard K. Sandwell's documentation, *The Musical Red Book of Montreal* (Montreal: F.A. Veitch, 1907) is rich in concert programs, but in many cases only the date, place, and performers are identified, since the program was no longer available.
11 For comparison, in the USA the C-major Symphony—first performed in 1839 in Leipzig by Mendelssohn—was introduced in 1851 by the New York Philharmonic under Theodore Eisfeld, the *Unfinished* in 1867 by the Theodore Thomas Orchestra, according to Mueller, *The American Symphony Orchestra*.
12 Review by 'Cherubino' [pseud.], *Saturday Night* (17 May 1902), 7. [*Ed.*]
13 The performance was given by members of the Women's Musical Club of Toronto, joined by Leo Smith on cello and a Mr. Bounsall on double bass; it took place on 6 February 1913 in the Conservatory of Music Concert Hall. [*Ed.*]
14 Maud McLean, *A Responsive Chord: The Story of the Toronto Mendelssohn Choir, 1894–1969* (Toronto: Toronto Mendelssohn Choir, 1969), 59.
15 *The School* 16/ 2 (October 1927).
16 A concert performance in Toronto, by Canadian artists, of Schubert's opera *Die Freunde von Salamanka*, 1 April 2012, was described by the presenter, Opera in Concert, as the work's Canadian premiere. [*Ed.*]
17 Otto Erich Deutsch, ed., *Franz Schubert: die Dokumente seines Lebens und Schaffens*, vol. 2 (Munich and Leipzig: G. Müller, 1914); rev., augmented ed. translated by Eric Blom as *Schubert: A Documentary Biography* (London:

Dent, 1946). Otto Erich Deutsch with Donald R. Wakeling, *Schubert: Thematic Catalogue of All His Works in Chronological Order* (London: Dent, 1951). [*Ed.*]

18 H. Plunket Greene, "Songs as the Singer Sees Them," Schubert Number of *Music & Letters* 9/4 (October 1928), 317, quoted in Maurice J.E. Brown, *Schubert: A Critical Biography* (London: Macmillan 1958), 346.

19 These three master's theses were each completed in the year cited. [*Ed.*]

13
Taking Stock of Canada's Composers from the 1920s to the Catalogue of Canadian Composers *(1952)*

This paper was given at the multidisciplinary conference "The Adaskin Years: A Celebration of the Arts in Canada 1930–1970" at the University of Victoria in March 1988, and subsequently published in *A Celebration of Canada's Arts*. The composer Murray Adaskin and his wife the singer Frances James inspired the conference, which they both attended. HK gives here his most extended memoir of his first assignment in musical lexicography, the CBC's *Catalogue of Canadian Composers*, second edition, 1952. Its breadth and comprehensiveness invited criticism and even ridicule, as evidenced in the quoted parody by Chester Duncan. HK refrains from listing Duncan's scholarly and musical qualifications (a professor of English at the University of Manitoba, Duncan was also a pianist and had composed a number of songs and piano pieces), though he does point out Duncan's own entry in the *Catalogue*. The "joke" entry which Duncan cooked up in fact closely resembles the actual final entry in the *Catalogue*, on Peter Zvankin of Winnipeg.[1] The first edition of the *Encyclopedia of Music in Canada*, 1981, met with similar comment from a critic in Britain, who ridiculed both its details of musical life in Medicine Hat, Alberta, and even the town's name, illustrating how strange and obscure the concept "music in Canada" has often seemed to those outside the country.[2]

This topic, which may well suggest a technical discussion of bibliographic methodology, focuses on the stock taking of Canadian composers and

---
A Celebration of Canada's Arts 1930–1970, ed. Glen Carruthers and Gordana Lazarevich (Toronto: Canadian Scholars Press, 1996), 15–26; republished by permission of Glen Carruthers

their works from a functional and historical point of view. My own perspective of musical scholarship supports the view that it is necessary to stress the intimate connection between fact gathering and ordering on the one hand and the search for musical values and the fulfillment of historical needs on the other.

Most of the work done by musical researchers—call them musicologists, historians, music scholars, or whatever you wish—has or should have three dimensions. In simple language, these are: 1) to clean up; 2) to search for gold; and 3) to observe connections.

1 To clean up is to assemble and verify the *facts* and to arrange them in some order. (To determine, for instance, the order in which universities introduced Canadian music courses into their curricula, or in exactly which year early in this century the Canadian composer Edward Manning wrote his splendid piano trio.)
2 To search for gold is to judge the *value* of the music so that the good will be performed, become known for its beauty and its effect on the soul, and may become an inspiration for future composers.
3 To observe connections is to investigate the *effect* of one event, or current, or person upon another, the interrelationship of a given culture or society and music within it—in short, the dynamics of musical history.

The musicologist who does not keep all three dimensions in mind can get into deep trouble. To engage in nothing but the assembling of facts without concern for values and relationships will never lead to wisdom; to philosophize about music without having at one's disposal a large bagful of solid information will soon lead to woolly thinking; and not to be searching for beauty, depth, and excellence in composition, but to lavish as much time on bad music as on good music, just "because it is there," does no service to one's community.

With respect to historiography in Canada, why did stock taking of Canadian compositions become a necessity in the second quarter of our century? What has it revealed and what good has it accomplished? Let us step back, for the sake of comparison, to the late nineteenth century. To idealize the situation a little, in Europe at this time there was a fair balance between the amount of new music composed and the time available to performers to examine it. Since music stores were as abundant as record stores are today, it was simple to browse through the latest crop of published compositions and pick out what seemed worthwhile to study at home. There was also a balance between the number of good new pieces and the opportunities to program them in concerts. Sooner or later every new work was performed, and further performances depended mostly on its merits as perceived by current taste. In this happy situation, dictionaries, historical or biographical studies, and even publishers' catalogues served mainly to document and reinforce what was already known, and only secondarily to initiate performances.

By the early twentieth century, the situation began to change in many ways. A multifaceted aesthetic and stylistic revolution was underway, based on the belief among younger composers that tonality's potential had been exhausted, as had the opulent sound and monumentalism of the previous century. This revolution estranged a part of the concert audience on whose response performances and publication depended. There was also a remarkable geographical expansion: countries that had been on the periphery of Western music—for instance, many in Latin America, in the Far East and, of course, Canada—now became participants and produced talent that deserved to be heard. These aesthetic and geographical factors increased the amount of music being written and waiting to be sifted through by performers.

In the same period sound recording and radio broadcasting were invented. They not only reached a larger audience, and reached this audience more frequently than did concert performances, but also made dissemination more competitive and more complex. To become known to broadcasting executives, in one's own and in foreign countries, and to break into the world market of sound recordings became of vital interest to composers. Conversely, radio programmers and record producers were faced with the task of choosing program material from a bewildering amount and variety of old and new music.

And, to focus on Canada, there was a growing national pride in homegrown products, intellectual as well as material. By the end of the Second World War this pride had translated into the active support of young talent. The need for a road map through composition-land became a keen one, so that "producers" and "consumers" of compositions could find one another.

This need was strong in all countries newly entered into the arena of Western concert music. The old countries had well-established music publishers with worldwide connections, such as Boosey and Hawkes, G. Ricordi, G. Shirmer, B. Schott's Söhne, and Universal Edition, who circulated thick catalogues and, in many cases, sponsored magazines devoted to contemporary music, and who by diverse other means saw to it that their composers were performed. The same countries also produced most of the musical reference books, including *Grove's*, *Riemann's*, and *Larousse*.

The newer countries had little access to this promotional apparatus. The old *Grove's* and the other dictionaries offered only cursory coverage of the peripheral countries. Pazdirek's huge *Universal-Handbuch der Musikliteratur aller Zeiten und Völker* (1904–1910, in thirty-four volumes) combined the listings of all current music publishers' catalogues—but not a single one from Canada. Add to that the complexity of many new scores, which made selection of works for performance through score reading difficult. No longer was it enough for a publisher to send samples of new publications to conductors and performers, counting on their eagerness to enrich their repertoire. Selecting music for performance became less and less a matter of the performer sifting through scores and more one of organized promotion. By mid-century what got performed and promoted depended largely on competition juries, selection committees, and promotional essays. That is where the "national inventory" came in: it attempted to impose an orderly and democratic procedure on the selection process and to inform objectively who the composers were, what they had written, and where their scores could be obtained. It thus facilitated balanced program-building. In short, self-help had become a mandatory method by which the smaller or newer countries could hope to obtain a hearing for their music, both at home and abroad. The taking of inventories had become an historical necessity.

I have selected for brief discussion two essay-type surveys of Canadian composition, which appeared in 1929 and 1942 respectively. Augustus Bridle, best remembered as the *Toronto Daily Star* music critic, wrote a survey called "Who Writes our Music?" in *Maclean's* 15 December 1929. (It's a kind of piece that would be unimaginable in the *Maclean's* of the 1950s or today.) He discussed more than fifty composers, old and young, Canadian-born or immigrant, strung up in catalogue fashion, his account bristling with titles, brief characterizations and miscellaneous information. However, Bridle's survey is not altogether without generalizations. For instance, he found that Canada's popular songs derived from Tin Pan Alley, its futuristic pieces from Europe, and its classics from dead men. What a strange juxtaposition—Tin Pan Alley, Europeans, and dead men! He was aware of the difficulty in getting music published and, hence, the dependence of each composition on performance to become known. He divided Canadian composers into French-Canadians and "others," a matter largely of having studied in Paris rather than Germany. (One cannot blame Bridle for not getting to know a great part of the music he lists—that is the common problem of all who survey any branch of literature.) Though basically uncritical, Bridle did recognize talent, such as Healey Willan and Rodolphe Mathieu, but composers of excellence and part-time writers of children's songs, marches, and anthems were paraded together in no fixed order. He deserved high marks for locating so many composers in 1929, but essentially he reinforced the image so common among the musical public, that Canada as yet had produced little in quantity and importance.[3]

While, in 1929, Bridle was concerned primarily with fact-gathering, thirteen years later the Quebec periodical *Culture* featured an article by Sir Ernest MacMillan, a man well qualified to distinguish between the good, the mediocre, and the poor, and to pay attention to musical values and interrelationships.[4] Perhaps this explains why Sir Ernest MacMillan presented only two dozen names in his survey of anglophone Canadian composers, although he probably had more contact with Canadian musicians from coast to coast than anyone else. The four choral and church music composers he named were Healey Willan (1880–1968), Alfred Whitehead (1887–1974), William Henry Anderson (1882–1955), and Hugh Bancroft (1904–1988); the four writers of songs and instrumental music were Leo Smith (1881–1952), Frederic Lord (1886–1945), Arnold Walter (1902–1973), and Donald Heins (1878–1949). He gave a quick nod to Albert Ham (1858–1940), Luigi von Kunits (1870–1931), and Augustus Stephen Vogt (1861–1926). He also talked briefly about some dozen younger men, and no doubt he knew many others. Still, his inability or unwillingness to mention more names can be linked, in part, to the lack of an inventory of composers. Was he aware, for instance, of the large output of W.O. Forsyth (1859–1937) and the more than competent works of Herbert Sanders (1878–1938), Douglas Clarke (1893–1962), or Allard de Ridder (1887–1966), and of the expatriates Clarence Lucas (1866–1947) or Edward Manning (1874–1948)?

MacMillan's perception of interrelationships led him to argue that music could not but develop more slowly than the other arts in Canada and that the role of folk song as an inspiration and encouragement for the flourishing of art music was significantly limited in Canada. He concluded wisely that "We cannot by [thinking] produce a national music; all we can do is to create an atmosphere in which a strong musical personality can express itself creatively and naturally.... [Art] has a way of emerging at the most unexpected places."[5] But MacMillan made no mention of one of the main reasons for the retarded development of composition in Canada: the lack at Canadian music schools of teachers familiar with and devoted to the new compositional techniques of Hindemith, Schoenberg, *Les Six* of France, Bartók, or Stravinsky. This undoubtedly *was* one of the main reasons for the slow development of contemporary music in Canada.[6]

The "Brown" CBC Catalogue (1947)

Various countries have published catalogues of their composers, with the emphasis on works rather than biographies. One example is Claire R. Reis' *Composers in America*[7] (editions 1930, 1932, 1938, 1947), which became an important model for the CBC's *Catalogue of Canadian Composers*, issued in 1947. The Canadian project took a long time to get going. As early as January 1940, John Adaskin of the CBC's Toronto Program Department sent out letters beginning "We have been asked to compile a list of Canadian composers of serious music, whose works have been published or recorded."[8] I do not know who had done the asking and why the project did not come to fruition. As the CBC's correspondence files reveal, in the following years the subject of gathering lists of composers, as well as the scores and recordings themselves, came up frequently among executives, sometimes at the request of the Wartime Board of Information. The main initiative came in the winter of 1942–43 and the person entrusted with the task of compiling a list of Canadian music was Captain J.-J. Gagnier, regional director of music at the Montreal offices. By late 1943 Gagnier had contacted 255 musicians and received 155 replies. Most of the information gathering was completed by 1944, but there was a shortage of secretarial staff for this particular task. After more than a year of inactivity, the unedited files were sent (early in 1946?) to the Toronto office of Jean-Marie Beaudet, the CBC Supervisor of Music, where they were typed out with hardly any updating or verification. The result was the distribution of 300 mimeographed copies of the *Catalogue of Canadian Composers* in 1947.

This list of the works of 238 composers, living or recently deceased, was a tremendous step forward in the documentation of Canadian music. It had an electric effect on conductors, other performers, and on the composers themselves, for seeing their list of works and biographical data in print boosted their morale and opened career doors. As someone who arrived in Canada in 1940 and knew almost nothing about Canadian composition until I heard Healey Willan's *Brébeuf* in 1944, I can confirm that browsing through the *CCC* was a revelation *and* an education. But the "Brown Edition" was several years out of date upon publication and new composers popped up every month, especially among returning soldiers. The CBC devoted a series of recitals to many of them and issued a few record albums. Composers' stories and photos were highlighted in magazines and some of their new music was even published. It was an exciting time for Canadian music.[9]

The "Green" CBC Catalogue (1952)

I now come to the central subject of my paper, the second and enlarged edition of the CBC's *Catalogue of Canadian Composers* issued in 1952—the "Green Edition."[10] About this I can speak from personal experience. On 1 May 1950, I had started to work in the CBC Toronto Music Library as a music clerk. Since my first assignment—to weed out duplicate parts from printed dance orchestrations—was completed in six weeks, my boss, Erland Misener, supervisor of the music library and of copyright clearance, suggested an update of the *Catalogue of Canadian Composers*. Canadian composers appeared with increasing frequency on the copyright clearance sheets that came to Misener's office, and the questions "Who is Canadian?" and "Who has composed what?" and "Who is affiliated with CAPAC and who with BMI Canada?" and "Who lives at what address?" became of acute importance in the CBC's internal operations. The decision to update was taken very lightly. Misener went to Geoffrey Waddington, the CBC's music adviser, and to one or two other executives, none of whom was too concerned that the production of what would probably be the CBC's largest book publication up to that point was assigned to one of its lowliest employees, with an annual salary of $1,750. But I was very happy to undertake such an interesting task, which I eagerly started in the second half of June 1950, my second month of employment. Waddington was the formal supervisor of the project and my questionnaires went out in his name.

A word about my approach. About 1950 there appeared to be, in musical style, a complete break with what had gone before because of the sudden burst on the Canadian scene of avant-garde music. It was hard to imagine Canadian music without the "revolutionary" Violet Archer

(b. 1913), Jean Coulthard (b. 1908), Jean Papineau-Couture (b. 1916), Harry Somers (b. 1925), Jean Vallerand (b. 1915), John Weinzweig (b. 1913), and many other young composers. We seemed to witness *the* beginning of Canadian composition; until then Canada seemed to have been merely a haven for semi-retired British organists and Paris-trained harmony teachers who dabbled in composition in their spare time, writing in an outworn idiom. The main purpose of the new edition certainly was to take stock of exciting new creativity. But I was aware of respectable composers from earlier generations, from Calixa Lavallée (1842–1891) and Guillaume Couture (1851–1915) to Clarence Lucas and Wesley Octavius Forsyth, and I felt it would enhance Canada's musical image to demonstrate that, in fact, there had been a century-old tradition of composing. Why not chronicle or at least index Canadian music from the beginning of written composition to the present? Apart from showing that Canadian music had a past as well as a present, this would make all kinds of studies and analyses possible and broaden the choice of music for performance. Indeed, because of its historical dimension, the book may have been one of very few attempts anywhere to document the entire compositional output of a specific country.

The historical material was compiled largely from whatever research I had done before joining the CBC. Because Quebec had evinced more interest in its musical past than had any other province, that material came largely from Quebec sources, such as the *Dictionnaire des musiciens canadiens* of 1935.[11] Other sources included the *Canadian Annual Review*, *Maclean's* or *The Year Book of Canadian Art*. My work certainly fell short of fulfilling its goal—today twice as many nineteenth-century composers could be listed. Later, when I began to collect whatever pre-1950 sheet music I could find, I was amazed at how little of it had been listed in the book.

Composers were canvassed by questionnaire in the summer of 1950. I found new names by reading, listening to the radio, and often by recommendation or hearsay. By October 1950 the essential work was done, although supplementary research led me to visit Ottawa, Montreal, and Quebec early in 1951. Not only did the CBC executives take the assignment somewhat lightly, but I must admit in retrospect that I worked too quickly. Too readily did I accept each composer's choice in providing either a detailed or a selective list and I failed to get back to many of them to fill in gaps in dates and timings of compositions, gaps which now look embarrassing.

By the spring of 1951 the manuscript was ready. Now the practical aspects of publication had to be considered. Production costs were estimated at $2,700, and after selling an estimated 600 copies at $3.50 each, the cost to the CBC would be below $900. In any case, the matter was referred to the head office in Ottawa where it probably was put at the bottom of the decision pile. The delay that had played havoc with J.-J. Gagnier's effort threatened to plague my own. Nothing happened for a few months. Then one day—12 July 1951—I had occasion to see Sir Ernest MacMillan, by then the "elder statesman" of Canadian music, who was very interested in the progress of the project. He was dismayed to hear that my work was gathering dust and already getting out of date. "Do you mind if I do something about this?" Sir Ernest asked, and I didn't mind at all. Five days later a memo arrived from Donald Manson, the CBC's acting general manager in Ottawa, giving the green signal but noting that "there should be no actual costs to the CBC." The Toronto staff were more than a little surprised. What we didn't know was that on the very day of my visit Sir Ernest had written a letter to Manson in which he emphasized the importance of the project and concluded, "If the CBC is unable to undertake this sponsorship I should like to feel free to explore other possibilities."

With the help of two senior staff members of the Press and Information Services in Toronto—Bob Bryden, who did the technical editing, and Tom Fairley, who helped polish my prose—the manuscript was readied for the printer. It came off the press on 8 January 1952. One thousand and thirty copies were printed, and by the summer of 1956, four-and-a-half years later, 709 copies had been sold or given away. In 1972 the book was reprinted by the Michigan publisher Scholarly Press, Inc.

Critical Reaction to the CBC Catalogue of 1952

The older composers were pleased to see an updated list of their works. For many younger ones, such as Harry Freedman (b. 1922), Serge Garant (1929–1986), François Morel (b. 1926), Harry Somers (b. 1925), and Gilles Tremblay (b. 1932) it was the first listing of their works in a reference book. I remember one composer even taking the trouble to drop in at the CBC Music Library just to meet me and pay his respects. His name was Murray Adaskin.

Reviewers were kind. "Eye-opener," "a counting of blessings," "Canada coming of age musically," were typical phrases. They were surprised at the number of composers: 356 in total, 118 more than in the first edition. Of these 356, about 275 were still alive.

As in the case of the first edition, the question of fact-gathering versus evaluation loomed large. To include or exclude composers according to the quality of their work, though desirable, was impractical since very few of the works were available for inspection; comprehensiveness could be the only goal. There was general agreement among critics that too many people had been included: amateurs, writers of a handful of songs or anthems, purveyors of students' pieces, and so on. William Krehm criticized the Sears-Roebuck mail-order catalogue proportions and argued that the inclusion of everything and anything written by Canadians was doing irreparable harm to the cause of Canadian music.[12] As recently as 1974 Chester Duncan, the Winnipeg musician and English professor, called the *Catalogue of Canadian Composers* one of the funniest books written in this country—I am still waiting for my Stephen Leacock Award—and he even concocted a fictitious entry to illustrate what he meant, combining elements from various entries. It read as follows:

> Nicholas Tryad. Amateur musician. Played second clarinet in Russian Army Orchestra 1903–1907. Came to Canada in 1908. Took piano lessons from Mrs. Smiles in Moose Jaw, 1913. Now engaged in textile business. Started to compose at the age of fifty-five. Anthem: *God Guard Thee, Newfoundland!*[13]

Well, it's Chester Duncan who should get the Leacock Award! The truth is that, perhaps naively, I regarded the book as a documentation tool that should be as complete as I could make it, but never as a vehicle for propaganda, let alone chauvinistic propaganda. The real reason for including a certain number of marginal composers was that the book was intended, first of all, for the internal use of the CBC staff, by those responsible for programming, writing continuity, or determining performing rights credits. And it would surprise the critics to know how many of the marginal composers had written one or two pieces that had been performed by orchestras or had won prizes in respectable contests. (The late Peter Zvankin [1879–1975], a businessman and the main model for Chester Duncan's sample, wrote a poem for orchestra that was twice performed by the Winnipeg Symphony Orchestra.) Others had won a CBC songwriters' contest. So much depends on an inventory's purpose.

If the 1952 *Catalogue* was short on value judgements, its facts at least illustrated the growth of composition in a statistical way. Even if one omits those musicians whose output was very small, who wrote only functional pieces, or who were amateur composers, one is still left with about 250 people possessing a professional command of part-writing, no matter what the quality of their products. In rounded figures, fifty of these were born between the eighteenth century and the 1870s. Of the others, over 100 were born between 1880 and 1910 and had well-established careers by 1950. Those born during the next twenty years accounted for another 100—certainly a remarkable increase. In his review of the *Catalogue*, John Beckwith applied more stringent standards.[14] He counted thirty-eight "Grade A exportable" composers and another forty of primarily historical interest, or who were promising but still young, or were unknown to him.

A Stimulus to Re-evaluation

Frequent and varied use of the *Catalogue* was made especially by the CBC's program staff, but also by recitalists and conductors planning programs or building their repertoire, and by journalists and students looking for information, tracing stylistic or teacher-to-pupil influences, or analyzing compositional trends.

Because of its obvious strength in listing the music between the two wars, the 1952 *Catalogue* also revealed that the mature composers of the 1920s, 1930s, and 1940s, though less committed to composition as a full-time activity, included as many well-trained musicians as the generation following them. Perhaps the time has come to re-examine their music and to lay to rest the view that all that mattered in Canadian music began only about 1940.[15] The 100 years previous to that date did produce a number of gifted, well-trained, and even progressive composers, Canadian-born or immigrant. Not all were perpetual imitators of Tchaikovsky, Gounod, Grieg, and Elgar. The best music of Healey Willan and Claude Champagne (1891–1965) has always remained in the repertoire, and works by Colin McPhee (1900–1964, not included in the *Catalogue*), Rodolphe Mathieu (1890–1962), Alfred Whitehead, and Luigi von Kunits are heard from time to time, but there should be much that is worthy of an occasional performance in the music of Douglas Clarke, George MacKenzie Brewer (1889–1947), Edwin Collins (1893–?), Ernest Dainty (1891–1947), Alfred La Liberté (1882–1952), Frederic Lord, Léo-Pol Morin (1892–1941), Émiliano Renaud (1875–1932), Allard de Ridder, Herbert Sanders, Leo Smith, the expatriate Gena Branscombe (1881–1977), and a few others. For such a reassessment the 1952 *Catalogue* still remains a useful tool.

Such circumstances as inadequate performance and publishing opportunities apart, the real trouble with the older generation of 1940 or 1950 was not that it was behind the times, but that, stylistically, it belonged to the end of a period, the so-called late Romantic period, whereas the younger generation had the advantage of representing a radically new point of view, the advantage of greater relevance. The father-and-son clash typical of any two successive generations was aggravated by this accident of historical constellation. Indeed, a favourite assertion by some of the younger composers, that the old ones were not "creative," only expressed the arrogance of youth.

What was new in the young composers of the 1940s was a sense of fellowship, expressed in the founding of the Canadian League of Composers in 1951, and a determination to make composition their main occupation and to become aware of and contribute to recent international trends and techniques. They broke away from the fetters of cultural colonialism, the notion that everything important comes from abroad, that Canadian musicians are importers, never exporters. What was also of tremendous help was the creation, by and for Canadian artists, of national support and promotion systems, of which catalogues were an important part.

Successors to the CBC Catalogue

The 1952 *Catalogue* is badly outdated now, even in its nineteenth- and early-twentieth-century coverage. It still has the most detailed lists available for William Henry Anderson, Joseph-Arthur Bernier (1877–1944), Douglas Clarke, Edwin Collins, Chester Duncan (b. 1913) [d. 2002], Arthur Henry Egerton (1891–1957), Gordon Fleming (1903–1959), Jean-Josaphat Gagnier (1885–1949), Eugène Lapierre (1899–1970), Albertine Morin-Labrecque (1886–1957), and some others. However, a vast amount of earlier Canadian music has come to light since 1952. The bulk of it is utilitarian music for church, school, patriotic rally, dance hall, or band parade, but a fair percentage of it—for instance, works by Guillaume Couture, Wesley Octavius Forsyth, Clarence Lucas, Charles Harriss (1862–1929), Émiliano Renaud, Calixa Lavallée—would do honour to any keyboard or vocal recital (and in fact [such works] do appear with increasing frequency in concerts, on recordings and broadcasts). The main index to this music is the National Library of Canada's *Union Catalogue of*

Canadian Music Publications to 1950; its main promoter is the *Canadian Musical Heritage Society*, established in 1982.

The successors to the CBC catalogues of 1947 and 1952 were the Canadian League of Composers' *Catalogue of Orchestral Music* (1957), the various Canadian Music Centre catalogues (begun in 1963 but unfortunately not revised often enough), the CBC's *Thirty-four Biographies of Canadian Composers* (1964) and, of far greater importance, *Contemporary Canadian Composers* (1975), edited by Keith MacMillan and John Beckwith. This work, which appeared also in an enlarged French-language edition, *Compositeurs canadiens contemporains* (1977), featured the selectivity that the CBC catalogues so much lacked, and set a new editorial standard for handbooks devoted to Canadian composers. It includes 144 composers active from 1920 on. The *Encyclopedia of Music in Canada* (1981, 1992) / *Encyclopédie de la musique au Canada* (1983, 1993) provides complete lists for the most important composers and selected lists or summaries for others.

The years have also produced books to satisfy more specialized needs, enabling, for example, teachers and performers to locate compositions for a specific instrument, from a certain province, in a certain form, or of a certain difficulty (e.g., suitable for young people). Patricia Shand's *Canadian Music: A Selective Guide-list for Teachers* (Toronto, 1978), the *Répertoire des compositeurs du Québec* issued by the Montreal regional branch of the Canadian Music Centre in 1986, or *Composers of Atlantic Canada '81* [Halifax, 1981] are examples.

The responsibility for keeping track of Canadian compositions is now shared by several organizations: the Canadian Music Centre for concert music, beginning about 1940, published or not, the National Library of Canada for current publications (printed or recorded) in all genres and for historical material, published or not, and the *Encyclopedia of Music in Canada* for listings under composer and genre entries. Furthermore, the performing rights societies, CAPAC and PROCAN,[16] keep extensive files for the compositions of member composers, though these may be less useful to the outsider. These organizations are likely to remain the basic sources for information about Canadian compositions for a long time.

The Continuing Importance of Catalogues

Though there is still reason for individual composers to complain about the scarcity of performances, recordings, and publications (and, I would add, critical discussion), altogether Canada's composers are among the best documented in the world. I believe that all the Canadian catalogues discussed have provided factual information that has replaced hit-and-miss approaches to programming and promotion. Facts have enabled their users to "dig for gold" and to observe interrelationships. The best inventories cannot create a golden age; they do, however, support the flourishing of art. They are the maps that document where we have come from, show where we stand at present, and may point out directions in which to proceed. In recent years the promotion of Canada's economic and political interests through its cultural image has become an important strategy, and it is the information system that provides the guide to the proper presentation of the cultural products themselves.

Catalogues provide the factual element in the trinity of fact, value, and connections, which was mentioned at the beginning of this paper, although editorial policy can inject an emphasis on value and foster the analysis of historical dynamics. One could go even further. At a Canadian League of Composers conference in Ottawa on 21 June 1986, one of the speakers quoted a French music critic to the effect that "there is no longer a history of composition; there can only be a catalogue of compositions." That may be an exaggeration, but it does contain truth, and it is a warning to cataloguers to take their task very seriously and to be proud of their contributions to musical understanding.

NOTES

1. Duncan reprinted the critical passage, including the parody, in his partly autobiographical publication *Wanna Fight, Kid?* (Winnipeg: Queenston House, 1975), 68–69. [*Ed.*]
2. Martin Dreyer, "Canadian Music Explored," *The Musical Times* (August 1983), 483. [*Ed.*]
3. Bridle's survey was followed in 1936 by a somewhat similar effort by Lawrence Mason, in the form of a series of bio-bibliographical sketches of eighteen Canadian composers in the Toronto *Globe* from May to September 1936.
4. "Musical Composition in Canada," *Culture* 3 (1942), 149–153. [Reprinted in Carl Morey, ed., *MacMillan on Music: Essays on Music by Sir Ernest MacMillan* (Toronto: Dundurn, 1997), 102–8. *Ed.*]
5. Ibid., 153.

6 I should mention in passing that speculation about the future direction of composition and the discussion of nationalism versus internationalism were taken up by Montreal musicians as well, among them Léo-Pol Morin (1892–1941) (*Papiers de musique,* Montreal, 1930), Eugène Lapierre (1899–1970) (*Un Style canadien de musique,* Quebec, 1942), and Jean Papineau-Couture (b. 1916) [d. 2000] ("Que sera la musique canadienne?" *Amérique française,* 2, October, 1942).

7 Claire R. Reis, *Composers in America,* rev. ed. (New York: Macmillan, 1947). [*Ed.*]

8 The copy I saw is addressed to Hector Gratton of Montreal. Hector Gratton fonds, Music Division, National Library of Canada.

9 Meanwhile a more modest initiative had concurrently taken place. The Canadian Federation of Music Teachers' Associations, the umbrella organization of private music teachers, had arranged with Oxford University Press in Toronto to issue *A List of Canadian Music* in the summer of 1946, a booklet of 23 pages. It listed published and unpublished works by about 125 composers under such categories as "Piano Solos," "Two Pianos," or "Choral." Unfortunately there are no biographical notes, not even indications of year of birth or place of residence, and no details about any compositions, such as date, scoring, duration, except the name of the publisher. At least here were alphabetical lists, one of composers and one of publishers.

10 The "Brown Edition" and "Green Edition" catalogues are so named by HK here because of the colour of their respective covers. [*Ed.*]

11 Soeurs de Sainte-Anne, *Dictionnaire biographique des musiciens canadiens* [2nd ed.] (Lachine, PQ: Mont-Sainte-Anne, 1935).

12 William Krehm, "Canadian Composers' New Attack," *Saturday Night,* 67/24 (22 March 1952), 19.

13 Chester Duncan, "The Musical Life: Some Personal Notes," *Saturday Night,* 89/7 (July 1974), 39.

14 *TSO News,* 3/4 (May 1952), 8, 13.

15 George Proctor's *Canadian Music of the Twentieth Century* (Toronto: University of Toronto Press, 1980) is a step in that direction.

16 Merged as SOCAN in 1990.

14
A Selection of Correspondence

HK seems to have spent a good deal of time each day writing things down—notes to himself, lists, essays, excerpts from books or articles that interested him, and a voluminous professional and personal correspondence. His archival papers include four filing cabinets full of his writings, ranging from multiple drafts of his publications (up to five or six corrected drafts for each finished work; he also typically kept several copies of each publication) to mundane domestic trivia. From this vast trove, we have selected a few excerpts illustrating the range of his correspondence over the years. The first letter, written during a period of unemployment following graduation, is a good example of HK being "useful": he has the temerity to write to the eminent musicologist Willi Apel with a list of corrections to the *Harvard Dictionary of Music*, which Apel had edited. Next is an inter-office memo HK wrote to Robert Chesterman, a CBC Radio producer in Vancouver; HK's remarks characteristically range from Beethoven to contemporary music. And finally, HK's editorial scruples come to the fore as he demurs from signing on to the writer and journalist Peter C. Newman's plan for an open letter rallying the nation on the occasion of the 125th anniversary of Confederation.

1. HK to Willi Apel

Toronto 5, Ont.
                                                    December 27th 1949.

Dear Professor Apel,

    I acquired a copy of your excellent Harvard Dictionary (5th printing) [1947] last winter and am using it frequently and with great pleasure. I think I can best show my appreciation by listing a few minor errors which may not have been noticed yet and by making a few suggestions.

> Cadenza: Beethoven, last Piano Concerto, op.73 not op. 76.
> Concerto: Weber, op.32, 1812 not 1912.
> Serenade: Brahms, add op.11.
> Whole-tone Scale: Schubert (?). A descending whole-tone scale occurs in the C major Symphony, first movement, development, triplets in strings. However this is really a modulatory passage.
> Trumpet: Why [a cross-]refer[ence] to Bach Trumpet which in its turn only refers to Clarin trumpet?
> Chord: [Cross-]reference should be to Fourth, not Fourth-Chord which does not appear as [an] entry.
> Terzett: refers to Trio, but under Trio no mention of vocal music is done. In section 2) under Trio the trio of the march might be mentioned.
> Dominant: secondary dominants. Perhaps the German word Zwischen-dominante might be mentioned here.
> Parallel chords: sliding diminished 7th chords seem to be an exception in classical harmony, they occur e.g. in Mozart's c minor concerto, in Haydn and Chopin. (I mean exception to the prohibition of parallel seventh chords.)
> Fugue: description lacks reference to Coda.
> Editions, Historical: Section VIII. dall'Abaco: Ausgewaehlte Werke.
> Periodicals: Melos. This exists again. I have Heft 10/11, 14. (?) Jahr, Aug/Sept. 1947.
> > Canadian Journal of Music: existed till 1919 only. At present musical periodical and newspaper writing is at an all-time low in Canada, but in the past Musical Canada, Toronto 1906–1933, monthly, and The Canadian Review of Music and Art, Toronto 1942–1948, monthly, have been of some significance.
> Alalá: Obviously Galicia in Spain, not in Poland is meant, perhaps this could be stated.
> An article on the psychology of music might be useful.
> An article on Salon Music might deal with this phase of 19th century music.
> I would like clarification on the use of the treble clef for the violoncello. When is it a transposing and when a non-transposing instrument in the treble clef? In Schubert's op.99 the treble clef sections

for the cello obviously have to be transposed an octave down, like the tenor voice, while in op.100 they are written in concert pitch. The latter would appear to be the rule.

Canadian music: Some other sources are:

Létourneau, Omer, Histoire de la musique à Québec.

Spell, L., Music in New France in the seventeenth century. Canadian Historical Review, v.8. June 1927.

Encyclopédie Grolier, 1947, under Canada, Musique, written by E. Lapierre.

MacMillan, Sir Ernest, Music in Canada. London. Royal College of Organists. Calendar 1936–37.

I started this year to collect source material and facts on the history of music in Canada and have about 140 typed pages of notes and excerpts so far. In case you ever require information about the subject I shall be pleased to help you.

I hope that my suggestions may be of some little value.

Sincerely yours
[Helmut Kallmann]

2. Willi Apel to HK

December 30, 1949

Mr. Helmut Kallmann
Toronto, Ont.

Dear Mr. Kallmann,

A few days ago I received your letter, and I hasten to tell you that I am very grateful to you for your list of errors in the Dictionary. Some of these had come to my attention before, but others had not been noticed, and will be incorporated in the new edition which I hope to be able to bring out within a year or two.

If you will be good enough to send me a short article on Canadian music, I shall be very glad to include it (with proper reference to its author) in the new edition.

Thanking you once more, I am
Very truly yours,
[signature]
Willi Apel

[HK duly wrote a new entry on Canada for the *Harvard Dictionary* (the existing entry consisted merely of five bibliographic items, dating from 1925 to 1940) and sent it to Apel on 31 January 1950. The *Harvard Dictionary* went through seventeen printings up to 1966 (selling over 155,000 copies), but HK's corrections and his article on Canada (which he subsequently revised in 1965) were not included until the second edition of the reference work appeared in 1969, twenty years after this initial correspondence.]

3. CBC Inter-Office Memogram

To: Mr. Robert Chesterman
Producer
Vancouver

From: H. Kallmann
Supervisor of Music Library
Toronto

Message:

In your program notes about Beethoven's Op. 7 a few days ago there was some speculation as to whether the Countess Keglevics could have been in love with Beethoven, a possibility suggested by the feminine form of the nickname, <u>Die</u> Verliebte.[1]

I may be dead wrong, but in all the years I have known this nickname, I have never related the <u>Die</u> to anything but Die <u>Sonate</u>, not Die Graefin. Even if the lovelorn person portrayed in the finale was Beethoven himself, the nickname would most likely still be Die, not Der.

The performance was great, and in spite of the explainers of modern music who, like Mr. Hopkins in his present series,[2] read a devastating review of an early performance of Brahms' First Symphony and then claim that "today this music sounds very harmless," I cannot help feeling that this Beethoven man must be absolutely mad when I listen to the first movement. I pity the people to whom the late Beethoven quartets or the Brahms symphonies present no listening problems. I can still be shocked by Eroica chords, but very little by some of our avant-gardists who forget that Webern did it all 50 years ago. Sorry for getting carried away. I do enjoy your programs when I listen.

Date July 6, 1966

4. Peter C. Newman, circular to all members of the Order of Canada, forwarded to HK by Judith A. LaRocque, Secretary to the Governor General [Ramon John Hnatyshyn] on 21 August 1992

ORDER OF CANADA—STATEMENT
A COMMUNITY OF DREAMS

"The mind supplies the idea of a nation," mused André Malraux, the French philosopher. "But what gives this idea its sentimental force is a community of dreams."

That image of Canada as "a community of dreams" is particularly relevant at this time in our history when the nation's continued existence seems threatened.[3]

Those of us fortunate enough to have been recognized by our peers and honoured by having received an [appointment to the] Order of Canada feel duty-bound to speak out at this perilous moment. Without in any way endorsing the many and shifting political positions that are in play, we wish to reaffirm our faith and belief in this great country of ours.

The Order's motto, after all, is "they desire a better country." We do—and we believe that a better country will emerge and can be perpetuated if every citizen rededicates him or herself to the ideals that allowed us originally to forge a nation across this huge chunk of geography.

We may be a loose federation of wildly diverse regions, but there is a quiver of common intent that has held us together for 125 years—and will continue to do so, if we allow ourselves to seize the future that can and will be ours.

If you would be willing to endorse this general statement of intent that would be published as a full page advertisement, including your name as one of its supporters, please let me know.

It is my hope that we can generate enough interest and raise the necessary funds, to run this ad in The Globe and Le Devoir, at a time when the national debate on Canada's future might most benefit from such a declaration.[4]

Should you be willing to make a financial contribution, please send along a cheque payable to the Council for Canadian Unity, which will allow for tax deductibility.

I do hope to hear from you.

Peter C. Newman

P.S. Please write. There is no simpler or more direct way for you to endorse the feeling that you "desire a better country."

5. HK to Peter C. Newman

August 30, 1992

Dear Mr. Newman,

Rideau Hall has sent me a copy of your recent draft statement "A Community of Dreams."

While I agree with the sentiments expressed and would endorse a reworded statement, I find the present text ineffective and not worth the expense of a full-page ad. This motherhood statement is vague and completely lacks punch. The threat should be spelled out—is it failure of an agreement on the constitution, is it US imperialism, is it world rule by transnational corporations?—and so should be the concept of "rededication." Merely to exhort people to be good citizens and to realize how lucky we have been just won't do.

Sincerely yours
Helmut Kallmann, CM

P.S. We met when we were guest speakers at the "Adaskin Years" conference in Victoria in March 1988, following one another.

NOTES

1 According to Beethoven's pupil Carl Czerny, Beethoven was in love with Graefin [Countess] Babette Keglevics, dedicated the Piano Sonata in E-flat major, Op. 7 to her, and nicknamed it "Die Verliebte" ("The Loved One"); see *Thayer's Life of Beethoven*, rev. ed. by Elliot Forbes (Princeton: Princeton University Press, 1964), 292. [Ed.]

2 The reference is to the British composer and conductor Antony Hopkins, whose BBC radio program *Talking about Music* was aired weekly throughout the 1950s and 1960s. [Ed.]

3 Newman is undoubtedly referring to a general sense of unrest in Canada at the time over the failure of the Meech Lake Accord to be ratified in 1990, a rising tide of support for the separatist movement in Quebec, and the polarizing debate over the Charlottetown Accord, which would be defeated in a national referendum on 26 October 1992. [Ed.]

4 The proposed full-page advertisement appeared in the *Globe and Mail* and *Le Devoir* on 17 October 1992, in the week before the vote on the Charlottetown Accord, carrying the names of some 700 Order of Canada members. [Ed.]

15
Mapping Canada's Music: A Life's Task

Guido Bimberg (full name Sir Graf Guido von Bimberg zu Lenninghausen) is a German music scholar who has taught around the world and has edited books on Russian and German music. After visits to several branches of the Canadian Music Centre and guest appearances at various Canadian universities between 1992 and 1994, Bimberg decided to edit a collection of essays on Canadian music, the first such book to be produced in Germany, or indeed in Europe. The project was of much interest to HK, whom Bimberg in his introduction [p. 5] calls "Nestor der kanadischen Musikwissenschaft" ("Nestor of Canadian musicology," referring to the ancient Greek king who was famous for his wisdom and eloquence). In this, the first essay in Bimberg's volume, HK reflects on his nearly fifty-year involvement in Canadian music studies. The book appeared as volume 25 of a Canadian Studies series produced under the aegis of the University of Augsburg's Institute for Canadian Studies. A projected second volume on Canadian music never materialized before the series ended in 2001.

The Impetus

All I wanted was to gain more insight into Beethoven's personality. I had plowed my way through three volumes of his letters in Prelinger's edition[1] and was now, in the summer of 1948, reading through the second

---

Guido Bimberg, ed. *Music in Canada / La Musique au Canada: A Collection of Essays*, vol. 1 (Bochum: Universitätsverlag Dr. N. Brockmeyer, 1997), 11–34

appendix. There, underneath a letter to the composer from a visitor to Vienna, it stared at me in clear print, "Theodor Molt, music teacher in Quebec, North America" ["Musiklehrer in Quebec in Nord Amerika"], December 1825.

"A music teacher in Quebec in 1825, but that's impossible!" was my immediate reaction. I thought the eldest of the teachers I saw around the Royal Conservatory of Music of Toronto, men born in the 1870s, surely belonged to the first or, at most, second generation of music teachers in this new country.[2] Yet here was someone by the name of Molt who taught in Quebec City a century earlier!

What was the story behind this man? Other Beethoven literature provided details about Molt's visit to the composer, and of these I will mention only that Molt, who had first settled in Quebec in 1822, returned there in 1826 with a Beethoven manuscript in his hands, the canon "Freu' Dich des Lebens," WoO 195. Rather, what piqued my curiosity was the Canadian aspect of the episode. Although I had arrived in Canada in 1940 as one of some 2,000 interned refugees from Germany and Austria, our camps were enclaves of European culture, for three years linked to Canadian musical life only by radio broadcasts of the Montreal and Toronto orchestras and recorded music programs. We knew little about Canada's history.

By the time I entered the University of Toronto in 1946 I had gathered my first impressions about current musical life. Although a strong wartime morale booster, music making had been downsized, but now that the nation had returned to civilian life it was raring to emerge stronger than ever. I heard a lot about music's future. Thus, in Quebec a series of state conservatories expanded or opened, in Toronto plans matured for a senior school with master teachers, a professional opera school, and a new course for future school music teachers. Composition teachers versed in contemporary idioms at last assumed university positions. Professionalism seemed just to arrive. Indeed there was a flurry, if not an explosion, of talent and activity. And what about the past? One didn't talk about that. In my three years of music history classes under three different professors, Canadian musicians, past or present, were never subjects of discussion or even mention. Anything of importance, as though by definition, had to take place in Europe or the United States. Music in Canada "had no past" apart from folksong, and in any case one was too busy to celebrate old heroes. True, the Hart House String Quartet of Toronto, and the Montreal Opera Company were memories of older music lovers; true, a Kathleen Parlow or a Rodolphe Plamondon had won acclaim abroad, but there had been a long succession of shipwrecked orchestral and operatic enterprises—backwoods enterprises typically led by organists who found themselves suddenly in front of an orchestra and who hated what little contemporary music they knew. Or so one was told.

Till the end of the war, music was taught at some dozen universities with curricula (at least in Anglo-Canada) perpetuating the time-honoured British system emphasizing complex tonal harmony, fugue and orchestration, but not teaching research techniques, contemporary idioms or much else useful for entering the profession. Little wonder that many young composers resented the conservative academics and part-time composers whom they identified with the age of Elgar or Tchaikovsky, instead placing Schoenberg, Webern, Bartók and Stravinsky on their banner. As if to confirm this negative view of the Canadian past, the CBC's epochal *Catalogue of Canadian Composers* (1947) with its generous coverage of living composers disregarded almost all those who had died.

Beside the music teacher of 1825 with Beethoven's manuscript in his hand, one other signpost made me suspicious of this negative view of Canada's musical past. My *Baedeker's Canada* of 1907 contained a number of city maps that displayed an "Opera House" in a prominent location, those of Hamilton, Ottawa, Saint John, Toronto, Vancouver and Winnipeg.[3] What cities, if any, had opera houses in 1948?

On the following pages I would like to trace my exploration of a vast virgin territory, beginning with the search for information, and continuing with the exploitation of that information in a number of major projects. It is very much a story of one thing leading to another—one lacuna after another prompting me to step into yet another field, gathering, interpreting, and disseminating information. With each step I realized more strongly how unaware Canadians were of the musical element in their own past, a past that should become as familiar as Canadian painting and literature were. As the years went by I was able to encourage others to participate in research and historiography. And finally in this essay I will reflect on some insights and lessons my search has yielded over a span of nearly 50 years.

The Search

The Christmas holidays of 1948 approached and I must have been well caught up with school work, for spontaneously I began to indulge my curiosity about Canada's musical past. A small step I thought, just preparing one more "set of notes" as I had done in so many classes. I wrote down at random all the musicians' names I could think of—I still preserve the list of hardly a hundred. I then extracted individual and other Canadian entries from *Thompson's International Cyclopedia of Music and Musicians* (a quite substantial coverage) and many other dictionaries and encyclopedias, Canadian or international. I took notes from the music reports in the *Canadian Annual Review*, *Le Bulletin des recherches historiques* and other periodicals, placing my sheets in folders marked Performance, Education, Composition, Trade, and Bibliography. Although locating or compiling a bibliography and checking through item after item is the recommended way of beginning any research, I found more information (and more enjoyment!) by random browsing in certain sections of the university and public libraries.

I obtained precious information also through correspondence, for example on early nineteenth-century musicians from Gérard Morisset, curator of art works at the Quebec Museum, in 1950, and later from Lucien Brochu and Léo Roy, also of Quebec City. On occasion I combined business or holiday trips with research and visits to local libraries, leading musicians and old-timers, for example, in Montreal (CBC Music Library, Bibliothèque nationale du Québec, Eugène Lapierre) and Ottawa in 1951, in Quebec (Séminaire de Québec, Université Laval, Henri Gagnon) in 1952, in Vancouver (Jean Coulthard and Vancouver City Archives) in 1954 and 1957 and the Maritimes (J. Russell Harper at the New Brunswick Museum, Phyllis Blakeley at the Archives of Nova Scotia and Harry Dean at the Maritime Academy of Music in Halifax) in 1955.

Soon four observations imposed themselves. The first was that no coast-to-coast survey of any historical depth had yet been attempted. "Writers on music in Canada are handicapped by the lack of a comprehensive body of readily available factual material," I complained in March 1950.[4] Only folk music collecting was thriving. True, Marcelle Rousseau wrote a master's thesis, "The Rise of Music in Canada" (1951) for Columbia University but she did not continue her investigation; Jean MacMillan had prepared a basic bibliography in 1940;[5] and Kathleen M. Hobday had compiled a comprehensive directory of Ontario music organizations in 1944–45.[6] At the turn of the century, Anglo-Canadians had produced a rash of countrywide surveys and stocktaking (Susie Frances Harrison "Seranus," 1898 and ca.1909, Edouard Hesselberg ca.1913, the several *Yearbooks of Canadian Art* and others).[7] However, these writings rarely had a historical perspective of more than a few decades.

Inevitably my quest for the earliest documented mentions of music guided me to La Nouvelle France, a rewarding quest, for it led to my second observation, that musical activity among the colonials was much older than Canadians seemed aware of. "Performances and experiments are labelled 'first in Canada' that may have had forerunners in a long forgotten time,"[8] I commented. Molt, it turned out, was an important pioneer but not the earliest of our musicians. In fact, French motets had been sung in Quebec in the seventeenth century and French keyboard music played in Montreal in the mid-eighteenth century. Older than expected also was the documentation of musical history by Quebec writers, beginning about the middle of the nineteenth century. In distinction to the survey writers in English, the chroniclers either delved into the distant past—Ernest Myrand in *Noëls anciens de la Nouvelle France* (1899 and later editions)[9] and Ernest Gagnon in *Louis Jolliet* (1902 and later editions), an account of the seventeenth-century explorer and organist[10]—or they recorded personal reminiscences (Nazaire LeVasseur, Gustave Smith, or Henri Têtu).[11] They tended toward writing monographs (Eugène Lapierre on Calixa Lavallée, the composer of "O Canada," or Léo-Pol Morin, *Papiers de musique*)[12] or biographical sketches in periodicals such as *L'Action nationale* and *Qui?*

The horizon widened. I found that in Quebec City there had been orchestral subscription concerts with music by Haydn, Mozart, Pleyel and their contemporaries in the 1790s. In the following century band music and choral singing were thriving, operatic troupes and many world famous artists visited Canada (if only as a side trip from the USA), while Canadian singers achieved fame in European opera houses. Philharmonic societies and *unions musicales* blossomed forth not only in major cities but in such unlikely places as Nanaimo, BC (1888) or Joliette, PQ (1892). In Vancouver, the Canadian Pacific Railway opened an Opera House in 1891, only five years after the city's incorporation, with a US touring company performing *Lohengrin*, although most of the Baedeker's opera houses rarely offered anything but vaudeville, operetta and public meetings. Some features seem distinctly Canadian. Ensembles toured to distant settlements; women composers and performers played a larger role than in Europe; and music competitions on the thinly populated Prairies provided occasions for travel and festivity which built a great community spirit. Such observations belie the time-honoured assertion that pioneering forced people to concentrate entirely on material tasks and left little time for cultivating the "finer things" in life. After all, people had plenty of time for religion and for sports, and in the long winters farm work was less demanding. Vendors of reed organs and pianos certainly did a booming business all over the country and organist-choirmaster after organist-choirmaster achieved fine results with previously untrained voices. Leaving aside the refinement of skill and taste, the appetite for music was whetted rather than stultified by pioneer conditions. If professionalism seemed to emerge but slowly outside the older cities, this had less to do with a lack of desire for art than with the musicians' problems of making a living in a thinly populated land.

I learned a third lesson. Music in early Canada was not exclusively of the oral tradition. It was and still is a widespread assumption that before the twentieth century Canadian music was predominantly folk music, fiddle music, hymns, plainchant and Indian drumming. It is quite likely that even in the mid-nineteenth century Canadians were as familiar with tunes by Handel, Haydn, Donizetti or Verdi and the parlour music of the day as they were with folk music and hymns.

Compiling extracts from so many scattered sources soon expanded my notes into five or six alphabetically arranged loose leaf binders, filed by topic and individual name.[13] My work also prompted a fourth observation: I found innumerable discrepancies in dates, name spellings and other information. Slowly I began to develop an instinct and a lasting skepticism for the reliability of specific writers and compilers of reference material.

First Applications

I don't remember when I first mentioned my investigations to others, but early in 1950 I submitted my still meagre files to Sir Ernest MacMillan, the dean of my faculty, who made some pencil additions to my pages and thought that mine had to remain a labour of love for the moment, but that the time would come when my expertise would be in demand. About the same time John Beckwith, then public relations officer for the Royal Conservatory, asked me to write an article on my work for the *Conservatory Bulletin*, a sort of rationale and program for my work. [The article is reprinted here; see pages 35–38.]

It did not take long to become known as a specialist. I began to work as a music clerk in the CBC's Toronto Music Library in the spring of 1950. A few months later I was assigned to revise the CBC's 1947 *Catalogue of Canadian Composers*.[14] In the course of this work, in December 1950 I wrote a number of letters to institutions that might hold Canadian compositions.

But since my title of "music clerk" carried no weight, I had these letters signed by my boss, Erland Misener, the "supervisor of music libraries and copyright clearance." Shortly afterwards, an answer came from Honorius Provost, associate archivist at the Séminaire de Québec, stating that the Séminaire owned Joseph Quesnel's operetta *Colas et Colinette* and a music theory book by Pierre Lagacé, adding that furthermore Mr. Misener should consult Henri Gagnon, Marius Barbeau and—one Helmut Kallmann of Toronto as experts in Canadian composition. I had arrived!

I started the revision of the *Catalogue* with the ambitious goal of documenting composition in one country from its very beginning to the present year, something possible only in a young country like Canada. It was a fishing expedition which drew attention to the new burgeoning of composition and provided coverage for many musicians of the past, especially from the Province de Quebec with its more adequate historical documentation. However, as I will stress later, I had no inkling of the surprising quantities of earlier publications and manuscripts.

It was just weeks after joining the music library when the telephone rang and the manager of the University of Toronto Press bookstore, Alfred E.H. Petrie, invited me at Sir Ernest's suggestion to discuss writing a book about music in Canada. I was stunned. I had thought of assembling data for a history, but not of writing that history myself. However, after I drafted a chapter and an outline of the structure, the Press encouraged me to go ahead. My work suddenly assumed a practical purpose.

Naïvely I had assumed that I could transform my notes into a book in a few months. As it turned out, with the demands of a fulltime job, with the need for additional research and with many, many interruptions, writing dragged on for about nine years. *A History of Music in Canada 1534–1914* finally appeared in 1960.[15] The difficult part had been not the research but the turning of data into prose and the lining up of items in logical sequence. I experienced very much what Pierre Berton, the noted popularizer of Canadian history, told a *Globe and Mail* interviewer: "All narrative writing ... is a series of scenes. Half the battle is the order of scenes. Half the battle is the bridges."[16] Exactly. Forcing multi-dimensional connections between different subjects and concurrent trends into a linear straitjacket is a difficult task. I had to type over many pages five or six times, just to make sentences flow one into the other and to find the clearest expression of an idea. However, to describe the lessons I had to learn in writing and research techniques would take another article, so I will say no more about those aspects.

Lacuna after Lacuna

As the fifties wore on, one project led to another. Each step in my work revealed another lacuna of research and publication. Coverage of Canada in current reference works? Haphazard and slipshod. A comprehensive bibliography of books and articles? Not in existence. Biographies? Three or four. Printed orchestral scores and piano music? A slow beginning. Recordings of concert music? Not even a dozen. A survey of music library holdings? No initiative taken yet. Deposits of the papers of deceased musicians and the files of organizations? A few in libraries, archives or churches, but rarely catalogued or publicized. An iconography of Canadian paintings with musical subjects? Not to be found.

The Canadian Music Council (of which I became an individual member in 1951) was anxious to remedy the overall situation. It published an essay volume, under the editorship of its chairman, Sir Ernest MacMillan, *Music in Canada*.[17] I was asked to write the chapter on "Historical Background," a sort of trial run for my *History*. When the Council launched the *Canadian Music Journal* in 1956, Geoffrey Payzant, its editor, asked me to review and list music periodicals of the past.[18] When Arnold Walter, founding president of the International Society for Music Education (ISME), needed a survey of "Audio-Visual Aids to Music Education in Canada" (1957), he saddled me with the task.[19] The new Canadian League of Composers asked me to be their archivist and to edit a *Catalogue of Orchestral Music* (1957).[20] Indeed, once my interests were known, requests for articles and information became frequent and have never stopped. Almost all I have written has been commissioned.

Some lacunae I tried to fill on my own initiative since they stood in the way of completing my book. An analysis of dozens of reference books prompted me to criticize Canadian coverage in the fifth edition of *Grove's Dictionary of Music and Musicians* (1954)[21]—entries on MacMillan and Healey Willan were a good twenty years out-of-date—and, to prevent similar slights, to offer lists of suggested entries and my collaboration to *Die Musik in Geschichte und Gegenwart* (MGG) and *The Harvard Dictionary of Music* (1969 edition).[22] The MGG article on "Kanada" (1958) was the first historical outline of music in Canada in any encyclopedia; I revised and updated it in 1995. I also developed a long lasting correspondence with the ace of music lexicographers, Nicolas Slonimsky, then editor of the current editions of *Baker's Biographical Dictionary of Musicians* and *Thompson's* (*The International Cyclopedia of Music and Musicians*), updating Canadian biographies and reporting on premieres. When the *Dictionary of Canadian Biography* began to appear in 1966, I remained for many years the sole contributor of musical entries, largely concerning early Quebec musicians.

For the International Association of Music Libraries someone had to mobilize Canadian membership. I acted as liaison for a dozen years and submitted lists of recent Canadian publications for the *"liste sélective"* of IAML's periodical *Fontes artis musicae*. I undertook to locate Canadian-held copies of music and music literature printed before 1800 in any country for its *Répertoire international des sources musicales* (RISM). RISM was my strongest IAML involvement, and occupied me from 1953 until my retirement in 1987. I obtained listings through correspondence with libraries and individual collectors and the occasional visit to older churches and archives. The total number of 2,800 items (to 1987) cannot compare with the wealth found in European countries, but it did locate a few volumes from the 16th century and it opened the door to Erich Schwandt's and Micheline Vézina-Demers' in-depth exploration of the treasures at the Archives des Ursulines de Québec and (with cooperation of Lucien Brochu and Claude Beaudry) at Laval University. Later I advised IAML on the setting up of the RIdIM (*Répertoire international d'iconographie musicale*) project in Canada since I had already compiled my own inventory of Canadian pictures with musical contents. Later still I was a consultant when RIPM (*Répertoire international de la presse musicale*) was initiated.

Collecting Canadiana

My research and knowledge of earlier Canadian music throughout the 1950s had been based on words rather than scores or recordings, with the notable exception of such scores as Couture's *Jean le Précurseur* and keyboard pieces by W.O. Forsyth, Calixa Lavallée and Clarence Lucas. On the whole however, compositions remained titles only; descriptions and judgments in my writings were based mainly on the comments of earlier writers.

I stumbled into yet another preoccupation with Canadian music. One day in 1959 Sybille Pantazzi, librarian of The Art Gallery of Toronto, informed me that she had found an old album with Canadian music at the auctioneer John Britnell's store and had hidden it on a bottom shelf so that I would still find it the next day. I picked it up for $2.50. In it I found

J.P. Clarke's cycle of songs *Lays of the Maple Leaf,* one of only two known copies of this largest Canadian sheet music publication to 1853. And during a random visit to a second-hand bookstore I acquired an equally rare copy of Clarke's *Canadian Church Psalmody* of 1846 for $1.25. I began visiting the annual Toronto Symphony Orchestra rummage sales and although I thought my first acquisition, H.J. Fulmer's "Wait Till the Clouds Roll By" in an edition "for the patrons of the Bon Marché" Toronto dry goods store, was a little below my standards of taste, I recognized that along with the dross would come the gold. I decided to keep this music for the day that our National Library would open a music department. Over the years I visited antique and secondhand bookstores, rummage sales, and private individuals who had heard of my interests and by 1972 I had assembled some 1,000 pieces, all of which were then placed in the National Library of Canada along with some 680 programs, 260 periodical issues and 2,000 press clippings.

At the same time I built a modest historical collection at the CBC Toronto Music Library, anticipating its use for radio. Such an opportunity arose when in 1965 James Bannerman and I designed a thirteen-week documentary series titled "Music in Canada." Years before, I had obtained on microfilm all the Lavallée music I had traced in the major libraries, and photocopies of the two Quesnel operas I had first inspected at the Séminaire de Québec. Alas, the CBC couldn't be stirred to perform this music and it was only R. Murray Schafer's initiative in the Ten Centuries Concerts (1962–67) that finally led to a revival of *Colas et Colinette* and other historical pieces.

Controlling my accumulation of old Canadian sheet music and exploring the holdings of major libraries in New York and Boston, the poetry collection at Brown University,[23] the CBC Montreal Music Library and the Toronto Public Library and a few private Toronto collections inevitably led to listing such music and learning about composers and publishers. What surprised me was that after dozens and dozens of pieces, I rarely came across the same one again, and if I did, it would differ in cover design or colour. It became obvious that the total production must have numbered in the hundreds or thousands and that my coverage of historical composers in the 1952 edition of the *Catalogue of Canadian Composers* was one-sidedly concentrated on Quebec. This experience suggested an ideal Centennial-of-Confederation project for the Canadian Music Library Association (CMLA): an inventory of "Canadian Music Publications to 1921" (later extended to 1951). After much discussion a committee designed a "data sheet" since the standard cataloguing format would not allow the description of details such as illustrations, dedications, or occasions for composition. As it turned out, the sheets later would be consulted by many researchers in search of pictures for books and exhibits or of information about printing or publishing history. They were filled in by CMLA members and stored at my home in unique copies filed by composer. However, a published byproduct, *Musical Canadiana: A Subject Index*,[24] enabled concert organizers, performers and researchers to find music titled after or dedicated to Canadian places, dignitaries or events, pieces like "A Trip to Niagara," "Vive Laurier" or "La Confédération Quadrille."[25]

On my move to Ottawa in 1970 the data sheets were deposited at the National Library which took the project under its wing, adding thousands of entries from its own collection and from copyright entry listings. Eventually each sheet (21,000 in 1996) was photocopied so that four files existed, according to composer, title, publisher and year of publication. The files are in constant use but have been available only in Ottawa. At long last, conversion to an electronic data base began in 1995 in collaboration with the Canadian Musical Heritage Society, extended also to pre-1952 manuscripts. This conversion will permit wide distribution and feature additional access points for searches. Although my participation is now limited to critical advice, the whole project remains my special pride and joy.[26]

Parallel with our cataloguing of sheet music I began a card index of early music publications in volume form—church music, songbooks, instruction books, the earliest dating from 1800. Supplemented by titles listed by Conrad Laforte, John Beckwith[27] and others, it remains the largest inventory of its kind and is also housed at the National Library. The listing of historical Canadiana remains the Music Division's responsibility, of current legal deposits that of the National Library's Bibliographic Services, and of contemporary concert music that of the Canadian Music Centre.

A Lonely Task No Longer

After publication of my *History* in 1960 there followed ten years without a major project but with many smaller ones, some of which I have just referred to. In those years I investigated more thoroughly certain interesting phenomena and personalities, for example, the music of the Children of

Peace at Sharon, Ontario (having made the first recording of their barrel organ in 1956), the plate number practices of certain publishers, or the careers of James Paton Clarke, Joseph Quesnel, Calixa Lavallée (and the different editions of "O Canada"), Theodore Molt and Gustave Smith. I researched a number of programs for Ten Centuries Concerts and carried out a survey of Canadian-built instruments in museums and churches.[28] In my only labour in the field of folk and aboriginal music, I compiled an all-round bibliography for the Canadian Folk Music Society (now Canadian Society for Traditional Music), later deposited in the National Library.[29]

It became too much for one person to carry out.

I had over the years made many contacts to obtain or provide information. John Beckwith, Elmer Iseler, Victor Feldbrill as critics or conductors had championed Canadian music from the beginning of their careers in the late 1940s, but Willy Amtmann was one of the very few engaged in historical research, writing his doctoral dissertation on musical life in New France (1956).[30] Others with a historical bent were librarians, and in 1956 Ogreta McNeill of the Toronto Public Music Library, Lucien Brochu of Laval University and I founded the Canadian Music Library Association already referred to. A section of the Canadian Library Association, it served to establish a working relationship between music libraries and to carry out bibliographic projects on a nationwide scale.[31] The latter included the inventory of published music described above, a *Union List of Music Periodicals in Canadian Libraries* and *A Bio-bibliographical Finding List of Canadian Musicians*.[32] The *Finding List* was the outcome of my analysis, over the years, of dozens of dictionaries for their Canadian entries. It saved much time in picking the right dictionary for information, it provided access to even the most obscure musicians and helped to spot and investigate discrepancies. It was completed and edited with Melva J. Dwyer and Lucien Brochu.

Musical scholarship has risen at an accelerating speed since the late 1950s. First it had to do exclusively with European high art, since few professors cared about exploring Canadian composition. A decisive step in the direction of Canadian music studies was taken in the late 1960s with the introduction of courses or lectures in Canadian music at several universities. The pioneers included Murray Adaskin (Saskatchewan), Willy Amtmann (Carleton), Violet Archer (Alberta), John Beckwith (Toronto), Richard Johnston (Calgary) and Maryvonne Kendergi and Lyse Richer

(Montreal). This trend reflected the Centennial wave of patriotism, and also the missionary work of the Canadian Music Centre (founded 1959), but my own explorations and publications provided some essential teaching tools.

Not only did the choice of Canadian subjects for theses become frequent, graduates and graduate students—Dorith Cooper, Beverley Diamond, Clifford Ford, Frederick and Sharyn Hall, Elaine Keillor, Bruce and Kathryn Minorgan, Carl Morey, Lyse Richer, David Sale, Nadia Turbide among them—sought a means of comparing interests and establishing liaison. On 7 November 1970 some thirty young scholars met at the University of Toronto (during a conference of the American Musicological Society). Some had prepared *A Basic Bibliography of Musical Canadiana* (unpublished)[33] for the occasion and I had the opportunity to present a talk on "Canadian Tasks for Musicology" in which I pointed out the benefits of research to Canadian music and the advantages to the investigator of working in one's own locale, often in dialogue with living subjects. I appended a list of some thirty suggested topics.

My longest and closest working relationships were with two teams of three. With John Beckwith and Keith MacMillan, my working relations began about 1947 and 1952 respectively. Beckwith and MacMillan worked together on *Contemporary Canadian Composers*,[34] and the three of us advised on the Canadian coverage of *The New Grove Dictionary of Music and Musicians* (with Beckwith as liaison with Grove's editor) but what bound us together was the goal to promote the recognition of Canada as a musical country. Our specialties were different. MacMillan, executive director of the Canadian Music Centre 1964–77, was an energetic organizer, salesman and catalyst, Beckwith a composer-explorer and teacher, myself a historian and collector. For years Beckwith and I read drafts of each other's articles to supply criticism, and often still we exchange prepublication copies. Research for history's sake alone is not Beckwith's first priority, it is typically tied to a creative or critical project. As a composer Beckwith treats discoveries of old Canadian music under the prism of twentieth-century techniques. As I see our relationship, with more time for research, I have done much of the grocery shopping and Beckwith much of the cooking, although his choices from the larder were always his own and as in the case of the music of Sharon, or Quesnel's *Lucas et Cécile*, they were separated by years. Both MacMillan, for whom I was "Mr. Music-In-Canada," and Beckwith have given me moral support and incentive over the years. Paul J. Green and Nancy F. Vogan, in *Music Education in Canada*, judged that the three are "regarded by many as the leading exponents of music in Canadian society."[35]

The "triangle"—a term we used as a verb to signify our final approval of an article—with Gilles Potvin and Kenneth Winters was about one specific project, the *Encyclopedia of Music in Canada / Encyclopédie de la musique au Canada* (*EMC*), to be dealt with later, and again we brought different interests and skills into play. Potvin had an intimate familiarity with musical life in the Province of Quebec through his work for the CBC in Montreal and a great general knowledge of singers and opera. Winters' great assets included the experience of a critic and a sure command of literary style; my contribution was largely in providing historical input, much of it from my previous research and in my experience in the architecture of reference books. Other productive relationships developed at the National Library. Maria Calderisi, in charge of the printed collection, became a close associate in collecting and controlling printed Canadiana, Edward B. Moogk applied a life's experience in collecting and researching Canadian 78 rpm recordings, and Stephen C. Willis did his part to enlarge and organize the manuscript collection. Calderisi's master's thesis on the history of Canadian music publishing and printing[36] was closely enmeshed with my own work; we also collaborated in the National Library's survey of music library resources.

Three Major Challenges

Much of my survey of music in Canada to the early years of our century came from secondary sources, primary ones being rarely available with exceptions such as the Voyer d'Argenson marches of 1791 which I located in 1950, the Quesnel manuscripts (1952) or the music files of the Vancouver City Archives (1957). Those libraries, churches and convents and even those archives which had holdings of musical interest kept them more often by default rather than policy. They lacked specialist staff to catalogue and provide physical care. Throughout my projects I became more and more frustrated by the lack of access to primary source material. In the mid-1960s I composed a prospectus for a central repository for musical documents—manuscript compositions as well as correspondence, scrapbooks, concert programs, photos and others, in addition to printed and recorded materials.

I submitted this to various institutions, among them the National Library of Canada. It happened that the National Librarian, Guy Sylvestre, having acquired the large group of manuscripts and personal memorabilia of the late Healey Willan, noted composer and church musician, decided that the time had come to establish a music division under the care of an expert in Canadian music. The dream of a national music collection that I had dreamt from the time the institution was opened in 1953 finally came true, and I was selected to be the division's chief. I assumed the position in April 1970.

I have described the division's organization, functions and holdings in *Fontes*[37] and here would rather sketch the collection's dynamic in fostering awareness of and work in Canada's music history and present. I was allowed to collect retrospectively and to expand the variety of media that together provide the country's musical memory—printed and recorded, published and handwritten, pictorial and artifacts, newspaper clippings, correspondence, diplomas and other ephemera. It was a golden opportunity to establish a "one-stop" research centre, to varying degrees a combination of library, archive, museum and documentation centre. There were certain limitations of scope in order to avoid duplication of the Canadian Museum of Civilization's folk music and ethnological collections and the Canadian Music Centre's library of contemporary concert music.

In twenty-five years the division has acquired the largest collection of musical Canadiana. It has become a preserver and facilitator that has attracted teachers of "CanMus" courses, graduate students, journalists, editors, biographers, broadcasters, filmmakers and plain music lovers. An outreach program provides exhibitions, both in Ottawa and travelling, publications, recordings and concerts.

Just as on the heels of my beginnings at the CBC I was invited to write a history of music in Canada for which I had intended merely to produce raw data, so within months of my beginnings at the National Library I was invited to discuss editing a reference book about music in Canada. The initiative came from a model patron of the arts, Floyd S. Chalmers, who was inspired to sponsor such a book by John Beckwith's 1969 polemic about Canadian music's "P.R. Failure" which had exposed the "appalling ignorance" of foreign reference books in matters Canadian.[38] Three editors were selected for the *Encyclopedia of Music in Canada (EMC)*,[39] Ken Winters, a Manitoban in Toronto with special responsibility for the English language texts, Gilles Potvin of Montreal for the French texts and I for the research aspect. As it turned out, the combination of anglophone, francophone and "new Canadian" was an effective one and we pooled whatever knowledge and skills we had—linguistic and informational. We assembled a wonderful team of assistants and worked with a supportive and non-interfering board that did wonders in the awesome task of fund-raising.

Again as in the earlier case, I had done a lot of the historical groundwork; in fact, I had worked on elements of *EMC* for twenty-two years without having a name for it or contemplating publication. As early as 1949 I had tried to persuade CAPAC, the performing rights society, that my notes might serve the compilation of "a handbook or encyclopedia of Canadian music." Twenty years later it was Chalmers who owned a match (to use an analogy), Beckwith who induced him to light it, and Keith MacMillan who showed him where to find kindling wood, in the Canadian Music Centre and National Library files and in my research notes. The bulk of the fuel would later come from several hundred contributors.

We decided early on that the book should have Canadian content only and that it should cover all facets of musical activity. On the occasion of publishing a second edition (1992 in English, 1993 in French, edited by Kallmann and Potvin) I reported about the many aspects of encyclopedia making in *Fontes*,[40] such as the breaking down of large subject areas into entries, the experiences in finding dependable contributors and obtaining accurate information. I will merely sum up the place of *EMC* in our musical self-knowledge. It was not only the first comprehensive Canadian inventory of one of the arts, but the first detailed lexicographic treatment of the music of any one country. Perhaps its most important aspects lie in the many memories it revitalizes, the connections it weaves, and the studies it may inspire. Above all it gives Canada a literary structure to absorb future developments in new editions. The documentation of music, by the National Library, the Canadian Music Centre and *EMC* is vitally important. After all, a few centuries from now people may remember Canadians through our literature, art and music rather than our politicians and CEOs—but only if the records of music and its history are available for inspection. Hence it is important to develop the tools of memory—libraries, archives, in particular scores, recordings and biographies.

After the verbal portrait of Canadian music provided by the encyclopedia, the logical next step was an anthology of the actual music. There were such models as Schering's and Apel's anthologies of Western music, and there was a *Music in America* anthology by W.T. Marrocco and

Harold Gleason (1964).[41] By the late 1950s I had drawn up general outlines of a Canadian volume for discussion with Beckwith. However, it was only in 1981 that Clifford Ford, a composer who had taught a Canadian music course at Dalhousie University, came up with a plan of action—and the prospect for some seed money. By 1982 five of us, including also Beckwith, Frederick A. Hall and Elaine Keillor, had formed the Canadian Musical Heritage Society (Société pour le patrimoine musical canadien). Later Lucien Poirier and Marie-Thérèse Lefebvre were recruited. All are devoted to the cause of Canadian music and sympathetic to nineteenth- and early-twentieth-century "Victorian" music. Ford as executive secretary has carried the brunt of the society's work, and I have been chair of the society since its inception.

Our work consists of combing through pre-1940 publications and accessible manuscripts, about half of them in the National Library, in order to select pieces either for their musical value or for their context in social history. With generous support from the Social Sciences and Humanities Research Council of Canada and other sources, we had published eighteen volumes by mid-1996 of a planned total of twenty-five.[42] All volumes combine critical editing with practical performance considerations.

The Canadian Musical Heritage / Le Patrimoine musical canadien (*CMH*) series of anthologies tries to undo the neglect of generations of Canadian composers which stands in contrast to our widely recognized and widely accessible visual artists and writers of the past. Much of the music in those eighteen volumes is more than competent and fully equal to that of minor composers of Europe and the United States. I am thinking of certain pieces by the Canadian-born Guillaume Couture, Gabriel Cusson, Wesley Octavius Forsyth, Calixa Lavallée, Clarence Lucas, Ernest MacMillan, Edward Manning, Rodolphe Mathieu, Joseph Vézina or Ernest Whyte and the immigrants Antoine Dessane, Joseph Quesnel, Alfred Whitehead and Healey Willan.

In Retrospect, What Have I Learned?

Since I began looking into Canada's musical past, almost another half century has become history, a period which has produced more Canadian compositions and more performers than the previous three centuries together. And with this half century the work of the historian itself has become history. While contributing to shaping the narrative of Canadian music history, my views and methods themselves have been shaped by history. I will focus this review on my 1960 *History* because I consider it my basic breakthrough in mapping Canadian music history, even though in *EMC* I refined and supplemented many of its assertions.

In hindsight, what would I change in a second edition of my *History*? I will leave aside the four-page list of corrections and new discoveries or conclusions in the 1987 reprint and the question of whether indeed I would undertake a second edition. I would like to begin with a few specifics before turning to general aspects of writing history.

The most important development since the 1950s is that a multitude of Canadian compositions of all eras is now available for critical review and that there is more precise documentation of the different literatures cultivated in performance, from hymns, anthems and plainchant to opera, oratorio, parlour song and dance music. I would no longer be obliged to deal with "musical life" at the expense of "music." This might go some way to satisfy Joseph Kerman's call that musicologists should break loose from positivistic fact gathering and devote more effort to critical appraisal.[43]

Assuming that my *History*, or anyone else's, would be stretched to cover the entire twentieth century, it would be time for a reassessment of pre-1940 composition. The appearance of a group of Canadian composers about 1940, rejecting the late-Victorian models of their teachers and hitching on to contemporary schools marks an important point of departure indeed—the establishment of composition as a career rather than as a sideline, the teaching of contemporary techniques and the adoption of orchestral writing as a main vehicle of expression. But modernism, it will be found, had struck much earlier than 1940, in Humfrey Anger's *Tintamarre* (1911) with its tone clusters, in Rodolphe Mathieu's atonal *Trois Préludes* of 1912–15, or in Colin McPhee's Piano Concerto No. 2 of 1924, to name a few examples. The *CMH*'s revival of these and the composers mentioned above[44] disproves the belief that professionally qualified composers came on the scene only about 1940.

Interdisciplinary studies were not yet quite in fashion in the 1950s. My *History* did treat music too much in isolation; only in *EMC* (under "Art, visual") did I touch on parallels with art. Parallels should also be drawn with literature, and not merely with regard to poetry settings and specific instances of cross-fertilization, but also to the problems, directions and peak achievements of each medium as a whole.

A regrettable weakness in my *History* is the briefness of the chapter on "Music in New France." It was written early in the process, when I expected the whole book to be much shorter. This lack of proportion troubles me not only because there was much more to say, but also because most of it I knew and could have written at that time. I believe I have explored more contemporary records of and quotations about music in New France than anyone else before or since, but I did not publicize many until the *Dictionary of Canadian Biography* and *EMC*. It explains the assertion in a recent publication[45] that the scholarly study of music in New France has "just begun" and that five scholars recently have discovered traces of the School of Versailles in works by Nicolas Bernier, André Campra and others, when in fact my work for RISM in the mid-1950s was the lever that produced a listing (supplied mainly by Lucien Brochu) of that music, a list which was then made accessible to other scholars and which has long since been integrated in the RISM volumes.

As to the general aspects of writing Canadian music history, a competently thought-out text has to do justice to three elements: facts, values and relationships. In blending these elements, the narrative has to force multi-dimensional reality into the linear medium of language and to seek compromises between the side-by-side and the before-and-after.[46] The time-tested methods are chronology and division into chapters; the juxtaposition and interplay of these elements depend on the skill of the historian.

The gathering, validating and selecting of facts and their interpretation as to their significance and long-lasting value cannot be treated as two successive tasks. I was wrong, in the Introduction to the *History* (p.6), to expect that evaluation should wait until the facts of "what actually happened" were available.[47] As E.H. Carr has pointed out, the two phases always go hand in hand: "the historian is engaged on a continuous process of moulding his facts to his interpretation and his interpretation to his facts,"[48] and indeed, that is how my writing proceeded in practice.

When it comes to identifying lasting values, the question of relativity arises. I believe that there are two opposite positions. The older view holds that artistic value exists objectively *sub specie aeternitatis*—Palestrina is good music whether you are a sixteenth- or twentieth-century listener, whether you live in Italy or the Far East, because laws of aesthetics (e.g., proportion and balance), acoustics and physiology are universal. More recently relativism has held sway in the context of multiculturalism. In its moderate form it maintains, as Warren Dwight Allen did in his *Philosophies of Music History*, that "Modern musicology is concerning itself with all the forms and styles of musical communication man has employed *at any time and in any culture* ... [Allen's italics]"[49]—a precept applied in

EMC on a one-country scale. In its less reasonable form it seems to hold that since all musical likes and dislikes are subjective and rooted in a specific culture, therefore the value of any kind of music is none other than the degree of satisfaction and pleasure it provides to its own audience (which in the case of popular culture translates into record sales profits as the yardstick). The most inane pop music in this view is deemed as worthy of musical (as distinct from sociological) study as the music of Palestrina! Surely one must distinguish between a descriptive study of global music "at any time and in any culture" and its evaluation; surely one must be aware that art of one age and society can appeal to other ages and societies when education and effort are applied.

The relationships (a term embracing influences, constellations, dynamics of change) are largely questions of hegemony. Which influence is stronger than which other influence, and exactly how does it work? One important tool for bringing order to such a quest is the tracing of patterns and themes. If traced carefully, these can clarify; if not, they may oversimplify or mislead.

The traditional patterns and themes revolve around stylistic characteristics, schools of composers, their great masters and other dominant characteristics grouped in chunks of time, currents, counter-currents, sub-styles and so on. More recently historians have placed these developments within larger cultural and social contexts, including the impact of technology and economics. But many other themes can be traced. Beverley Diamond in her analysis of the underlying values and assumptions of three histories of Canadian music offers interesting suggestions for alternative "narratives" although she avoids committing herself to any.[50] Some themes—and I have added a few—deal with hegemonies or concentrations of power and influence, Montreal vs. Toronto, music business (mass entertainment) vs. aesthetics as shapers of taste, Canadian-raised and immigrant composers, conflict and conciliation between economic and autonomous musical forces, town and country opportunities for music making, oral and printed dissemination, mutual contacts between vernacular and cultivated traditions (to use H. Wiley Hitchcock's terms) or gender relations. Indeed some of these themes are traced in the three histories Diamond has analysed; others could be added. I once heard Virgil Thomson suggest that composition alternates between periods of growing complexity and the reassertion of simplicity, certainly a worthwhile proposition to explore. In fact, the possibilities for tracing themes in isolation or interaction are endless.

Mapping Canada's Music: A Life's Task

Is it justified to rewrite the history of music in Canada from such viewpoints? That depends, in my view, on making a distinction between historical studies with well-defined limited perspectives and full-fledged histories. Some themes lend themselves perfectly well to historical studies—the roles of the oral, notated and recorded dissemination of music, or the participation of women in musical activities—but I cannot see them as backbones for a global account of Canada's (or probably most other countries') musical history. Nor should interdisciplinary approaches swallow up investigation of each discipline by itself. The essential focus of music history should remain composition, with its style varieties, aesthetic credos, mutual influences, its strong personalities and successive chronological points of division as ordering factors. However, Canadian music historiography should increasingly embrace native, "ethnic" and various vernacular forms of music. Canada has always been a laboratory for the study of musical transplantation and adaptation, and the recent waves of immigration from dozens of countries provide new vistas for such studies—and indeed for new avenues in composition. Here is a special niche for Canadian music historiography.

I can do no better to sum up my view of the essential patterns in Canadian music history than to quote a passage I wrote some twenty-five years after the *History*, dealing with the period to World War One:

> Music, this is certain, did not grow from a single seed into a complex plant; rather it was nourished by an accumulation of different traditions—the songs and dances of the native peoples, the hymns, chorales, and anthems of the Methodists, the Mennonites, and songs and bagpipe music of the Highland Scots, the European repertoire of piano and flute music within the reach of amateur performers, not to forget parlour ballads and tunes from popular operas. These forms and genres of music came to the colony fully-grown; indeed, instead of taking root, they often deteriorated because of a lack of teachers and a dearth of printed scores to maintain the traditional skills and repertoires. The growth that did take place in the colony itself expressed itself in the building of a framework supporting musical activities—"philharmonic societies," instrument manufacturing, music publishing, private and school teaching. Under colonial conditions the important changes in musical taste and practice were not so much self-propelled as they were introduced from the outside by new immigrants, by imported sheet music, and by visiting star artists. And yet, subtle modifications of the inherited or borrowed traditions did occur, due to the mixing of people with different traditions, and also to budding consciousness of a new society with its own identity.[51]

Epilogue

The newcomer to a city needs a street map, the native rarely does. It is no surprise that a newcomer should have been curious to find out the who of music's personalities, the what of activities, the how of working connections, and the why of importance. From childhood I have been a compulsive mapmaker, both in the literal and the applied senses, but perhaps that is merely one way in which the human quest for order expresses itself.

I could have explained my motivation for exploring Canadian music history as a gesture of gratitude for fate having dumped me in Canada. Successful immigrants often claim to have been inspired by gratitude to do a good deed for Canada, but I distrust that assertion. I believe the fun in doing congenial work comes first; awareness of "paying back" develops only as the work comes to a close; knowledge and love of country arise through one's work. It was the chance to explore and discover that spurred me on, the fun of locating and fitting together the pieces of a jigsaw puzzle, the move from chaos to order. Through my quest I have come to admire and love Canadians, rather than the other way around.

The best reward for my labours is that others have taken up the task, independently or with my help. Many were among the 530 contributors to the second edition of the *Encyclopedia of Music in Canada*. Gradually my self-imposed responsibilities have slipped into the hands of younger scholars, some with the librarian, archivist and historian training not available in my student days. None will have to do the digging I had to do, but they may re-examine, re-evaluate, deepen and broaden. I have no intention to retire from Canadian tasks but I feel free now to devote some time to non-Canadian interests that had been placed on the backburner in 1949.

Over the decades I extracted information about Theodore Molt from at least 20 sources, but still gaps remained in his biography. In 1995, the year of his 200th anniversary, I had an opportunity to visit Molt's birthplace, the municipality of Gschwend in the vicinity of Stuttgart. The local worthies—historian, schoolteacher, musician and even the mayor—turned up to present me with photocopied documentation of the young man's career as soldier and school teacher and to discuss family members and residences. In turn they listened eagerly to what I could tell them about Gschwend's distinguished son and his career in faraway Quebec and Vermont where he had found a new life.

And not to forget, the manuscript of Beethoven's canon "Freu' Dich des Lebens" has been a treasured possession of the National Library's Music Division since 1979.

NOTES

1 Fritz Prelinger, ed., *Ludwig van Beethovens sämtliche Briefe und Aufzeichnungen*, 3 vols., (Vienna and Leipzig: C.W. Stern, 1907); *Nachträge*, vol. 4, (1909); *Nachträge, Erläuterungen*, vol. 5, (1911). The correspondence with Molt is in vol. 5, item 1298. (I made a keyword index of which I can supply copies.)
2 For example the pianist Frank Welsman (1873–1952) and the violinist Frank Blachford (1879–1957).
3 In cities and towns of Victorian and early twentieth-century Canada, the civic auditorium or hall was often called the "opera house." It hosted lectures, rallies, and sometimes concerts, but almost never operas. [*Ed.*]
4 Helmut Kallmann, "Canadian Music as a Field for Research," *Royal Conservatory of Music of Toronto Monthly Bulletin* (March 1950), 2. [The essay is reprinted here; see pages 35–38, *Ed.*]
5 Jean Ross MacMillan, "Music in Canada: A Short Bibliography," *Ontario Library Review* 24 (November 1940), 386–96. [*Ed.*]
6 Kathleen M. Hobday, *Survey of the Musical Resources of the Province of Ontario* (Toronto: Department of Educational Research, Ontario College of Education, University of Toronto, 1946). [*Ed.*]
7 Susie Frances Harrison, "Historical Sketch of Music in Canada," *Canada: An Encyclopedia of the Country*, vol. 4, ed. J.Castell Hopkins (Toronto: Linscott, 1898), and "Canada," *The Imperial History and Encyclopedia of Music*, vol. 3: *History of Foreign Music*, ed. William Lines Hubbard (New York: I. Squire, ca. 1909); Edouard Hesselberg, "A Review of Music in Canada," *Modern Music and Musicians*, ed. Louis C. Elson, Supplement (New York: University Society, 1912; supplement 1913); Augustus Bridle et al., "Music," *The Year Book of Canadian Art 1913* (London and Toronto: J.M. Dent and Sons, 1913), 61–148; Campbell McInnes, "Music in Canada" (113–21), Marius Barbeau, "French and Indian Motifs in our Music" (123–32), and Augustus Bridle, "Composers among Us" (133–40), *Yearbook of the Arts in Canada 1928/1929*, ed. Bertram Brooker (Toronto: Macmillan, 1929); Ernest MacMillan, "Problems of Music in Canada," in *Yearbook of the Arts in Canada 1936*, ed. Bertram Brooker (Toronto: Macmillan, 1936), 185–200. [*Ed.*]
8 Kallmann, "Canadian Music as a Field for Research," 2.

9 Ernest Myrand, *Noëls anciens de la Nouvelle France: étude historique* (Quebec: Dussault & Proulx, 1899); 2nd ed. (Quebec: Laflamme & Proulx, 1907). [*Ed.*]

10 Frederick Ernest Amédée Gagnon, *Louis Jolliet, découvreur du Mississipi et du pays des Illinois, premier seigneur de l'île d'Anticosti: étude biographique et historiographique* (Montreal: Librairie Beauchemin, 1902; 2nd ed. 1913; 4th ed. 1946). [*Ed.*]

11 Nazaire LeVasseur, *Réminiscences d'antan: Québec il y a 70 ans* (Quebec City: Charrier, 1926) and "Musique et musiciens à Québec: souvenirs d'un amateur," a series of forty articles published in the monthly journal *La Musique* [Quebec City] between 15 January 1919 and 22 December 1922; Gustave Smith, "Souvenirs et relations de voyages (1824–1856)," ms in LAC and "Du mouvement musical en Canada," *L'album musical* [Montreal], thirteen articles appearing in instalments between December 1881 and December 1882; Mgr. Henri Têtu, "Impressions musicals," a series of articles in *Action sociale* from 13 March to 25 May 1915. [*Ed.*]

12 Eugène Lapierre, *Calixa Lavallée: musicien national du Canada* (Montreal: Granger Frères, 1936); 2nd ed. 1950; 3rd ed. (Montreal: Fides, 1966); Léo-Pol Morin, *Papiers de musique* (Montreal: Librairie d'action canadienne-française, 1930). [*Ed.*]

13 There are 43 as of 1996 although since 1970 most of my research material is filed at the National Library of Canada or in the Encyclopedia of Music in Canada files.

14 Helmut Kallmann, ed., *Catalogue of Canadian Composers*, rev. and enlarged edn (Toronto: Canadian Broadcasting Corporation, 1952).

15 Helmut Kallmann, *A History of Music in Canada 1534–1914* (Toronto: University of Toronto Press, 1960).

16 Val Ross, "Captain Canada at 75 Face to Face," *The Globe and Mail* [Toronto], (7 October 1995), C1.

17 Ernest MacMillan, ed., *Music in Canada* (Toronto: University of Toronto Press, 1955).

18 Helmut Kallmann, "A Century of Musical Periodicals in Canada," *Canadian Music Journal* 1/1 (Autumn 1956), 37–43 and 1/2 (Winter 1957), 25–36.

19 Helmut Kallmann, "Audio-Visual Aids to Music Education in Canada," ISME series *Technical Media in Music Education*, mimeographed (n.p., 1957). [*Ed.*]

20 [Helmut Kallmann, ed.,] *Catalogue of Orchestral Music* (Toronto: Canadian League of Composers, 1957). [*Ed.*]

21 Helmut Kallmann, "The New *Grove's*: Disappointment to Canada," *Saturday Night* 70/23 (12 March 1955), 25. [The review is reprinted here; see pages 39–42, *Ed.*]

22 Regarding HK's contributions to *The Harvard Dictionary of Music*, see his correspondence with Willi Apel published here on pages 183–85 [*Ed.*]
23 The Harris Collection of American Poetry and Plays, Brown University, Providence, Rhode Island; this is one of the five largest collections of sheet music in the United States.
24 *Musical Canadiana: A Subject Index*, compiled by a committee of the Canadian Music Library Association (Ottawa: Canadian Library Association, 1967).
25 The pieces are by William J. Cornish, Alexis Contant, and Léon Casorti respectively. [*Ed.*]
26 See the Library and Archives Canada website "Sheet Music from Canada's Past," which covers sheet music publications up to 1921, at http://www.collectionscanada.gc.ca/sheetmusic/index-e.html. [*Ed.*]
27 Conrad Laforte, *La chanson folklorique et les écrivains du XIXe siècle (en France et au Québec)*, Collection Ethnologie québécoise: cahier II, Les Cahiers du Québec 12 (Montreal: Éditions Hurtubise HMH, 1973); John Beckwith, "On Compiling an Anthology of Canadian Hymn Tunes," *Sing Out the Glad News*, CanMus Documents 1 (Toronto: Institute for Canadian Music, 1987), 3–32. Includes "Appendix, Canadian Tunebooks, and Hymnals with Music, 1801–1939: A Checklist," 30–32.
28 Helmut Kallmann, *Canadian-built 19th Century Musical Instruments, a Check List* (mimeographed, 1965); 2nd ed. (Edmonton: Edmonton Public Library, distributed by the Canadian Music Library Association, 1966).
29 The folk music bibliography covers the literature and recordings up to about 1970 and is stored as a card file in the Music Division of the National Library of Canada.
30 Willy Amtmann, "La vie musicale en Nouvelle-France," D.Litt. thesis, Université de Strasbourg, 1956; see also his *Music in Canada 1600–1800* (Cambridge, ON: Habitex, 1975), expanded and translated as *La musique au Québec, 1600–1875* (Montreal: Éditions de l'Homme, 1976). [*Ed.*]
31 In 1971 it became the Canadian Association of Music Libraries (CAML) and affiliated with the International Association of Music Libraries.
32 *Union List of Music Periodicals in Canadian Libraries*, compiled by a committee of the Canadian Library Association (Ottawa: Canadian Library Association, 1964); supplement, 1967; 2nd edn, Larry C. Lewis, ed. (Ottawa: Canadian Music Library Association, 1981). *A Bio-Bibliographical Finding List of Canadian Musicians and Those Who Have Contributed to Music in Canada*, compiled by a committee of the Canadian Music Library Association (Ottawa: Canadian Library Association, 1961). 2nd edn, *Musicians in Canada: A Bio-Bibliographical Finding List / Musiciens au Canada: index bio-bibliographique*, Kathleen M. Toomey and Stephen C. Willis, eds. (Ottawa: Canadian Association of Music Libraries, 1981); the coding system of the second edition made it less attractive for quick consultation.

33 Frederick A. Hall et al., compilers, *A Basic Bibliography of Musical Canadiana*, typescript (Toronto, 1970). [*Ed.*]
34 Keith MacMillan and John Beckwith, eds., *Contemporary Canadian Composers* (Toronto: Oxford University Press, 1975).
35 J. Paul Green and Nancy F. Vogan, *Music Education in Canada: A Historical Account* (Toronto: University of Toronto Press, 1991), 322.
36 Maria Calderisi, MMA thesis, McGill University, 1976; published as *Music Publishing in the Canadas 1800–1867 / L'Édition musicale au Canada 1800–1867* (Ottawa: National Library of Canada, 1981).
37 Helmut Kallmann, "The Music Collection of the National Library of Canada," *Fontes artis musicae* 34/4 (October-December 1987), 174–84.
38 John Beckwith, "About Canadian Music: The P.R. Failure," *Musicanada* 21 (July-August 1969), 4–7, 10–13; expanded and reprinted in *Music, The AGO and RCCO Magazine*, 5/3 (March 1971) 33–37, 56.
39 Helmut Kallmann, Gilles Potvin, and Kenneth Winters, eds., *Encyclopedia of Music in Canada* (Toronto: University of Toronto Press, 1981) / *Encyclopédie de la Musique au Canada* (Montreal: Fides, 1983); Helmut Kallmann and Gilles Potvin, eds., *Encyclopedia of Music in Canada*, 2nd edn (Toronto: University of Toronto Press, 1992) / *Encyclopédie de la Musique au Canada*, 2e édn (Montreal: Fides, 1993).
40 Helmut Kallmann, "The Making of a One-Country Music Encyclopedia," *Fontes artis musicae* 41/1 (January-March 1994), 3–19. [Reprinted here on pages 103–24 *Ed.*]
41 Arnold Schering, ed., *Geschichte der Musik in Beispielen* (Leipzig: Breitkopf and Härtel, 1931); Archibald T. Davison and Willi Apel, eds., *Historical Anthology of Music*, 2 vols. (Cambridge, MA: Harvard University Press, 1946, 1950); W. Thomas Marrocco and Harold Gleason, eds., *Music in America: An Anthology from the Landing of the Pilgrims to the Close of the Civil War, 1620–1865* (New York: W.W. Norton, 1964). [*Ed.*]
42 The final volume (vol. 25) appeared in 1999; in addition, a two-volume *Historical Anthology of Canadian Music* was published in 1998. [*Ed.*]
43 Joseph Kerman, *Contemplating Music* (Cambridge, MA: Harvard University Press, 1985), *passim*.
44 See the reference above (page 205) to Couture, Cusson, Forsyth, etc. [*Ed.*]
45 Marie-Thérèse Lefebvre, "The Role of the Church in the History of Musical Life in Quebec," *Canadian Music: Issues of Hegemony and Identity*, ed. Beverley Diamond and Robert Witmer (Toronto: Canadian Scholars' Press, 1994), 67.
46 I am aware that new technologies have made multi-dimensional histories a possibility, e.g., by adding sound to text, or by presenting text in vertically and horizontally arranged boxes giving the reader choice in the order of progressing from one unit to another.

47 This Introduction is reprinted on pages 43–47. [*Ed.*]
48 Edward Hallett Carr, *What Is History?* (London: Macmillan, 1961), 24.
49 Warren Dwight Allen, *Philosophies of Music History* (New York: American Book Company, 1939), 342.
50 Beverley Diamond, "Narratives in Canadian Music History," *Taking a Stand, Essays in Honour of John Beckwith*, ed. Timothy J. McGee (Toronto: University of Toronto Press, 1995), 273–305. The three histories that Diamond examines are Helmut Kallmann, *A History of Music in Canada 1534–1914* (Toronto: University of Toronto Press, 1960); Clifford Ford, *Canada's Music: An Historical Survey* (Agincourt, ON: GLC, 1982) and Timothy J. McGee, *The Music of Canada* (New York: W.W. Norton, 1985).
51 Helmut Kallmann, "Music in Upper Canada," Nick and Helma Mika, compilers, *The Shaping of Ontario: From Exploration to Confederation* (Belleville, ON: Mika Publishing, 1985), 220–27.

16
The Matter of Identity

Invited by Carl Rosenberg, the editor of *Outlook, Canada's Progressive Jewish Magazine*, to contribute a think piece, HK produced this article, which later appeared in a German translation.[1] In his retirement years, HK reflected on the extraordinary, often tragic, twists and turns of his early life: the interruption of his family life and education; his internment by the British even though, like so many other "enemy aliens," he had more experience of the Nazi menace and was as a result more solidly anti-Nazi than many of his warders; his eventual adoption of not only Canadian residence and citizenship but a career devoted to the study and documentation of Canadian music. Between 1996 and 2004, HK edited and circulated entirely on his own initiative ten issues of an "Internees' Newsletter," keeping his aging fellow-survivors of the Canadian wartime internment in touch with news of each other's activities. Sojourns in Europe renewed his feelings of belonging to a German cultural heritage: these included vacation visits to Germany in 1962, 1971, 1994 (on the invitation of the Senate of Berlin, extended to ex-Berliners persecuted by the Nazis), and 1995 (as a speaker at the opening of an exhibition concerning the former Jewish residents of Berlin-Schöneberg); Austria in 1997; and Germany again in 2002. He regularly conversed in German with Traute Weinberg, the companion of his last decade. The "long form" of the Canadian census, starting point of his commentary, was abolished by the Canadian government as a cost-saving measure just before the census of 2011: such questions are no longer asked.

Outlook, Canada's Progressive Jewish Magazine 39/4 (July/August 2001), 15–16; reprinted by permission of Carl Rosenberg, editor

What is my identity and what does identity mean? I was born and raised in Berlin in a liberal German-Jewish family. I left by *Kindertransport* for London in 1939, and was interned and sent to Canada in 1940 with over 2,000 other refugees. Of these, some 900 settled in Canada in the late years of the war.[2] By now I have lived in Canada for over sixty years, and during my employed life I have devoted nearly all my time, research and writing to matters related to music in Canada. If national identity were simply a matter of choice I would be happiest to be nothing but a Canadian.

But the recent Statistics Canada Census (long form) inquired about my ethnic origin and my religion. Should I answer Jewish and Jewish? And here I get in a conflict not only with the census designers but with a majority of Canadian Jews with ancestors in Eastern Europe who feel themselves an ethnic unit even more than adherents of a religion.

Ethnic origin: for generations my ancestors have spoken nothing but German, the few Hebrew phrases my parents knew from prayers were learned by rote; they could hardly translate them. In my case ethnic origin involves not only language (including a lifelong accent)—all the books I read in my youth were written in or translated into my mother tongue—but also folksongs, and a cultural and geographical environment. What else does "ethnic" mean? To be honest, I put down "German" on the census form.

Religion: the Census form (question 22) asked for one's religion "even if the person isn't practicing." I answered "Jewish," because I have a certain interest in the history and sociology of religion, though from childhood I went to synagogue only when pushed, and in Canada only for weddings or funerals. Why does the Census want to bolster numbers by including non-believers?

Is an identity necessary? Is it a matter of personal choice, or is it an objective fact independent of my will, Jew-German-Canadian? I can distinguish three kinds of identity: involuntary, forced and voluntary. Involuntary identities are one's mother tongue, one's family, childhood and early environment. My fellow ex-internees all remember identities forced upon us—assuming the names of Sara or Israel in 1939 and a year later being designated "Enemy Aliens—Prisoners of War, Second Class." Voluntary identity is one's decision to identify with a circle of friends, a spouse, a profession, a political party, a system of philosophy, a club, a city or a country.

As human beings we always remain tied to our youth. What then has happened to our ties with the German and Austrian countries of our birth?

The Matter of Identity

Among my fellow ex-refugees, I have observed a great variety of attitudes. It depends very much on the relative strength of memories of either a happy home and youth's irrepressible zest for life, or the suffering under Nazi brutality. It depends also on how successfully we have started a new life in Canada or elsewhere, and how "realistic" and adaptable a personality we have.

Realists live in the present. They suppress the memory of horrible experiences, refusing to visit Germany, speak German, or take an interest in German affairs. I can understand and respect that. I have less sympathy for those who consider every last German a former Nazi supporter. I think of the thousands of non-Jewish spouses who stuck to their Jewish partners, of the staunch non-Jewish anti-Nazis I met in internment, of men such as Thomas Mann, Pastor Niemoeller or Carl von Ossietzky—more than a tiny minority. For the thousands who cheered Hitler and his parading troops there were thousands who stayed at home or were locked up in concentration camps.

Many other ex-refugees are neutral. They return once to the town of their birth, talk German when necessary, but have no inner need to associate with the people or their culture. But scratch beneath the surface and you will find the Viennese fond of his opera and his dialect or the Berliner glorying in his theatres and his local jokes. Their mental equipment still reflects Germany, whether they like it or not.

My own view of the German connection is more positive. I have never tried to force myself to adopt or abandon an identity. I have drifted where fate took me, to Canada, to Toronto, into a career specialty, even a happy marriage. I do not want to erase my fond memories of my family and my many anti-Nazi friends, my early summer holidays, my love of Berlin geography and dialect. I do not, cannot deny my strong German, nor my somewhat weaker Jewish roots.

Although in the decades after the war I was reluctant to visit Germany, I did build cultural and personal links and read German books. Since my retirement in 1987 I have done what I could to document my years in the public and Jewish schools and to trace childhood friends. I have visited Germany several times and get along with most people; I enjoy the scenery and feel that this country belongs to me. Like so many Canadians I have dual, though unequal, identities. I look on German history in a perspective of hundreds of years. It embraces more than just the age of the Brownshirts. Hitler could not wipe out the integral role in Austro-German culture of Heinrich Heine, Moses and Felix Mendelssohn, Karl Marx,

Gustav Mahler, Sigmund Freud, Max Liebermann, Max Reinhardt, Kurt Weill, Albert Einstein and many others. Why should I not feel connected to their country? The life of Jews in Germany has seen high as well as low points. Both must be remembered, both are part of my heritage.

German Jewish liberals in my childhood considered themselves German by nationality and ethnicity, Jewish by religion. Along came the Nazis and said, "Once a Jew, always a Jew," the Jews cannot be Germans. Some Jews, especially the Zionists, agreed. The division has stuck. Many of the exiles look at their roots too negatively, behaving as though Hitler had won. Hitler almost defeated the Jews under his control, but only almost. Don't we know that he lost the war, that we are not only victims but victors? We have every reason to mourn our dead and remember our suffering, but even more reason to celebrate our long history with its achievements thanks to the mixture of Jewish and German roots.

It has been said that the German-Jewish symbiosis ("union between organisms each of which depends for its existence on the other"—*Concise Oxford Dictionary*) came to a tragic end in 1933. As Rabbi Gunther Plaut (Leo Baeck Memorial Lecture 36, 1992) put it: "They [the Jews] wanted to embrace the German spirit and failed. In the end they returned to their own roots." Did they really fail? On German soil, probably, but on a world perspective, the German-Jewish spirit has survived and pervades a huge post-expulsion literature, scholarly, belletristic and journalistic, written by writers rooted in German education: one can see it in our writings, our teaching, our outlook on life. Even though we have become Canadians, Americans, British, Israelis, Latin Americans and citizens of many other countries, with one foot most of us still stand in the homeland, no matter that some may deny it. The Jewish refugees have transplanted much German thought and knowledge throughout the world. It's almost like our revenge on the Nazis: they were unable to stifle the German in us "non-Germans."

Those who were rooted in German education are now in our seventies or older. After us a new generation of German Jews will take our place. Whether they will feel themselves as Jews in a religious or historical sense or whether former Christians and former Jews will have lost a distinct identity (intermarriage becoming the rule), all this cannot be predicted. But a new generation descended from Jews will assume a role in German society, different from the old one, vital nonetheless. The German-Jewish spirit will live on!

There is no sense denying this; it always hurts me to hear my fellow exiles talk about "them" (the) Germans and "us" Jews, as though one necessarily excludes the other. We were both at the same time. In the last analysis our identity is none but that of human beings, who like all human beings are born into an environment, a culture, an age, but we do not belong unalterably, because of DNA or the mystique of "peoplehood," to one or another community, beyond our awareness and our daily life.

I can live very well outside a pigeon-hole, outside an either-or identity. I have adapted to life in Canada, but probably 80% of the music I know and love is German or Austrian. I enjoy a dozen other identities—for instance, I prefer the company of progressive persons and I have a minor interest in modern Jewish history. However in the last analysis I am just myself—a human being exposed to various societies, cultures and countries and I can live very well, thank you, without fitting any single classification.

NOTES

1 "In Sachen Identität," *Berlin Aktuell, Zeitschrift für exilierte Berliner* 69 (June 2002), 19–21. [*Ed.*]
2 An account of HK's experiences with the *Kindertransport* and as an internee in Canada is given in German in Gerd Braune, "Flucht ins Ungewisse: Kindertransporte retteten viele jungen Juden vor den Nazis: zum Beispiel Helmut Kallmann," *Frankfurter Rundschau am Wochenende* (19 June 1999); the article is available online at http://www.hgoe.kuen.bw.schule.de/eengine/index.php/hgoe08/geschichte_entry/26/. [*Ed.*]

17
At Home with the Kallmanns: A Schöneberg Family in the 1930s[1]

HK maintained a lifelong correspondence with many of his neighbours and schoolmates from pre–Second World War Berlin, and shortly after the war ended he was able to obtain photos of people and places he had known. He formed a collection of his own scholastic records from the elementary school (*Volksschule*) and high school (*Hohenzollern-Gymnasium*) he attended, as well as documentation about his father, including his father's LL.D. dissertation (1896, University of Göttingen) and other writings. Among the "other writings" are the 1936 article mentioned here, "Vom Geiste der Bibel" ("Of the Spirit of the Bible"), and the *Kindertagebuch* (Children's Diary) begun in the 1920s.[2] Though he may have long intended to write a full account of his immediate family and many relatives and their tragic wartime disappearance, the impetus to do so was an invitation from Ursula Schroeter of Kunstamt Schöneberg, the arts centre of his native district in Berlin, to contribute to an exhibition of the lives of exiled and expelled former citizens. He wrote the essay in German in 1992, and in 1993 he sent a copy of it to the Center for Jewish History in New York (the essay is available in German, along with an English précis of it, on the Center's website at http://access.cjh.org/643464). On 30 May 1999 HK was present in Berlin for the opening of the Kunstamt exhibit *Exil: Flucht und Vertreibung aus dem "Bayerischen Viertel" (Exile: Flight and Expulsion from Berlin's "Bavarian Quarter")*, and he was subsequently an interviewee for the documentary film *Geteilte Erinnerungen* that arose out of the exhibition. In 2001, with the help of Traute Weinberg, he made this English

---

Previously unpublished typescript, 1992/2001

translation and circulated it to friends.³ In 2002 HK had a plaque mounted in the Jewish Cemetery in Berlin-Weissensee, commemorating Arthur, Fanny, and Eva Kallmann, as well as many other close relatives who perished during the Nazi era.

Introduction

Solid, educated, and law-abiding—these three qualities characterize the circle of Germans of Jewish ancestry into which I was born in August 1922. The first ten years of life are the most decisive ones for anyone, and I had the good fortune to enjoy a very happy upbringing with emotional stability as part of a close-knit family, and to be given a European education and outlook on life.⁴ Certainly even as a child I sensed that it was a difficult time for our family, indeed for all Germans and many other nations. Thrift guided all decisions and every adult conversation proclaimed that in earlier times, before the war, "everything had been better." Yet one also lived in the belief that thanks to the Weimar Republic, justice, equality, and reason would prevail in the end.

This report about my family during the years of the Nazis will contain little that is sensational: until October 1942 (the time of the deportations) there were no arrests, no shouting, no thrashings, no need to hide, and, as far as I could learn as a child, no slandering. (I am sure that I do not have to emphasize the fact that many horrible things were kept from the children's ears, that I did not understand the full seriousness of a great deal that happened, and that I have forgotten much in the intervening years.) On the other hand, something else that was just as characteristic of the rule of the brown tyrants—the "dummen Jungen" (rowdies) as my father called them—was the gradualness of the steps against the Germans of Jewish descent, the almost imperceptible progression from one mean thing to another, until at the end nothing but the death sentence remained. Yet at the same time, what is surprising in retrospect is that almost until the deportation in October 1942, the old habitual forms of life were maintained: social contact with Jews and Christians, birthday parties, theatre and concert visits, excursions, even short vacations.

About the years before Hitler I want to sketch only the most essential points. From about 1903, when the apartment building was new, to December 1932 my father (Dr. Arthur Kallmann, born 1873) had lived with his parents (until their deaths in 1917 and 1919) and his youngest sister (of four) Marie, at Bamberger Strasse 6, a quiet street in the attractive

"Bavarian Quarter" of Berlin. My mother (Fanny, née Paradies) moved in upon their wedding in December 1919. My sister Eva, born in 1921, and I, born in 1922, spent the first decade of our lives there. The building is still standing.

My father had maintained his law office in an apartment at the busy intersection of Bülowstrasse 85, at the corner of Potsdamer Strasse, since early in the century. As a consequence of the economic downturn he gave up the office about 1931 and entered into an office partnership with his colleague Dr. Adolf Eisenmann at the corner of Potsdamer and Winterfeldt Strassen. But that measure too did not result in the necessary savings and so we searched for a combination of home and office. Eventually we found it at Geisbergstrasse 41, on the third (by Canadian count fourth) floor, across from the large W30 post office.[5] The busy pedestrian traffic was favourable for a law office. The building had an elevator, and the U-Bahn (underground) was around the corner. The apartment had seven large rooms and the "half" maid's room. [See page 138 for a floor plan of the apartment.]

Clouds Appear on the Horizon

It's easy for me to talk, because I slipped through World War Two without hearing a single shot, without starving, and my three years of internment in Canada were closer to a summer camp than a prison, but I am grateful to my fate for having been raised precisely in the twenties, that hopeful decade in German and Jewish history when Germany became a democratic republic, when for the first time Jews felt truly emancipated, and when Berlin grew into a cultural centre without parallel. I had the fortune to put down my roots in a liberal and upright family. But the hope that with the Republic there would come a more democratic and more humane Germany was disappointed: for German Jews the twenties were not the beginning of their final emancipation but its end.

"Write him and he'll have to mend his ways"

It is early 1933. The grownups talk about very important matters. Serious, exciting matters. The Nazis have taken over the government. They plan evil. They lock up their opponents, they rule with orders and scaremongering, they are brutal and without mercy. Some people are sent to a camp (Sonnenburg I believe) where they are tormented and beaten. The greatest enemies of the Nazis are the communists, the objects of their fiercest hatred the Jews. But as organizers of parades and festivities—in this they are great, as even their opponents admit. "If Hitler is such a bad person, then write him a letter and explain to him how bad he is. Then he will have to mend his ways," I as a ten-year-old advise my parents. Soon there is a day of boycott during which Jewish lawyers may not enter the law courts. "But, papa, if you simply walk up the steps to the law court, how can anyone stop you?"

The Notary Sign Is Stolen

One morning in 1933 or 1934 one of us notices that my father's notary sign with the Prussian eagle is missing from the railing in the front garden. Overnight it has been unscrewed and stolen.

Herr Engwicht Disappears

A portent of the dark future is a rather disquieting phone call from Mr. Engwicht, who up to this point in 1933 has given my father more work than any of his other clients. It is late evening and he calls from one of the big hotels. He has met some foreigners, possibly Dutch people, and they work out some grand business plan. Something very important and urgent. My father advises them lengthily over the phone. Engwicht and his people will either call back or come to us around midnight. My father waits for a long time. No further phone call. Did Engwicht explain later on? Was he going to mock my father, or did the contract come to naught? I know only that something was fishy.

The Law Practice Goes Under

Other Jewish lawyers are soon forbidden to practise; only those who fought at the front line in the First World War and those with many years of practice are allowed to continue in a limited way.[6] My father belongs to the latter, though he was not a combatant in the war. Now he represents only Jewish clients. The office secretary, Fräulein Fohgrub, stays another year or two; later we children sometimes have to help (e.g., typing legal documents or expediting letters). Day after day the government law gazette prints new laws, laws which have simply been proclaimed without parliamentary debate, laws that trample on procedure and decency. My father is incensed. Jewish lawyers now form "cartels," groups of four who meet on occasion and discuss events. Eventually my father is no longer allowed to plead before a judge, can only advise his clients. Then, about 1937 or 1938 that too stops.[7] For him, there is no other means of earning money, as he has now turned sixty-five.

The Collapse of the Family Begins

August 1934. The children come home from school. Aunt Jenny Kallmann has died today, we are told. What, so suddenly? She wasn't reported sick! Well, that's how it goes. That's all we are told. (Children's diary, kept by my father from 1921 to 1942; entry for August 1934:) "The children accept news of Jenny's death silently but without special signs of emotion." The parents travel to Eisenach where the aunt has lived for years, a difficult, lonely, and unhappy person. They make the arrangements customary in a case of death and go for an enormous walk, to Thal and back. It is supposed to have been thirty-five km.

One day we visit the Heinrichs, cousins of my mother. I am twelve or thirteen and am very impressed by Leo Heinrich. Not because he was decorated with the Iron Cross in the war, but rather because here is an adult who asks me about my interests and fascinates me with his conversation. A few months later I hear that Leo Heinrich is dead. Why, how? Well, he just died.

Aunt Jenny is dead; Aunt Marie Kallmann, supervisory social worker for war widows and dependents in the district of Tiergarten, and Aunt Else Paradies, social worker in the infant's care department in the district of Lichtenberg, are let go with a small pension. Aunt Else Joachim, the dreamer, has problems with her husband, the bon vivant, after thirty-five years of marriage; soon she leaves him. Every few days she arrives unannounced at our door, and pours out her heart. "Max is hysterical again," she whispers to my mother. Besides, she misses two of her three children: the daughter is in Paris, the older son in Zlin, Bata's model city.[8] I overhear talk that the children, in their twenties, take sides for or against father and mother, and quarrel with one another. So, that's what adults are like among themselves. How nasty, I say to myself.

Illness

At least harmony exists among the four of us, the Kallmann parents and children. But towards the end of March 1935 my father suddenly becomes ill. Indigestion, constipation. Perhaps an intestinal flu? My mother's cousin, Dr. Max Heinrich, examines, consults a specialist, Dr. Neumark.

The two call on professor Albert Salomon, an old friend of Max Heinrich. An operation is required immediately. Off in the ambulance to the clinic at Leibnizstrasse. Mother goes along. Are we ever to see father again? Aunt Marie stays with us children and prepares a soup instead of dinner. We eat in silence. In the afternoon news comes: intestinal blockage; cancer (but that we were not told). It had been caught just in time. Two further operations. Three and a half months in the private clinic. A nurse stays with our father day and night, Margarete Heenes from Hersfeld. She believes the sun turns around the earth and Germany around Hitler, but she provides loyal care. Father asks me to look up the opening of Beethoven's Sonata Op. 54. The themes of all the other thirty-one he can remember, but not this one. In July he returns home. Professor Salomon has saved his life. A permanent wound requires daily cleaning and bandaging by my mother. He has lost strength, has aged; the daily routine is dictated by the wound. Can one get cancer from worrying?

The Immediate Family

Father

All showing off, all snobbery was foreign to my parents. To display wealth and status was not their way. I learned only much later from my cousins that grandfather Kallmann had been a banker, if only in a small town. My father had let out only that grandfather had owned a grain silo. On the contrary, my father was always anxious to impress others with his *lack* of wealth. We were always used to his moaning and sighing—"Oh, god, what's going to become of us?" or "I don't know how we shall have the means to live through next month." If one of his sisters came with a pair of socks as a birthday gift he scolded her: "I forbid presents. You know, I can't reciprocate. Those times have passed."

My father was the true scholarly type, the opposite of a bon vivant. He made life hard for himself, didn't indulge in anything except for the occasional concert or theatre visit with my mother, or the Sunday excursions (religiously observed if the weather was nice) and (until 1930) summer travels to the Baltic Sea or the Alps. Later on we children went only with mother or her sister to inexpensive places.

The mere thought that our father would have gone to a bar for a glass of beer or taken us to a candy store is almost unimaginable. The only gifts he gave were books. On our Sunday trips to the Grunewald, sandwiches and cutlets were taken along; only on long excursions did one go to a local inn for coffee and cake. His old hat and coat, his old boots remained the "new" ones for years, and only urgent pleas by our mother made him accept a replacement. His microscopically small handwriting, slicing up incoming envelopes to use as note paper, turning off the lights when he left a room for only a minute—these habits surely were more than typical German thriftiness. Was it fear of impoverishment, or simply a hereditary trait?

On the other hand, our father was extremely generous in the time and interest which he showed towards the children. He unsparingly provided stimulation, explained, reminisced about his own youth, made us think and expand our knowledge by the use of jocular questions, almost always in informal conversation at dinner, on saying goodnight, on our walks or when making music. In music we never had another piano teacher; especially the duet playing of orchestral music, in which he encouraged me, was to be of fundamental importance in my career as a music librarian and historian. In all this he acted less the authority imparting knowledge than as a fellow learner. Unless he was busy in his office, we had access to him at any time. He was no disciplinarian; he exuded authority through his learning, his dignity, his seriousness. He did not punish, but his annoyance amounted to the same when we could not provide an answer to a simple question. How often did he tell me when I could not master a Latin construction: "Just think a little! You know that very well!" He also got angry when we used coarse German, *Dreck* instead of *Schmutz*, or *schmeissen* instead of *werfen*.[9] Then he might ask: "Tell me, what does your father do?" and I would answer with a smile "He drives a garbage truck."

Despite his moaning and his pessimism my father had a quite cheerful nature within the inner family circle, always ready for a little joke. He had pet names for all sorts of people: his clients Pinkus Fluss (river) and Simon Tenzer were Pinkus Fluvius and Simonides; Aunt Ziele (Cecily) was Aunt Cyliax, her sister Marie Levy was Marie le Vieh (cattle); his colleague Edmund Meyer was Munio Meyer; my friend Günter Pohland was Junker Pohland (a name supposedly in Goethe's *Faust*);[10] my classmate Helmut Pessen was called the Great Classmate because he was not only very tall but also the best in class. When Aunt Else Paradies once again had spent money lavishly he spoke of the Paradisian vein (inherited from Grandfather Paradies). He had a knack for writing funny verses for us children and his toasts at family weddings were full of humorous allusions. His sisters would then admiringly whisper to one another "Arthur sparkled with wit once again."

In music too our father loved turns of melody that expressed playful well-being (e.g., bars 82–90 in the Larghetto of Beethoven's Second Symphony, bars 174–181 in the first and bars 70–77 in the third movement of Schubert's "Great" C-major Symphony, and a certain figure in Mendelssohn's Overture *Die Heimkehr aus der Fremde* (*Son and Stranger*). Were his groans a ruse to conceal his natural cheerfulness, or was the gaiety a cover for his worries? Which was his real self? I could never tell. I only know that as far as the fate of the family was concerned, his pessimism was triumphant, more so than he could have imagined, on account of his trust in German law, and his belief that despite the despotism and recklessness of the Nazis there would still be boundaries of conscience and law. But the impertinence, the lack of mercy, and, worst of all, the utter lack of humour of the "dummen Jungen" knew no limits.

The humanist high-school education (Latin—Greek—French) which teaches that great art outlasts millennia had made our father immune to currents of fashion. He was certainly familiar with Freud's theories, or told us about the new fashion for streamlined design, but currents such as cubism, twelve-tone music, or the movies he regarded with the puzzlement of an outsider, even though he was not dismissive of them. Max Joachim had taken him to the cinema once, but there was nothing but commercials. Never again waste time on that! To participate as partisan or disciple in one current or another of the turbulent cultural life of the twenties was not his way. He would rather open his Goethe and looked for spiritual guidance to Beethoven. His collection of scores began with Bach and ended with Brahms.

Our father blossomed in his immediate family, in his piano music, his books, his walks, his German law, his love of his homeland. A few times in the late 1930s he gave up what he loved most after wife and children: playing the piano. "My mind isn't tuned for entertainment any longer," he would reply when questioned. Whom did he punish with this protest except himself? Only constant persuasion made him resume playing, with urgings such as "We all love to listen to it," or "The children should get to know good music."

When he joined a discussion at all, whether among friends or with pen and ink, it probably was on a subject of jurisprudence or in defence of the Jews. Typically what seemed of importance to him was some minor observation, some small point that the prominent spokesmen had overlooked. To others some of his opinions may have seemed of minor relevance; they might politely comment "yes, yes" but did not take much notice. His great pleasure was to check on an incorrect literary quotation or a dubious historical date, or to disentangle the confusing statements of some philosopher; this he did on his weekly visit to the Wilmersdorf library in the former Joachimsthal high school.

It is probably superfluous to mention that his Germanness had nothing to do with doctrines such as "We Germans are the greatest of peoples," "Military officers are the ideal of humanity," or "It is a duty to obey"; rather it consisted in experiencing the landscape of his homeland, in developing a taste for great works of art, in contributing to one's own subject (he was the editor of the *German Jurist's Calendar* [originally *Weber's*] 1906–1914 and 1930), and above all, in cultivating the mother tongue and living a clean life.

(Supplement: More about My Father)

I meant to say only as much about my parents as is necessary to understand their behaviour in these horrible years. Perhaps the characterization of my father turned out somewhat one-sided in consequence. But since I have started to draw the picture, I should continue. Have I created the impression, for example, that he looked down on popular entertainment? That was true, as far as the hit parade and salon music was concerned, but he was not above delighting in popular, even coarse literature. For instance, he submitted samples of Berlin slang to a newspaper, collected by his sister Marie in her practice as social worker.

It was characteristic of the age that the male of the household had little to do with practical matters—it is thanks to their maids that thousands of men could be intellectually productive beyond their occupation. If at all, my father appeared in the kitchen only to call his wife to the phone. Otherwise the weekly winding of the pendulum clock and the occasional adjustment of a piano hammer were about his only practical activities.

I have already hinted at the ascetic side of my father. He disdained candy and it is almost impossible to imagine him playing a card game. He resisted such modern inventions as the fountain pen or the radio; only the children had a simple camera and a small metallic gramophone, and the headphone radio was a present of little interest to him.

He walked where someone else would have taken public transit. This kept him slim and kept his heart in good shape, a decisive factor in his 1935 illness. In the thirties his hearing deteriorated a little and a little dot swam around in his field of vision—but only after much prodding could he be moved to see a doctor. That the piano was not tuned for years certainly was misplaced thrift, as it hurt the formation of my ear training and musicianship. Only upon the pleading of his sister Marie was the piano overhauled in 1933.

Along with this having-to-be-pushed went a certain irresponsible boldness. From Ehrwald in 1928 he went up the Zugspitze (Germany's highest mountain) on the cable car with our host, but Herr Schennach came back by himself, which gave us quite a shock. The Doctor had told him the last piece he would be able to manage by himself, he need not be driven. Nighttime had already fallen when he arrived back in good humour, completely unaware of possible dangers. Another time, our father told us, his train had stopped in Breslau for about twenty minutes and during this time he figured out down to the second how much sightseeing he could do. Usually he was not punctual because he did not want to believe that the time had run out. He also was quite a good swimmer—and more daring than he should have been. My timidity in physical exercise I must have inherited from my mother.

My father lacked *chutzpah* completely. He would never have advised a client to go ahead with a lawsuit if there was no chance to win, just so he could charge his fee. Indeed, in 1991 a cousin of mine who was already grown up when I was a child told me that my father always charged his clients the lowest possible fee that he could manage.

My father's musical taste was formed during a time of great upheaval where the disciples of Liszt/Wagner and Brahms fought for or against the "music of the future" or absolute music. He definitely preferred the intimate, warmer romantics like Chopin, Schubert, and Schumann to the boastful and noisier music (he knew little of Brahms); he criticized Liszt because of his tingling and clattering and Wagner because of his racket and his bragging (Wagner's anti-Semitism he seemed to have overlooked). He called these elements "music for the not so musical," not quite fairly. Ringing, loud noises were definitely not to his taste. At the end of a piece, say a Beethoven sonata, he would leave out the final fortissimo chords. Big noises were unnecessary and unpleasant. His playing certainly was distinguished by a soft, singing sound. Yes, like Glenn Gould later, he accompanied his own playing with purring or humming. As a young man he had visited Leipzig and used the opportunity to visit the old Carl Reinecke (who in 1902 had retired as the director of the Conservatory) and played for him. Reinecke confirmed that he had rarely heard such a beautiful touch.

It should be added that my father voted for the State Party (liberal democratic) whereas my mother and aunts tended towards social democracy.

Mother

Our mother (born 1894) was 21 years (and one day!) younger than her husband. She was born and grew up in the area between Stettiner Bahnhof and Weidendammer Brücke. The address of Grandparents Paradies changed frequently: Invaliden, Elsasser, and Chausseestrassen. Only about 1914, four years after my mother left school, did the Paradies family move to a new apartment building in Halensee, Johann-Georg-Strasse 12. Mother's school had been the Luisenschule in Ziegelstrasse, and even if I did not possess her autograph book, I still could quote the names and sayings of some of her teachers. Like my father she had been a good student and after her last regular year she had attended the additional "Selekta" class.

Following that she was sent to Lausanne, Switzerland to attend a so-called "Pensionat" or finishing school, but had to return soon after because of her father's illness (diabetes). She later became a student at Alice Salomon's school for women social workers. During the First World War she worked for the Austrian Women's Aid society.

It is difficult to describe or sketch my mother's special attributes. She was much more practical and down to earth than her husband with his idiosyncrasies. I believe that if we had followed her inclination, we probably would have emigrated in the middle of the thirties, but where to? She was neither aggressive nor passive, not loud but also not too quiet; she was not highly educated but still very knowledgeable. She was very industrious, modest, reliable, and always tolerant. Most of all I remember her as a peacemaker who had a good relationship with everyone in our family. Her good advice was always in demand and respected. These were the typical characteristics of a trained social worker. If somebody needed help, she was always ready to assist. She was busy enough but still found time to collect money for the Jewish social welfare organization. She was definitely stricter in her behaviour towards us than our father and it was she who occasionally disciplined us or (rarely) withdrew privileges. For me she was everything you could have wished for in a mother; whenever it was called for she warned, encouraged, corrected, consoled, scolded, reprimanded, yielded, helped, rebuked, explained—sometimes patiently, sometimes losing her cool, but always loving and participating.

For relaxation our mother liked to read a novel. On Sundays she preferred sometimes *not* to participate in a family outing; instead she loved to go out on a weekday afternoon with a girlfriend or cousin to spend a couple of hours in a coffeehouse. I believe she attended lectures at the Education Department of a Jewish college. Furthermore, Eva and I occasionally went along with her to events of the Jewish Kulturbund (theatre, opera, concert).

Under the influence of my father, and due to the enormous hardships, my mother exercised great frugality, which was not part of her own upbringing. She was very dependable, she never used any make-up, never smoked, and showed plenty of patience with the fairly aggressive tenant, Frau Sturmfels, who tried to take over the reins in our kitchen. She definitely was not shy to speak her mind, and when our concierge used rude language, she told her: "But Frau Blachmann, you are a lady, you don't talk like that." That got a quick response. One of my mother's typical expressions used to be "I wasn't born yesterday" (*Ich bin doch keine geborene Doofritzki*).

The Children

Jewish parents suffered horribly from the knowledge that they had brought their children into a world where there was little hope for the future, and where untold disaster was looming. Gone were the hopes of belonging to the German majority as equals. The danger for their children was not only to be excluded from any professional education, but also to become pariahs. If young people constantly hear that they are inferior and not able to play among others as an equal, if they are treated like outcasts, then the danger of permanent psychological damage is a constant threat. If parents did not prepare for emigration immediately or in the near future, then there was very little they could do to protect their children from harm. Attending school was still allowed, but the prospect of training for a career was almost hopeless. It was still possible though to give their children some general instruction and stimulation, for example visits to museums, good reading material, theatre, knowledge of their own environment, information about their family's history, etc. The great experiences of youth were still open to us: exploring the features of our own city and the surrounding province of Brandenburg, getting to know a particular symphony or opera, or enjoying a play by Molière or Shakespeare.

Our father, in his own particular way, did everything he could to give us as many cultural impressions as possible. It would have been nice if he could have sent us from time to time to a non-Jewish theatre or to the opera when it was still allowed. Maybe he avoided the expense or he preferred to guide our cultural education according to his own ideas.

I have talked about my schooling elsewhere. Here I will only record that in 1927 and 1928, Eva and I started respectively at the twelfth and thirteenth elementary schools on Hohenstaufenstrasse. Eva continued in 1931 at the Chamisso Lyzeum (a high school for girls) at Barbarossa Platz, and I was transferred to the Hohenzollern Gymnasium (for boys) on Martin-Luther Strasse (1932–1938). My sister moved on to the Jewish home economics school in 1937 and to the Jewish Kindergarten Seminary in 1938; in that year I was forced to leave my school and switched to the high school (for both sexes) of the Jewish Community on Wilsnacker Strasse in the Moabit district of Berlin.

If they made any mistake, it is my feeling that our parents failed to instill in us greater self-reliance, so that we would have been able to make our own decisions. The children were to remain naive as long as possible, whether in politics, shopping, or sex education. It was probably right not to rush ahead, but if the parents' timing is off, then classmates and other contemporaries will likely give youngsters the wrong ideas. In any case, their attempts to shelter us to a certain extent from the political danger succeeded only in part. Extracts from the Children's Diary show our reactions clearly:

> 28.4.1933: "Both are learning about the measures against Jews, especially Jewish lawyers, but don't show any agitation. Helmut is often offended by the anti-Semitic remarks of older students, but still returns home in high spirits. For the moment they are both allowed to continue with their schooling."
>
> Late August / early September 1933: "I say to Eva, I am sad that you have to live in such horrible times for Jews! She replies, yes, but one can't do anything about it!"
>
> 26.8.1934: "In response to Marie's comment that 'every word (of the government) is a lie,' Eva replies 'you can't say that: a *word* cannot lie, only a *sentence* can.'"
>
> Late 1935: "When I got stuck in the elevator with Eva, she showed no fear, but rather was amused." (Not of political significance, but characteristic of youth nonetheless.)
>
> 12.1.1936: "When I walked to the Stadtpark with both children, Helmut maintained that the European powers had no right to take

land away from other peoples (e.g., Italy from the Ethiopians). Might makes right."

23.3.1937: "Eva hears of the recent death of this (religion teacher) Dr. Cohn, and reports the news without seeming to be very moved; she is always averse to sentimentality or romanticism." (We were typical Berliners!)

My father is surprised at our nonchalance. Children are not as affected by events as are adults, they don't know as much about politics, they live in a world of their own—thus he may have tried to explain things to himself. Was it really so? I believe we did know quite a bit, because at school we saw more Nazis day after day than did the adults. We children, more than our parents, were discriminated against in words and deeds. I rather think that our nonchalance was a bit of a protest, "Do you adults have to talk all the time and endlessly about politics and be upset all day? There are other things in life! Your worrying about us only makes us nervous."

We children were different from each other: Eva was socially more mature, showed more courage in sports, belonged to a Jewish youth group (beginning in 1934), and read more novels than I, but her piano playing never went beyond the simplest songs. From an early age she hoped to work with children (like Aunt Else, the former social worker who was an infants' welfare nurse in Lichtenberg), and had an aversion to office work. She had a good figure, was balanced and modest, and would have made a good wife and mother. Late in 1935 the *Kindertagebuch* records: "Her attitude is German-Jewish; she enjoys her youth group and synagogue visits."

On the other hand I didn't make myself heard in a group decisively enough to make an impression and remained a shy listener on social occasions. In the physical training classes at school, which amounted to tests of courage, I was quite inhibited (though I enjoyed running and climbing). I much preferred to spend my leisure time with three or four good friends (with non-Jewish as well as Jewish ones, right up until my emigration) and was never at a loss for how to occupy myself. In my elementary school days I sat for hours bent over the atlas or a city map, absorbing the position of cities, the course of rivers, the boundaries between counties and provinces, the street patterns. At the age of seven I had memorized all the Berlin streetcar routes (some seventy) and all the stations of the U- and S-Bahn. Later I occupied myself, depending on the inclination of my pals, with the drawing of fantasy city (transit) maps, with the design of school class timetables and railway schedules, collecting and swapping stamps, or compiling lists of the works of Mozart and Beethoven. I practised the piano, accompanied Peter Ball in violin sonatas by Mozart and Schubert, and tried to compose music.

But we did not just sit indoors all day; over the years we travelled on almost all streetcar and bus lines, from Müggelheim to Waidmannslust, from Klein-Machnow to Heinersdorf; we sketched the track layout of the Lichtenberg streetcar barn (the largest); we stood at the corner of Potsdamer and Lützow (twenty-two lines) or at the Berlin City Hall (sixteen lines) and noted down all passing streetcars; we knew exactly which cars were stationed in the Belziger Strasse barn (i.e., 6201–6210). When my father heard of such nonsense he grumbled "I wish the boy would occupy himself with more spiritual matters." He was largely right, for like so many other pupils I occupied myself with history, mathematics, or French more from fear of failing than from true thirst for knowledge. It is also true that once I had found something that fascinated me, whether Mozart's music (which after all was something spiritual), the secrets of the BVG (Berlin's public transit company), or years later, the history of music in Canada, I could never indulge in it enough and would have loved to forget everything else. Nevertheless, my friends and I had a good look at our hometown and walked a lot, all the while breathing fresh air and exercising our memory.

Would I have spent my free time differently under normal circumstances? My hobbies corresponded exactly to my sensibilities and needs, but they also reflect the fact that I was excluded from other activities, such as school excursions or visits to the main theatres and concert halls. (It remains a puzzle to me why today so many teenagers are at a loss to occupy their free time sensibly, since there is an infinite variety of valuable but harmless fields of interest. Is it essential to live in a metropolis and to have a stimulating father?)

I should like to mention the names of my friends at this point. Peter Ball, son of a Jewish lawyer who had to give up his practice about 1934, was in my school class for six years in the Hohenzollern school. He then went to the Kaliski (Jewish) school and emigrated to New York in the fall of 1938. He died as a young medical doctor in 1957. Peter and I shared both musical and geographical interests. Now to mention the two non-Jewish friends: Günter Bein lived in the same building, Bamberger Strasse 6, until our families moved in 1932 in opposite directions. For four years we were in the same public school class of Herr Oppermann and were inseparable playmates. Even after we moved we met about twice a week while attending different high schools. Only when we were 14 or 15 did our interests and our milieu change so that our meetings became less frequent. After 1939, I did not resume contact with him until 1962. At that time he was a news reader with the radio and had a reputation as a cabaret director and actor. Later he was with Südwestrundfunk in Baden-Baden, where he died in 1972. Günter Pohland joined my class in 1935 and for three years we sat on the same bench. How much Latin and mathematics we copied from each other! Pohland, Ball, and I had a friendship which grew from our common interest in the BVG streetcar and bus routes and vehicles. Pohland's father was a bus driver and thus we knew about route changes, internal timetables, and other corporate secrets. We typed our own magazine, the *Verkehrswochenschau* (Weekly Transit News). Pohland stuck close to his Jewish friends; his father was obviously an anti-Nazi. Since Günter lacked his left hand from birth, he was exempt from physical training but had to participate in the German Youth (a subdivision of the Hitler Youth for boys aged 10 to 14). If he had to visit us in his brown shirt, he always apologized. He kept visiting me up to the week of my departure and after the war I immediately contacted him. We maintained contact until his death in 1986 and since then I have exchanged mail with his widow. During the Nazi period, he once told me, his father had been a communist, but not after the war.

The Circle

Our family was large, our acquaintances numerous. My father had more than twenty cousins, my mother about fifteen, nearly all in Berlin. Home visits were limited to only a few; the others met mainly at weddings and funerals.

Since long before my birth and up to the days when my parents and sister were deported in October 1942, a Christian person always lived with us, either a maid, old Ida, or the subtenant Marie Reuter. There never was a gap between "us" and "them," a feeling of being different.

Closest to us was Ida Brandt. Ida (or Idchen)—her surname was never mentioned—was born in 1853 in Kreuzburg in Silesia and was hired as nanny by my Grandparents Paradies in the 1890s. When the children had grown up and the parents had died, she stayed on from 1925 as the housekeeper for my Aunt Else. Both moved about 1928 to a new housing block on Pommersche Strasse. Ida was a substitute grandmother and thoroughly spoiled us. When my aunt was forced to give up the apartment about 1934, eighty-year-old Ida moved into our maid's room. A year or two later she moved into an old-age home and I can still remember how hard my mother and aunt struggled for permission to stand by her as "next-of-kin" in the week of her death in 1938. The difficulties probably were not due to anti-Semitic but rather to bureaucratic reasons, because the rule allowed only blood relations to be present. But finally the request was granted.

That Ida thought nothing of the Nazis goes without saying; she was a social democrat of the old school who pictured how it would be once the workers would rule and the rich had to work. When Hitler's name came up, she would promptly say "I spit on this thug" and called him the "Hergelaufene" (intruder). She also made fun of the old emperor—"Heil dir im Siegerkranz, Pellkartoffeln mit Heringsschwanz"[11]—and liked to take shots at "better people." It is possible that I picked up more ideology from Ida than from my reticent parents.

Frau Auguste Bahr-Brauer also loved us like a grandmother. The widow of a builder in Danzig, she came to us from earliest childhood once or twice a year to mend and alter bedsheets and clothing on the sewing machine. That was always a festive day because Frau Bahr (when she married again in the 1930s she added the name Brauer) could talk so amusingly about her other clients—"Oh, dear Lord, the old Frau Neumann, how much she has suffered, I'm telling you, and she was always so good to the poor, yes, giving them so much. Well, and then she got it with the kidneys, no, what a good woman that was." We children enjoyed teasing her until she threatened us: "Don't be so naughty, Evchen and Helmi, or the bogeyman will get you!" When we could no longer afford the maid, my mother took me along to Uhlandstrasse 124, explained the situation to Frau Bahr, and begged her to help with the housework twice a week. Although this was a bit below the dignity of her social rank, the good woman agreed without batting an eyelid.

The maids changed frequently until 1926, when Johanna Hensel (from Biesenbrow near Angermünde) came; she was twenty-one years old at that time. We loved Johanna and she loved us, especially our mother. I can still see the tears in her eyes when she parted from us in 1932. She returned to us briefly in 1934. When she was sick later on, after she had a baby, my mother cared for her intensively, giving her advice and help. Later we found a place for her as the housekeeper and companion to one of my aunt's fellow social workers, the "half"-Jewish Gertrud Höniger; she remained in that apartment until after Höniger's death. Johanna was a modest, genteel person; to the end of her life (1994) we exchanged birthday and Christmas greetings.

Between Johanna and Mrs. Bahr-Brauer (as household helpers), Mrs. Helene Lange from Ruppiner Strasse helped with the cleaning a few times a week. This was the time when our new apartment had to be put back in shape, and when the Nazis came to power. A robust working-class woman with the ebullient speech of a true Berliner, I remember her as a well-read, highly politicized woman with a thirst for knowledge, who hated the Nazis.

Similarly bold language was used by Herr Ludwig, whose dairy store was next to Büttner's. "Everything is supposed to be better now. I just don't notice any sign of that yet. Butter gets scarcer all the time. One can't eat guns and lies." Thus it went all day unless an unknown customer entered the store. I visited the Ludwigs in 1962. He showed me a spoon, part of the silver cutlery my mother had sold him cheaply so she didn't have to hand it in to the Nazis. During the war Herr Ludwig had a run-in with the Gestapo, but he survived.

Margarete Fohgrub, the daughter of an elementary school teacher from Trebbin, was my father's office secretary for about eight years until 1934 or 1935, when the practice had shrunk so much that he could not continue to employ her. A little later she became Mrs. Moder and with her husband moved to Falkensee, outside Berlin; they then moved in the 1950s to Buschkrug, a west Berlin garden suburb, where they were living when my wife and I visited them in 1962.

Fräulein Reuter moved into the maid's room in 1937 (not to be confused with the Reuter family to be discussed shortly). She called herself Mary and was in her mid- to late forties. If I recall correctly, she worked in a pawnshop on Marburger Strasse. After the war she married a Herr Koglin and lived on Frankenstrasse.

The Neighbours in the Apartment Building

We were lucky to have found our apartment. Of the ten apartments in the building, four were empty in 1932. The manager, Herr van der Riesen, was glad to have found occupants. The rooms were large, the back corridor almost fourteen metres long. Next to us a divorced Jewish woman moved in with her somewhat unruly son and her brother, the jurist Lefebvre. On the second floor the homeopath Buchholz received a stream of patients, and next to him lived the Baroness Jutta von Dallwig, who was kindly disposed toward us. One hardly ever saw the Buchholzs. As it transpired, his wife was Jewish and her mother, who lived with them, was deaf (which protected her from my piano playing). Further down there was an elderly couple named Cohn from Mannheim, elsewhere a Fräulein Mühlpfordt, who rented out rooms. Above us was the office of the Society of Loyal Upper Silesians, which eventually bought the house.

A Quote from Goebbels: "Today we don't need a commentary on Faust*"*

On official holidays our Geisbergstrasse was not exactly a sea of swastika flags. There was even one house, at No. 39, without any; that's where the employees of the Soviet Embassy were quartered. One of the most ambitious flags was that of Miss Toeppe, a retired piano teacher who kept house with an elderly Viennese singer, Miss Rausch. We avoided Toeppchen and Räuschlein ("potty" and "stupor") as best we could. But in the winter of 1936–37 the Nazi flags disappeared and one day Miss Toeppe spoke to my father: she could hear our piano playing through three floors and would be interested in my progress. The reason for her change of mind soon became apparent. She had written a commentary on Goethe's *Faust, the* definitive commentary, as she vouched herself, moreover the first in which the text was black and the commentary red. Since she couldn't find a publisher for this commentary, she approached Dr. Goebbels directly and asked for his support in publishing this deed for German culture. Goebbels did answer her, but not the way she expected: such a commentary we don't need today. Frl. Toeppe was enraged: imagine, we don't need Goethe! Now she no longer needed Goebbels. And she was through with the Nazis.

I was asked to play for her. My father selected the first movement of Beethoven's *Tedesca* Sonata, Op. 79. The day was 14 February 1937. But unfortunately I was insufficiently prepared and Miss Toeppe judged right away: he isn't mature enough for this piece. But she presented two tickets to us for a piano recital by Else Blatt and soon after gave me a book from her bookcase: *Felix Mendelssohn-Bartholdys Briefwechsel mit Legationsrat Karl Klingemann in London* (Essen: G.D. Baedeker, 1909).[12] I entered: "from Frl. Margarete Toeppe, 21.2.1937." In the past fifty-five years I have often read in this book.

Grandmother Reuter

"Horst's grandmother always sends you her best regards," my mother wrote to me when I was in internment camp in the early 1940s. Horst Reuter was a day older than I and for seven years sat next to me on the school bench. His grandmother, probably the widow of an official or officer (correction: she came from a family of master chimney sweeps) owned the building at Geisbergstrasse 30, and his father was an unemployed bank employee, but our classmates teased Horst, because his father nonetheless owned an automobile. The Reuters, so I may guess, were typical conservative nationalist middle class, the kind that tried to adjust to the regime. Omi practised the Horst Wessel Song at the piano.[13] Horst's father joined the NSKK (National Socialist Automobile Corps). Horst, at fourteen or fifteen was sent to a residential school in the country, so he could be toughened. He was supposed to learn discipline and obedience as befitted a German boy. Although the Reuters seemed to adjust to the new regime, for Omi and Horst's parents this had nothing to do with the Jews they knew. Occasionally I was invited to help Horst with his homework and went home with a chocolate bar. Yes, I was a Jew "but exactly on account of that so intelligent" they imagined.

My mother's most devoted school friend from the Luisenschule was Erna Werner, née Kutschkow. In a letter to me dated 20.8.1946 she writes: "My husband had been removed from his office (Finance Office, Pankow District) because he had constantly refused to join the Party. Now he is back. They had made him serve in the police of the Neukölln district!!!" From a letter of 8.1.1947: "My husband was shadowed because he was known to be friendly towards Jews. It was his job to administer the (expropriated) real estate. They had made the fox the guardian of the chicken coop. He did whatever he could to salvage what could be salvaged for the Jewish owners and over time that could not remain hidden. Besides, I had resisted the request to work for my special 'friend' (Goebbels) in the Ministry of Propaganda and therefore didn't know whether I too was being observed." (The Werners' only child was killed on the eastern front at age 17.)

The Jewish Element

The Toronto rabbi Gunther Plaut (born 1912), who had grown up in Berlin, writes in his memoirs *Unfinished Business* (Toronto 1981, p. 35): "I was so to speak a Jew at home and a German in the streets."[14] I believe the opposite holds for my family and most liberal Jewish Germans: in our surroundings we were often identified as Jews and attacked, excluded, vilified, although admired by others. At home we read, according to age and taste, Goethe, Bismarck, Thomas Mann, Fritz Reuter, Selma Lagerlöf, Erich Kästner, Else Ury, or Karl May; we played Beethoven and Schumann on the piano; we were smitten with the beauties of the Bavarian Alps, the

Baltic Sea, or the Harz Mountains; we delighted in Berlin jokes and idioms; we planned excursions to Potsdam or the Löcknitz (a small river), or walked to Charlottenburg Palace or the Kreuzberg hill. The prints on our walls were by Dürer or of Greek sculptures.

This did not mean that we were trying to hide our Jewish roots. My father never thought of baptism; instead he gave up his desire to become a judge. If religion was something outgrown by scientific reason, there was no point in exchanging one for the other; it would have been cowardice to avoid exclusion by such cheap means. Religion was superfluous rather than burdensome, but the heritage of Jewish wisdom and culture was to be recognized as long as it made sense. Grandparents Kallmann were said to have belonged to the Reform congregation (minimum Hebrew, no hats; Canadian Reform Jews would have been called Liberal). As a member of the CV-Verein,[15] my father was engaged in fighting anti-Semitism; to name another example, he once presented me with Karl Emil Franzos's novel *Der Pojaz* on my birthday.[16] My mother came from a more conservative family; she fasted on Yom Kippur and lit Jahrzeit-candles in memory of her parents and her brother. This attested to religiosity less from conviction than from respect for her parents' beliefs. Very rarely did three or all four of us go to synagogue on a Friday evening or Saturday; probably always on Yom Kippur, New Year's day, and Hanukkah. Sometimes my mother lit candles on Friday evening and cut slices from a challah. As she said, this gave her a feeling of security because it reminded her of her childhood.

Yes indeed, one began to remember one's Jewish customs. The children were too old for a Christmas tree; we had one only in 1932. Attempts to celebrate Hanukkah or Passover were somewhat clumsy because we didn't know the procedures. Typical for our position between the religions was a remark in my letter to a friend, April 1938: "Friday night Seder (at home) and synagogue. Sunday many visitors and Easter eggs."

The Jewish confirmation (Bar Mitzvah) takes place on the thirteenth birthday. This didn't apply in my case because of my father's illness and recovery in 1935. As usual he maintained that we had no money for the party associated with the Bar Mitzvah. The religious aspect was of lesser concern. Perhaps the fact that Rabbi Dr. Swarsensky came from the village Marienfliess near his hometown of Stargard reconciled him. I myself had little use for religion as teaching or as ritual. The preparation demanded much coaching and memorizing, which I accepted as something unavoidable. The Bar Mitzvah finally took place in October 1936 in the synagogue on Prinzregentenstrasse, together with twelve other boys.[17]

Social Life

Visitors Come

Birthdays and other family gatherings were not only occasions for the exchange of experiences and political news (because my parents had lost the inclination to read the censored newspapers or listen to radio propaganda), they were a recital of complaints and miseries and an occasion to reminisce about better days; they provided relaxation, confidence, and an illusion of security: one realized that one was not suffering alone.

Such gatherings began with placing the tea cozy over the telephone—"one never knows." The themes of conversation which then unfolded were always the same four or five. Number one: the meanness of the Nazis. "Such a meanness has never occurred before—not in the whole history of mankind." One has lost his job, another was forced to sell his business at the lowest price, a third one was shadowed or interrogated and threatened by the Gestapo. Every guest has such stories to report. With indignation one remembers that my parents' cousin Fred Levy lost his arm in the World War, cousin Otto Moses went missing in the Battle of the Marne, cousins Kurt Joseph and Erich Loewenberg died at the front. And the grandparents invested large sums in war bonds, which were never paid back. That is the gratitude towards Jewish families! But one also talks about what the gentile neighbour or the coal delivery man said about Hitler the other day: well, there are still decent people. (Typical was the remark of one of my classmates: "If lies had short legs, Goebbels would have to crawl on his behind.")

Theme number two: "What's going to become of us?" The possibility of emigration and the chances of earning a living: for people over fifty, both are pretty much non-existent. "What should I do in Bolivia or Turkey; even in England I would not understand local literature," my father states on one occasion. Too late did my parents look for opportunities to emigrate. My mother had well-to-do relatives in the USA—the children of my grandmother's cousins—but they did not react, although they did help a few other relatives.

Theme number three: "Do you remember" (to be filled in at will, e.g., how grandma had sprained her ankle, that was in the year '03, still in the Elsasser Strasse, and then Aunt Marie dropped by in the afternoon and took offence because she wasn't invited for supper …), and Aunt Helene claimed, once again, that in Stargard she and Gretchen this-or-that had climbed over the roofs. That's all in your imagination, my father would retort, the older brother skilled in legal cross examination. No, insisted Helene, from the Nachtigallensteig one could jump sideways from house number five. I do remember. But my father maintains "impossible." (I went there in 1995 and found one possible roof!)

Theme number four: Stories of illnesses and news from the circle of relatives and friends. There is always a story about the doctor and the wrong diagnosis. In the end a famous professor is consulted and he says of course this must be treated quite differently and then the patient recovers immediately. (The story can also be told the other way, with the professor as the ass.)

Theme number five: Funerals. "I can still remember how he always said, you know he said: 'That's the way life is, isn't it?'" or something equally profound. "How was the attendance?" Attendance is the most important variable in any funeral analysis. And "still remember" is obligatory too.

We children listened silently and often amusedly not only to what was being said but to how it was said. At least the humorous side has remained more firmly in my memory. When a guest appeared with a small gift for our mother, it was always announced "instead" of something else. "Here is a box of pralines instead of flowers." "I bring you flowers instead of a pair of stockings." "This time I give you stockings instead of a box of pralines." And then, while coffee and cake were consumed at the large dining table, there were all those gestures, those introductory phrases, those interpolations, those self-confirmations. "Now, let me also say something," "Listen people, just imagine ... no you can't imagine," "Well, that's how it was, right, wasn't it so?" "Well, tell me, Herr Rechtsanwalt, am I not right? Now tell me, I am right, am I not?" "Don't mind, dear Fanny, if your old aunt tells you something." And Herr Ascher repeated for the third time "Yes, yes, yes, yes, Herr Rechtsanwalt, yes, yes, very nice" ("Herr Rechtsanwalt," even though they had been friends for more than thirty years), and later his sister Hetty Ascher would sound her customary "Jeorch, it's time to leave." (In the Berlin dialect, George becomes either Jeorch or Orje.) It was simply wonderful! Our father on his customary seat at the end of the table would listen in silence most of the time and announce himself with his characteristic clearing of the throat only when it was a matter of correcting some statement of fact or explaining a context.

"Uncle Horwitz is severely ill"—"Don't make jokes, it is much too serious!"

Many Jews took the Nazi movement too lightly at first and indulged in facile predictions and speculations—Hitler is much too stupid to set Germany to rights again; soon he will have exhausted his tricks. Then my father would scold: "A man who has achieved this degree of power cannot be without a certain talent. I'm afraid the man must be taken very seriously." Some Jews still lived it up, wrongly relying on the little money they possessed. Many tried to restore their psychological balance by telling jokes. This carefree attitude enraged my father. "There is no longer any reason to laugh" he would say when these jokes were told, that typically began "Hitler, Goebbels and Goering arrive at the gates of heaven," and end something like "'And who is that little Jew over there?' asked Saint Peter, looking at Goebbels" (as Goebbels could be taken for a Jew). Or a Nazi big shot instructs his gardener always to address him with "Heil Hitler!" The next day the gardener reports "Heil Hitler! The dog is dead." My cousin Gerhard, always an optimist, phoned one evening and said only five words: "Uncle Horwitz [i.e. Hitler] regrettably seriously ill," and then he hung up. Don't fool yourself, my pessimistic father would have thought. (There was talk at the time that Hitler needed a throat operation.)

The Poor Devils Show Up

The more the pressure from the outside grew, the stronger the cohesion within the Jewish community. In the 1930s impoverished and unfortunate acquaintances and relatives suddenly appeared. For example, Fräulein Neustadt, whom my mother had not seen for many years, but recognized one day on a shopping trip. She wore a shabby dress, was shapelessly corpulent and looked at us bashfully. Fräulein Neustadt, so our mother explained, came from an incredibly wealthy family, their real name had been Itzig, that worst nickname for Jews.[18] The wealth must have been lost in war bonds and the inflation years. She now had a small room in Schaperstrasse. "The Neustadt woman," as we heartless children spoke of her, appeared at our door now and then. "Mutti, the Neustadt woman is here again" we whispered into the kitchen. She hadn't eaten anything since yesterday morning and was in bliss when our mother offered her a bowl of soup or gave her an old piece of clothing, probably also a few coins. Once the Jewish community sent her to a Jewish convalescent home in Havelberg to recuperate, and she felt she was in paradise.

At Home with the Kallmanns

My Aunt Marie, the social worker, who was more at home at her desk than at the kitchen stove, took a course in a school for cooking and baking run by Oetker's (the baking powder company) in the mid-1930s and then took up a position as a housekeeper and companion with Prof. Bruno Güterbock and his wife, a couple who lived in the Nikolassee district of Berlin. (He had been a museum director, she had published a novel.) One day Aunt Marie was surprised to hear the cleaning lady sing while washing the stairs. This was a trained singer's voice! It turned out that Fräulein Koppel had been a singer (probably the first soprano in the choir) at the opera of Chemnitz and had been kicked out as a "half" Jew. Immediately my aunt arranged recitals in our apartment with my father at the piano. The guests were asked to contribute 50 Pfennigs to help Fräulein Koppel to get along. She sang Schubert, Chopin, Schumann, Bizet and other composers.[19]

Restrictions—Privation

As time went on, my parents gave up one comfort after another. After the folding of the *Vossische Zeitung*[20] there was no newspaper that my father cared to subscribe to; he borrowed old issues from his colleague Eisenmann, which I picked up and returned weekly to his home in Ansbacher Strasse; I believe it was the DAZ (*Deutsche Allgemeine Zeitung*). We never owned a radio, apart from one with headphones which hardly ever worked. My father did not want to hear the news distorted by lies and agitation; music on radio would keep him from playing the piano. Vacation travels were out of the question after 1932. My parents' bedroom was now baptized "the ice cellar" and heated only when one had caught a cold. We could no longer afford to keep a maid, so my mother had help only by the day. The smaller room near the entrance where Aunt Marie had lived was rented out from 1936, then the maid's room, and finally the large office as well as my room after I had left. Where one would have taken public transport before, one now walked. If I had to go to the vicinity of the Charlottenburg railway station (3.5 km) I had to walk at least one way, the other on a short-trip ticket. Food began to be in short supply all over Berlin in 1937, especially butter, and much to my regret—at the age of fifteen one does develop an enormous appetite—I had to be content with bread dipped in grease. Then Jews were ordered to hand over gold, silver, and jewellery and to deposit all stocks, shares, and investment papers with a certain bank. But all these restrictions were only trifles compared to what the war and the persecution were to bring after my departure.

Self-Preservation, Self-Deception, and Resistance

In retrospect many people have asked why the German Jews didn't resist, why didn't they act as the Jews in the Warsaw ghetto did later on? Why did you accept each blow, always grateful that the last one had not been harder? Was the nonchalance which my father noticed repeatedly in my sister such a passive acceptance? I do not know the answer, but I believe that this weakness of character, the lack of civil courage, the cult of obedience were precisely the middle class and the German element in us, just as it was with the non-Jews, the majority of whom failed just as badly. Canadian Jews of East European descent—for the most part of impoverished, proletarian origin—and certainly Israelis from diverse countries show much more elementary fighting spirit. The anti-Nazis from German working-class circles whom I got to know in internment camp, whether social democratic or communist, Jewish or gentile, were cut from a different cloth; many of them had risked their life in illegal fights against the Nazis.

But the behaviour of middle-class Jews was not quite that passive after all. The example of my parents shows that not everything was swallowed down, even though the protest was sometimes hopelessly naive, such as the belief that through proof of one's love of the homeland or by model behaviour one might impress the Nazis one little bit. One's devotion to Germany, one's faith in German law, admirable in and of themselves, were completely ineffective as an answer to the Nazis. Just as ineffective as the trust others had that their wealth would protect them.

My father's special attachment was to his hometown of Stargard. How he liked to talk about the marketplace where my grandparents had rented an apartment from the Piaschewskis and how the water was obtained still from a pump in the market in the 1870s. He told us about the river Ihna, the Madü lake or about their excursion to the village of Ball where the grandfather treated the children to a glass of sugar water. On a roll of thick paper in our bookcase there was a map of Stargard on which my father as a young man had coloured the buildings and green spaces. He wouldn't miss the opportunity to attend the tercentenary celebration of his school, the Peter Gröningsche Gymnasium, in 1931. The next year he contributed an article on "The Ihna as a Geographical Problem" to the periodical *Unser Pommerland*. Part of his purpose was to show how much Jews loved their home region. (The problem was that the Ihna came from a lake which in turn was fed by little creeks of different lengths. Which creek deserved to be called the Ihna, and how long did that make the Ihna? Different maps gave different answers.)

A Song for the Homeland

In certain years my father had musical ideas which he expanded into short compositions, but rarely wrote down. One of these ideas came to him in the 1930s. Critically planning each succeeding note, he expanded his idea slowly into a song without words. And what did he name this song with no lyrics, the one who had been cheated out of his homeland? It is called "German Homeland" and it is the only one of his pieces which is in my possession. I may say, despite its slow growth it is a unified whole. The entire piece develops out of the first bar in an arch of architectural logic.

I know that my father in sleepless nights or at daytime often composed letters if something weighed on his mind. Letters to Goebbels and other potentates. Letters in which he contradicted their lies matter-of-factly and lectured them on German law, letters which fortunately were never put on paper. Except perhaps one to his childhood friend Max Howe from Stargard, now director of spa facilities in Bad Salzelmen—what do you, Max, have to say to all the evil things that are happening to me and my co-religionists? I believe Howe answered briefly but was non-committal. Once, as we were walking along Motzstrasse between Eisenacher Strasse and the American church, my father confessed to me: "I am not a person whose nature it is to hate, but when I hear that Goebbels, I cannot control myself: this scoundrel I hate with a passion."

A Secret Trip of the Parents

One afternoon something disquieting happens. Nothing special really. The parents simply tell Eva and me, "We are going out for a few hours. We can't tell you where to, but don't worry, we'll be back." That the parents leave us alone is rare, but after all we are old enough. But that they would not tell us where they were going, that is frightening, even though they sounded quite reassuring. Have they been summoned by the Gestapo? Are they visiting an old acquaintance of whose existence we are not supposed to know—perhaps in an asylum? We could not guess and never found out.

Early in 1992 it suddenly dawned on me. I haven't got the slightest proof, but it would have been just like my father to do this. Werner von Blomberg was from Stargard, and five years younger than my father. He certainly had attended the same school. He became Minister of War and Commander-in-Chief of the Wehrmacht in 1935, and a General Field Marshal in 1936. He was devoted to Hitler but represented a different social stratum than the Nazis and quarrelled with Nazi big shots about retaining "half"-Jewish officers or something of that sort. It would have been just like my father to write to Blomberg, address him as a fellow Stargarder and schoolmate, tell him about the misery and finally ask him to use his influence to tell the Nazi leaders, enough now with persecuting the Jews, you are damaging only yourselves. Did Blomberg respond by arranging a private meeting? It would be hard to believe, but it is a possibility. As a matter of fact, Blomberg soon fell out of grace, supposedly because of his second marriage. (It would be more probable that my parents owned some property or investments, the sale of which should be kept even from their own children, as one kept one's finances a strict secret.)

A more public kind of protest is revealed in my father's article "Of the Spirit of the Bible," which was published on 15 August 1936 in the *Mitteilungen der Jüdischen Reformgemeinde zu Berlin* (pp. 86–87),[21] to my father's chagrin slightly abbreviated by the editor. He points out that the Bible has been for a millennium "one of the foundations of the religion of civilized mankind and thus also of the German people, whose greatest spirits have paid admiring homage to the Holy Scripture of the Jews. It was judged worthy of translation by Luther, and of praise by Goethe, Herder, and Humboldt; from it Hindenburg gathered his last religious edification (Book of Nehemiah, chapter 4, verse 11),[22] and thus the Bible is protected against the suspicion of ethical inferiority in any of its parts. Such a suspicion is extended quite often toward the figure of Jacob, but apparently in older times guided by a more primitive mentality his story had a different effect on people. Otherwise it would be incomprehensible why the given name Jacob is used so frequently in the south and northwest of Germany, in Holland and England."

The controversial admonition "An eye for an eye, a tooth for a tooth" my father views in the light of comparative law as historic progress from "Eyes for an eye, teeth for a tooth." He also quotes "He who beats or curses his parents, who abducts people—see the most recent German criminal law!—or sells human beings, shall be put to death." Is this not meant as an irony at a time when in Germany human beings were abducted every day?

He explains that "the thought of being the 'chosen people' is not a Jewish particularity, but receives in the Bible a more articulate form than among other peoples. Just as in the Bible Israel is singled out from all others to spread the idea of a pure God among all of humanity, so also we know of phrases like 'proud as a Spaniard,' the 'sacro egoismo' of the Italian, the 'grande nation' of the French. China considers itself the 'Middle Empire,' the English and Americans are convinced that everything that happens to them and that they accomplish has never been achieved by any other nation. Theodor von Bernhardi at one time accused Turnvater Jahn 'of the national superstition of the Germans being a chosen people.'"[23] The reader to whose judgment the article is addressed must have asked himself, what would Bernhardi have made of Goebbels and the other Nazi ideologues?

Der Stürmer Feels Honoured

One day the telephone rings, "I should like to speak to the lawyer Kallmann." "Yes, one moment please." "This is Weiss, Berlin editor of *Der Stürmer* [the notorious anti-Semitic rag]. Our journal intends to publish an exposé of your client Simon Tenzer. He owns an apartment building on Ebertystrasse. We hear that he behaves impertinently towards his tenants and is altogether a crook. We are going to clean up there!" "All I can reply is that you have been given wrong information. I have known Tenzer for many years and can vouch that he is an honest and very good-natured landlord who is lenient if someone is sick and cannot pay the rent promptly; he also gives little Christmas presents to the children in the building." "Herr X has told us evil things about Herr Tenzer." (My mother sits next to my father, puts her hand on his as though to say: be careful, don't say too much.) "Oh, if you are depending on Herr X, I can only say, he has often been unwilling to pay his rent, often bothers the other tenants, and we have already sued him and won." (And so on.) "And by the way, your journal is completely unknown to me." Herr Weiss is impressed. "Well, then I am going to temporarily refrain from publishing the exposé. I have the honour!" (The tenant was a bad apple who thought his membership in the SA would protect him from paying his rent.)

Short Trip on Streetcar Line 57

One day my mother and the two children took the streetcar line 57 for a short-trip ticket from Emser Platz to Viktoria-Luise-Platz. We stand on the rear platform of the last car and wait for the conductor. He sees us but does not come to collect, probably chats with some passenger or other. Already the streetcar stops at our destination. We could get off without having paid. My mother knocks on the inner door and insists on paying the fare. She explains to us that she wants the conductor to know that people like us are honest.

"This woman is Aryan"

On Thursday, 10 November 1938 I go to the Jewish school in Moabit, as usual.[24] Only a few pupils and teachers are there. There is talk about the synagogues burning. Arrests have already begun or are to be expected. There is hardly any thought of teaching. We are advised to go home in small groups at staggered times. Men who have been warned in time go into hiding with female relatives or non-Jewish friends, or get lost in the Tiergarten or a forest or on a railway train. Since I am only sixteen and my father over sixty-five we are spared. My cousin Rudolf Lehmann, then thirty years old, drops by, walks from one relative to another. To my friend Peter Ball, recently emigrated to New York, I write on the Saturday: "On Thursday and Friday I didn't get around to writing, even though I wasn't at school on Friday. But so much is happening and everyone is so upset, so I have no peace ... It is up in the air as to what will happen with our school. Perhaps my class will never be together again in its totality." Soon after my mother goes to pick up clothing from a Jewish cleaner's, in the vicinity of Wittenbergplatz, near the corner of Bayreuther Strasse and Wormser Strasse, when a bunch of Hitler Youth storm into the shop to create havoc. When they notice my mother, their leader says: "Let this woman go, she is Aryan." (My mother had no "Jewish" features.)

Another example comes to mind. Dr. Max Heinrich, my mother's cousin, once returned home from a visit to us and at the Zoo station waited for his streetcar 72 or 93. Since he looked "Jewish" some SA-trooper pestered him. "I was a German soldier and wear the Iron Cross," said Heinrich, whereupon he knocked the lout down and jumped quickly on the departing streetcar.

Decline

My Departure

My departure by *Kindertransport* to England is set for 12 June 1939. In the weeks before I have to appear at government offices and agencies and make important purchases with my mother. Then I go for farewell visits to acquaintances and friends; others come to us, Christians as well as Jews. Frau Bahr-Brauer says: "Helmichen, just remain always as you are." Frau Goldstein lets me look through her music cabinet to pick out something. I select the piano reduction of *Fidelio* which still sits among my scores today. On 9 June my father and I play piano duets one last time, the slow movements of Haydn's symphonies 85 and 88. The next day we make a last excursion to the Grunewald forest, which had become a second home to us.

In order to keep emigrants on tenterhooks, the police will issue the passport only at the last moment, on the morning of the day of departure. My father and I walk to Kurfürstenstrasse, my last walk with him. The Gestapo man hands over the passport. My father asks "Don't you think it would be better if the boy passed his matric before he leaves?" My heart sinks. Will my father really decide to keep me at home? But the Gestapo man says: "No, be glad that he can leave."

Back at home my father wants to spend a few minutes alone with me. We sit in the breakfast niche of the dining room. How many times he must have gone over what he should impart to me at the end. But instead of spontaneously passing on wishes, requests, explanations, or instructions, or passing judgment on me, only generalities reach my ear. There is something artificial in this scene; it is almost embarrassing to have to do him this favour.

Minutes later the farewell to my sister follows, the taxi is called, and fifteen minutes later we are at the Lehrter Bahnhof. The last farewell from my parents is wiped from my memory. Soon the child emigrants enter the reserved coach and the train leaves. Meanwhile the parents have walked to the Invalidenstrasse and wave from the bridge. Standing close together, they form a unit to my eye; I know they will support one another. That is consoling. Then I introduce myself to the others in my compartment. One is called Hartmann from Chemnitz and turns out to be the younger brother of the Hartmann who recently joined my class in school.

At Uelzen and Soltau the Lüneburg Heath looks exactly like the coloured picture in my geography book. (Years later, travelling from Hamburg to Hannover it didn't look at all like the Lüneburg Heath.) In the late afternoon we arrive in Bremen where we are led to an emigrant's hall, fed, and lodged overnight. And thus ended the most decisive day of departure in my whole life.

Excerpts from the *Kindertagebuch* and from Letters to Canada 1940–42

I want to cite only excerpts from the Children's Diary my father kept—the *Kindertagebuch* (KTB)—and from letters which reached me in Canada via internment mail. The precise date on which one legal right after another was taken away from Jews and one burden after another was placed on them—the prohibition on telephoning, the Yellow Star, the ban on using public transportation, the limitations on shopping, the food rationing—all these have been described elsewhere. Unless otherwise marked, all quotes are from Arthur Kallmann.

> KTB, 29 March 1940. "29.2.1940 final examination by Oberschulrat (chief school official) Dr. Anders at the Jewish Kindergarten Seminary. He is praised highly by Eva."[25]
>
> Letter, 20 August 1940. "We are well, often have visitors, which don't make up for your absence and, when the weather is fine, we walk in the Tiergarten. With Eva I picked raspberries in the Grunewald bog and the three of us made the steamer trip which I had promised Mutti many years ago for her birthday. Aunt Helene has been living with us since the beginning of August; she sleeps in front on the chaise longue and will be restored to health once she receives orthopedic shoes."
>
> Letter, 9 November 1940. A.K. discovers his Greek readers and grammar, reads in them, then in Tacitus's *Germania* and three further volumes: *History of Stargard*, Balzac's *Femme de trente ans*, and Wölfflin's *Basic Concepts of Art History*.
>
> Letter, 18. December 1940. "Uncle Walter (Dr. med. Schwerin) has become a transport worker."
>
> Letter, 11 January 1941. "Our experience confirms that one can sleep at 6–7°C. and stay in the room at 13–14°. Telephoning has stopped as of the 1st of the month." He is reading Maupassant and Balzac. "Aunt Helene now has her orthopedic shoes."

Letter, 2 February 1941. "In bed I am reading Auerbach's *Barfüssle* and a very pleasant book by Yolanda Földes written in simple English, *The Street of the Fishing Cat*."

Letter, 9 March 1941. "Casting aside my declining principles I went to two concerts of the Kulturbund, a string quartet afternoon and the Symphony No. 2 by Mahler, for which my companion, Uncle Walter, had provided me with a musical introduction. I much enjoyed it."

Letter, 10 March 1941, Fanny K.: "Now the money for the valuables has arrived." (Crossed out)

Letter, 9 May 1941. Arthur K. has played Beethoven's last cello sonata with Clara Bussenius (neighbour and friend of Aunt Marie); with Rosenthal, the former concertmaster of the German Opera, he played violin sonatas by Brahms and Franck, but R. wants to be paid.

KTB, 28 May 1941. Parents are called to appear before the Gestapo.

Letter, 3 June 1941 (Pentecost). "We were rewarded by ideal beautiful weather; on Sunday we went to Pichelswerder; on Monday to Schlachtensee."

Letter, 12 June 1941. "Do you know M. Mitchell's *Gone with the Wind*? It took me exactly two months to read the 1000 pages in a good translation. It is one of the best shaped novels that I know."

Letter, 22 July 1941. Fanny K.: "We have made a few nice excursions … with Eva and Aunt Else Joachim in the Grunewald hunting for rasp-'bears'; we sailed on steamers which I love so much. The day before yesterday I went by steamer from Wannsee to Sakrow Lake with papa, sister Gerda and Fräulein Koppel."

Letter, 22 July 1941. "Experiences of your good mother in 1940 taught us the value of health. On 28 August 1940 Mutti suffered an incredible accident as she left the drying room [on top of the apartments under the roof] carrying the laundry basket in front of her. She stepped on a gap which she had not noticed was secured only by a weak sheet of tin, and fell through it to the fourth floor, in front of the door to the apartment of Frau Witzig, who lives above us. At first she was taken care of by Frau Witzig and Fräulein Mühlpfordt and others living above us, before I was called (you can imagine the fright all around). I then took her down in the elevator and speedily called for Dr. Priebatsch, who again showed his mettle. Mutti's strong nature and great luck—for she suffered no severe injuries—helped her to recover after several weeks, although until recently an occasional light pain reminded her of the fall. The financial aspect was covered by our landlord's insurance."

Letter, 22 July 1941. Eva: "I have two weeks' vacation now which I spend partly at home, partly outdoors (Wannsee, Potsdam, Grunewald, Müggelsee)."

KTB, 27 July 1941: "Excursions are becoming risky politically. The order to carry the Star of David is accepted calmly by Eva. She wears it without complaint."

Letter, 7 August 1941. Fanny K.: "We spent an especially beautiful day in Birkenwerder ..."

Letter, 5 September 1941. "For the third time I am playing through Chopin's Etudes in order, repeating each one three times. Despite their difficulties they are a great joy, only today it was a pain to play the longest one, truly a test of patience. I had to put off doing the repetitions."[26]

KTB, 16 November 1941. "Smell of gas in Eva's room at morning; in the course of the day it transpired that the homeopath Buchholz with his divorced Jewish wife and his mother in law have committed suicide." Probably the divorce was only pro forma so he could keep working for a while.

Letter, 30 November 1941. "We have many visitors, seeking advice or consoling us." Fanny K.: "Don't worry about us, we hold our heads high."

KTB, "On 1 December 1941 we receive a notice of eviction. On 2 December we all, including Helene, go to the Jewish Community office where we are told that the eviction has been postponed due to Eva's employment by the Jewish Community."

Red Cross Message to Canada, 8 February 1942. "Aunts Else [Joachim] and Marie [Kallmann] [transported] to Riga." [Our friends] "Fräuleins Landsberg are dead" [obviously suicide].

KTB, late March 1942. "Eva accepts all the shameful measures continuously taken against us with serene nonchalance."

KTB, 1 May 1942. Eva receives permission to use public transit.

The last entry in the *Kindertagebuch* stops in the middle of a sentence without a final period: "6 September 1942. Eva walks on foot to [the cemetery in] Weissensee to take part for the first time in a funeral, that of her young colleague Eva Ilsberg. She walks [about 11 km each way] with Rabbi Kempner and his wife …"

Farewell Forever

Next month, on 14 October 1942, the parents are deported to Theresienstadt, then Eva is taken away on 26 October, supposedly to Lodz, forever. My father had spent fifty-three years in Berlin without a blemish, forty of them in Schöneberg; my mother had been a model social worker. Now these righteous people are deported, like criminals. Except that criminals are usually tried before a court of law and only imprisoned for a good reason.

The End

My father died in Theresienstadt in March 1943. I have never found out anything about the fate of my sister.[27]

In her last postcard from the Schleuse checkpoint (an assembly area locked both from the inside and the outside) at the Theresienstadt camp my mother writes to Frau Sturmfels late in 1944 (undated): "My dear Frau Sturmfels. Once again I send you heartfelt greetings and a thousand thanks for all your love. I have also written to Ellen [Frau Sturmfels' daughter] to tell her that she doesn't have to worry about Helene. Please look after Fräulein Sternberg at the Home for the Blind and Frau Irma Rosenzweig, Hohenelbe J 38. Warmest regards, Fanny Kallmann." Then she is on the way to Auschwitz or Birkenau.

Frau Sturmfels, our Jewish subtenant, along with her "half"-Jewish daughter, was herself sent to Theresienstadt on 6 May 1944 and met my mother there again. She survived the war and reported to me on 6 November 1946: "After the parents and Frau Lehmann [Aunt Helene] were picked up together, your mother went with great confidence, whereas your father with his outspoken feeling for justice was very bitter and left the apartment only after much persuasion. I stayed behind with Evchen and Fräulein Reuter. Evchen still went to assist in the Jewish Kindergarten every day until she too was deported to Poland, fortunately together with all the other young girls from the Kindergarten. As much as I could, I helped her with the packing and to get through the difficult half hour when she took leave of her empty family home. But Evchen was a courageous human being, she left with a hope in her heart for a reunion with all her loved ones. Unfortunately it was not to be her fate; may God have granted her an easy death."

Disposal of the Furniture and Valuables

The apartment building at Geisbergstrasse 41 was bombed in the night of 22–23 November 1943 (as was my high school, the Hohenzollern Gymnasium). Letter from Erna Werner, 10 August 1946: "The house started to burn simultaneously on the stairs, the roof and the basement. The tenants stood on the opposite side of the street and had to look helplessly on, unable to do anything." They had stuffed the room rented to Fräulein Reuter "with your furniture so that your parents would at least find something, if they had come back."

Herr Ludwig of the dairy shop next door bought some cutlery, surely with the understanding that later he would sell it back. When I dropped by in 1962 he showed me a piece. Fräulein Toeppe had accepted the carpet from the room with the balcony.

Letter, 8 July 1946, from Günter Pohland, my friend from school, at Grunewaldstrasse 87: "Your parents must have trusted him [the caretaker Paul Bögner] somewhat because, as he told me, they burned all private and business papers of your father in the furnace room prior to leaving Berlin. The contents of the apartment were confiscated by the finance department and later were sold."

Letter, 6 November 1946, from Frau Sturmfels: "As far as I know the caretaker bought the piano and a few other things from the finance department, which had confiscated the apartment."

Fräulein Gertrud Höniger, Kurfürstendamm 231, formerly a social worker in Herzberge and a colleague of my Aunt Else Paradies in the borough of Lichtenberg, reported on 24 November 1947: "Both your parents were in Berlin longer than your Aunt Else under the well-known sorrowful conditions, which very much affected your father in particular. But I was able to spend a few restful and peaceful afternoons with them, enhanced by mutual interests and your parents' nice library. We [Frl. Höniger and Johanna Hensel] then moved the books to our apartment. I am very sorry to have to tell you that all those books and also the furniture which we stored were burned when our place was bombed out completely in February 1944."

The Werners visited the Geisbergstrasse apartment secretly until the end, under the pretext of visiting Fräulein Reuter, the Gentile subtenant.

(They actually became good friends.) Erna Werner writes on 20 August 1946: "An elderly lady [probably Frau Sturmfels] has told me that Frau Kallmann was moved from Theresienstadt in October 1944 in a transport probably to Auschwitz. It is so terrible that I have to write all this to you. Of your dear mother the old lady has said she was like a good angel, had helped everyone wherever she could and was very popular."

For years after the war the Werners helped me with my restitution claims, a complicated and time-consuming labour, and only in the last years, at my urging, did Herr Werner keep a small percentage of the payments. The Werners also sent me the jewellery which they had buried under a tree in a park.

Letter, 6 November 1946, from Frau Sturmfels: "In Theresienstadt everyone had to work. Your mother worked in varying capacities. First as a nurses' aid, at the end at the post office, work that quite appealed to her ... One day she was called up for the transport to Birkenau. She hoped this would speed up her release since she was coming back to Germany ... I accompanied her to the Schleuse checkpoint, from where the transport started. She was in good spirits. Several of the women that she had befriended were in the same transport, among them the wife of Dr. Pribatsch ... As I heard later, the entire transport is said to have been gassed."

Letter, 5 June 1947, from Frau Moder, née Fohgrub. "One day before your dear parents went to Theresienstadt, I visited them. Even before then your mother had given me a box with family photos and an album in which your father made notes about your and Evchen's childhood. Also a slim drawing pad which contains, I suppose, your first efforts at drawing. [Frau Moder sent these family documents to me in 1953.] ... From Evchen I still have a lot of toys passed on for my elder daughter ... My heart always saddens when I look at these toys and think of Evchen. She was such a good child and had to give up her life because of the Nazi scoundrels."

Why? Probably there is no answer to this question. And yet I cannot avoid ending with it. Why?

NOTES

1 Schöneberg is a district in south-central Berlin, south of the Tiergarten park and west of the former Tempelhof Airport (which closed in 2008). It is the birthplace of the actress Marlene Dietrich and the conductor

Wilhelm Furtwängler, and is the setting of the Berlin stories of Christopher Isherwood. From the turn of the century until the rise of the Nazis, many upper-middle-class Jews lived in Schöneberg, including Albert Einstein, Kurt Tucholsky, and Leo Baeck. [*Ed.*]

2 Aside from the quotations given here, further excerpts from this account of the progress of Eva and Helmut, maintained by Arthur Kallmann for almost twenty years, appear in translation in Dawn Keer, "Helmut Kallmann: An Account of His Contributions to Music Librarianship and Scholarship in Canada" (MLIS thesis, University of Alberta, 1991), 14, 17, 19, etc. [*Ed.*]

3 HK's written English was always impeccable. However, this translation of his own German text has a number of minor lapses from idiomatic English, which the editors have felt justified in changing, in each case checking the English translation against the German original. In no instances has the sense been altered, and the changes are no doubt fewer than the author himself would have made if preparing the essay for publication. [*Ed.*]

4 This outlook, these values might be summarized as follows, although they were never spoken. Yet they were obvious from the behaviour of adults:
   a. In one's profession one has to do one's best—an occupation is not just a time filler, not merely earning a living.
   b. One is supposed to be decent, useful, and helpful to one's fellow humans.
   c. Beyond this the purpose of life is to get to know, experience, and make one's own the most beautiful things on earth: natural beauty (scenery or natural events), the magnificent works of art, and the lofty thoughts (painting, architecture, music, literature, and philosophy).

   Are the values listed under "c" only the accidental ones of the educated class, as opposed to those of the consumer, the revolutionary, or the religious zealot, or are they of universal validity?

5 W30 was one of the main post offices; I believe it was the central office for stamp collectors for all of Germany. Next to it was the headquarters of the nationalist Kyffhäuser league (for war veterans), at the next corner the VDA (*Volksbund für das Deutschtum in Ausland*—Society for Germans Abroad) and the Scala (variety shows). Among the larger stores in the vicinity were the Pommersche Meierei (dairy chain) and Büttner's coffee store with a stuffed bear outside its door.

6 The exception for war veterans was introduced on the initiative of President Hindenburg; HK's father was allowed to continue practising law as an *Altanwalt* (Senior Lawyer), a category that included those who were called to the bar before 1914. See *Lawyers without Rights: Jewish Lawyers in Germany under the Third Reich*, exhibition catalogue (2000), 9, http://www.schildhaus.com/downloads/Brosch%C3%BCreLWR_USA.pdf (accessed 12 June 2012). [*Ed.*]

7 A general prohibition banning all Jewish lawyers from practising law came into effect on 30 November 1938; see *Lawyers without Rights*, 9. [*Ed.*]
8 The Bata Shoe Company was founded in Zlin in 1894; the Bata family planned to create an urban utopia in Zlin with housing, schools, hospitals, and social welfare programs that were considered progressive for their time; the plan was later copied in Bata company towns around the world (including Batawa, Ontario, founded in 1939). [*Ed.*]
9 *Dreck/Schmutz* = muck/dirt; *schmeissen/werfen* = chuck/throw [*Ed.*]
10 In the Walpurgisnacht scene of *Faust*, Mephistopheles refers to himself as "Junker Voland"; Junker denotes a member of the lesser nobility (equivalent to "squire"). [*Ed.*]
11 This is a mocking version of the old German Imperial anthem (sung to the tune of "God Save the King"); the true lyrics begin "Heil dir im Siegerkranz / Herrscher des Vaterlands!" ("Hail to thee in victor's laurels / Ruler of the Fatherland"). The parody could be translated as "Hail to you in your laurels of potato skins and herring tails." [*Ed.*]
12 This book (*Felix Mendelssohn-Bartholdy's Correspondence with Legation Counsellor Karl Klingemann in London*) was published on the centenary of Mendelssohn's birth. It remains an important source for Mendelssohn scholarship and has never been translated into English. Klingemann, Mendelssohn's closest friend, was a diplomat (stationed in London for over thirty years), poet, and musician. [*Ed.*]
13 *Omi* ("nanna") is a word German children use for their grandmother; HK is referring to Grandmother Reuter. [*Ed.*]
14 Plaut died on 8 February 2012 in Toronto at the age of 99, just four days before HK's death. [*Ed.*]
15 The Central-Verein deutscher Staatsbürger Jüdischen Glaubens (Central Association of German Citizens of Jewish Faith). [*Ed.*]
16 *Der Pojaz* (*The Clown*) was written in 1893 but not published until 1905, a year after Franzos's death; it is a *Bildungsroman* about an East European Jewish boy who dreams of a career in the theatre. [*Ed.*]
17 Prinzregentenstrasse synagogue opened in 1930 but was burned to the ground during the wave of destruction and terror that was unleashed on Kristallnacht, 9–10 November 1938. [*Ed.*]
18 At the time, 'Itzig' was a pejorative name used for all Jews. [*Ed.*]
19 This may have been the Lea Koppel, born 11 June 1905 in Berlin, listed as a singer in Theophil Stengel and Herbert Gerigk's Nazi-era publication *Lexikon der Juden in der Musik* (Berlin: B. Hahnefeld, 1941), column 141. [*Ed.*]
20 The *Vossische Zeitung* was a liberal daily newspaper published in Berlin and regarded as the national newspaper of record for Germany until it was forced by the Nazi party to close down on 25 March 1934. [*Ed.*]

21 The journal title could be translated as *Communications of the Jewish Reform Congregation in Berlin*. The journal ceased publication on 15 October 1938, and the congregation itself came to an end in 1939; see Simone Ladwig-Winters and Peter Galliner, eds., *Freiheit und Bindung: Zur Geschichte der Jüdischen Reformgemeinde zu Berlin von den Anfängen bis zu ihrem Ende 1939* (Teetz: Hentrich & Hentrich, 2009). [*Ed.*]
22 Nehemiah 4:11—"And our adversaries said, They shall not know, neither see, till we come in the midst among them, and slay them, and cause the work to cease" (*King James Version*). [*Ed.*]
23 Theodor von Bernhardi was a Prussian diplomat and military historian; Friedrich Ludwig Jahn, known as "Turnvater Jahn" ("Father of Gymnastics Jahn"), was a gymnastics educator and German nationalist. [*Ed.*]
24 During the night of 9–10 November 1938 (*Kristallnacht*) in Germany and Austria, hundreds of synagogues were destroyed, thousands of Jewish shops and properties were broken into and ransacked, and 30,000 Jews were arrested. In Berlin alone, some 12,000 Jewish men were sent to the concentration camps at Sachsenhausen and Buchenwald. As Hermann Simon has written, "There was nothing left for the Jews in the Reich to hold on to. Only downfall remained." See his "1938: The Year of Fate," in *Jews in Nazi Berlin: From Kristallnacht to Liberation*, ed. Beate Meyer, Hermann Simon, and Chana Schütz (Chicago: University of Chicago Press, 2009), 18. [*Ed.*]
25 This qualifying exam completed Eva Kallmann's certification process to become a Kindergarten teacher. [*Ed.*]
26 Even for professional pianists, playing three times through the entire twenty-seven études of Chopin requires both skill and stamina. [*Ed.*]
27 In a communication from the International Tracing Service of the Canadian Red Cross (18 July 1996), HK learned that Eva Kallmann was transported with other Jews from Berlin to "the East," probably Poland, on 26 October 1942. For only 10 per cent of those transported are there further records. [*Ed.*]

List of Helmut Kallmann's Writings

A list of HK's writings from 1949 up to June 1987 is available in *Musical Canada: Words and Music Honouring Helmut Kallmann*, ed. John Beckwith and Frederick A. Hall (Toronto: University of Toronto Press, 1988), 315–24. Dawn Keer, "Helmut Kallmann: An Account of His Contributions to Music Librarianship and Scholarship in Canada" (MLIS thesis, University of Alberta, 1991), 128–40, provides a somewhat more extensive list of HK's published writings from 1947 to the fall of 1990. The chronological list given below includes all of HK's published writings until his death. Entries below marked with an asterisk (*) are published in this book.

Music reviews for *The Varsity* [the University of Toronto student newspaper], 1947–49. Dawn Keer in her MLIS thesis, cited above, provides a selection of sixteen reviews (four from 1947, eight from 1948, and four from 1949). Original copies of all these reviews, which were written during HK's undergraduate studies in music at the University of Toronto, are available in the Helmut Kallmann archival papers, which are to be deposited in Library and Archives Canada in Ottawa.

"Canada on the Musical Map." *Music and Art* [Los Angeles] 3/8 (October 1949), 3.

*"Canadian Music as a Field for Research." Royal Conservatory of Music of Toronto *Monthly Bulletin* (March 1950), 2.

"Music in Early Canada [part 1]." *The Muse* [Toronto] 1/5 (April 1950), 2–3. Reprinted in *Music and Art* [Los Angeles] 4/5 (Fall 1950), 5.

"Music in Early Canada [part 2]." *The Muse* [Toronto] 1/6 (May 1950), 3–4.

"Canadian Music in the Nineteen Forties." *Music and Art* [Los Angeles] 4/3 (Summer 1950), 2.

Editor. *Catalogue of Canadian Composers*, revised and enlarged edition. Toronto: Canadian Broadcasting Corporation, [1952]. Republished St. Clair Shores, Michigan: Scholarly Press, 1972.

"First Opera Arrived by Stagecoach." *Globe and Mail* [Toronto], (8 July 1953), 15.

"Foreword." *Canadian League of Composers Concert Program*. Toronto, Eaton Auditorium, 28 November 1953. [A brief history of all-Canadian concerts.]

List of Helmut Kallmann's Writings

*"The New *Grove's*: Disappointment to Canada." *Saturday Night* 70/23 (12 March 1955), 25.

"Music Festivals in Canada." *The Annual Stratford Shakespearean Festival of Drama and Music 1955* [souvenir program]. Stratford: Shakespearean Festival Foundation of Canada, 1955. [26].

"Historical Background." *Music in Canada*. Edited by Ernest MacMillan. Toronto: University of Toronto Press, 1955. 10–31.

"Music in Canada and the Canadian Music Council." *Canadian Library Association Bulletin* 12/5 (April 1956), 178–80.

"A Century of Music Periodicals in Canada." *Canadian Music Journal* 1/1 (Autumn 1956), 37–43.

"A Century of Music Periodicals in Canada (Concluded)." *Canadian Music Journal* 1/2 (Winter 1957), 25–30.

"A Check-List of Canadian Periodicals in Music." *Canadian Music Journal* 1/2 (Winter 1957), 30–36.

Review of *Canadian Portraits: Famous Musicians—MacMillan, Johnson, Pelletier, Willan* by Louise G. McCready and *Musiciennes de chez nous* by Claude Gingras. *Canadian Music Journal* 1/4 (Summer 1957), 76–78.

"Today's Music Library Resources—Tomorrow's Music Library Services." *Proceedings: Twelfth Annual Conference*. Ottawa: Canadian Library Association, August 1957. 28–29.

"Der deutsche Beitrag zum Musikleben Kanadas." *Mitteilungen, Institut für Auslandsbeziehungen* [Stuttgart] 7/3 (July-September 1957), 200–4. [Canada issue; written 1955]

"Audio-Visual Aids to Music Education in Canada." International Society for Music Education series *Technical Media in Music Education*. Mimeographed. N.p., 1957.

Editor. *Catalogue of Orchestral Music*. Toronto: Canadian League of Composers, 1957. [Unsigned.]

"The Percy Scholes Collection: Nucleus for a National Library." *Canadian Music Journal* 2/3 (Spring 1958), 43–45.

"Canadian Music Library Association." *Feliciter* 3/9 (May 1958, Part 2), 7.

"From the Archives." *Canadian Music Journal* 2/4 (Summer 1958), 45–52. [Documents from BC archives selected with commentary by HK.]

Review of *Past and Present: A Canadian Musician's Reminiscences* by Louise McDowell. *Canadian Music Journal* 2/4 (Summer 1958), 81, 83.

"Kanada." *Die Musik in Geschichte und Gegenwart*, vol. 7. Kassel and Basel: Bärenreiter Verlag, 1958.

"Heintzman, Theodore August." *Encyclopedia Canadiana*, vol. 5. Ottawa: Canadiana Co., 1958.

"Musical Instruments, Making of," and "Music Composition," vol. 7. *Encyclopedia Canadiana*. Ottawa: Canadiana Co., 1958. Rev. ed. Toronto: Grolier, 1966 and 1975.

List of Helmut Kallmann's Writings

"From the Archives: Organs and Organ Players in Canada." *Canadian Music Journal* 3/3 (Spring 1959), 41–47.

Review of LP recording of *Bach: Concerto No. 5 in F minor* and *Beethoven: Concerto No. 1 in C major, Op. 15*. Glenn Gould, piano; Columbia Symphony Orchestra; Vladimir Golschmann, conductor. Columbia ML5298. *Canadian Music Journal* 3/4 (Summer 1959), 51–53.

A History of Music in Canada 1534–1914. Toronto: University of Toronto Press, 1960. Reprinted in paperback with corrections, 1969; reprinted in paperback with list of amendments, 1987. [*Introduction, 3–7.]

Review of LP recordings of Shostakovich *Symphony No. 6*, *Symphony No. 11*, *From Jewish Folk Poetry, Op. 79*, and other works by Russian and Soviet composers. *Canadian Music Journal* 6/1 (Autumn 1961), 40–45.

A Bio-Bibliographical Finding List of Canadian Musicians and Those Who Have Contributed to Music in Canada. Ottawa: Canadian Library Association, [1961]. Compiled by Melva J. Dwyer, Lucien Brochu, and Helmut Kallmann.

"From the Archives: The Montreal Gazette on Music from 1786 to 1797." *Canadian Music Journal* 6/3 (Spring 1962), 3–11.

"RISM Report about Canada." *Fontes artis musicae* 9/1 (January-June 1962), 21–22.

"The Siege of Quebec." Mimeographed program note. Ten Centuries Concerts, 9 December 1962.

"Papineau-Couture, Jean" and "Pentland, Barbara." *Die Musik in Geschichte und Gegenwart*, vol. 10. Kassel and Basel: Bärenreiter Verlag, 1962.

"Music." *1962 Britannica Book of the Year / The Year in Canada*. Chicago: Encyclopaedia Britannica, 1962.

"Music." *1963 Britannica Book of the Year / The Year in Canada*. Chicago: Encyclopaedia Britannica, 1963.

*"Joseph Quesnel's *Colas et Colinette*." Mimeographed program note. Ten Centuries Concerts, 6 October 1963.

Directory of Degree Graduates. Toronto: University of Toronto Music Alumni Association, 2 March 1964.

"CBC Seeks Antique Musical Canadiana." *CBC Times* 16/51 (20–26 June 1964), 8.

"History of Opera in Canada." *Opera Canada* 5 (September 1964), 10–12, 78.

"Music in Canada." *CBC Times* 17/46 (15–21 May 1965), 11–13. Abridged version reprinted as "Themes in Canadian History." *Bulletin: Royal Conservatory of Music* (Winter 1966).

"Music in Canada." Thirteen-part documentary series for CBC Radio [English network], written and arranged by James Bannerman and Helmut Kallmann, based on HK's book *A History of Music in Canada 1534–1914* (1960). Produced and directed by James Kent; aired Sundays at 7:30 p.m., beginning 16 May 1965. Also presented on the CBC French radio network

List of Helmut Kallmann's Writings

as *Chronique de la vie musicale au Canada*. French-language scripts by Andrée Desautels; aired Fridays at 9 p.m., beginning 21 May 1965.

"Joseph Quesnel, Pioneer Canadian Composer / Joseph Quesnel: ancêtre des compositeurs canadiens." *Canadian Composer* 3 (October 1965), 22–23, 36, 44.

"Heinz Unger†." *Zeitschrift für Kulturaustausch* [Stuttgart] 15 (1965), 291.

Canadian-built 19th Century Musical Instruments, a Check List. Mimeographed. Toronto: CBC Music Library, 1965. Second edition, revised, Edmonton: Edmonton Public Library, distributed by the Canadian Music Library Association, 1966.

"First Fifteen Years of Canadian League of Composers / La Ligue canadienne des compositeurs, quinze ans d'activité." *Canadian Composer* 7 (March 1966), 18–19, 28, 46.

Notice. *Canadian Library* 22/5 (March 1966), 357. [A request for materials for the CMLA Centennial Project, an index of music printed in Canada up to 1921.]

"Report of the Canadian Delegate from the International Association of Music Libraries (AIBM) to the Canadian Music Library Association: June 1966" and "CMLA Centennial Project—Music Printed in Canada up to 1921, Chairman's Report for 1965–66." *Proceedings of the 21st Annual Conference, June 19–24, 1966*. Ottawa: Canadian Library Association, 1966. 94 and 98–100.

"The Acceptance of 'O Canada' / L'adoption d' 'O Canada.'" *Canadian Composer* 8 (April 1966), 18–19, 38–39, 40–41.

*"Music Library Association Digs Up Our Musical Past / L'Association des bibliothèques musicales explore notre passé." *Canadian Composer* 11 (October 1966), 18–19, 28, 46.

"Vogt, Augustus Stephen." *Die Musik in Geschichte und Gegenwart*, vol. 13. Kassel and Basel: Bärenreiter Verlag, 1966.

"Dangé, François" and "Merlac, André-Louis de." *Dictionary of Canadian Biography*, vol. 1. Toronto: University of Toronto Press, 1966.

"Toronto's Music—Before 1867." Mimeographed program note. Ten Centuries Concerts, 8 January 1967.

"Compositions in Canada: 1867–1967." *The Telegram* [Toronto], 28 January 1867. [Special advertising section, Women's Committee, Toronto Symphony Orchestra Association.]

"Music in Canada, 1867, A Long Glance Backward / Musique au Canada, 1867, un long regard vers le passé." *Musicanada* 3 (July 1967), 5–6.

Musical Canadiana: A Subject Index. Preliminary edition compiled by a committee of the Canadian Music Library Association. Introduction by Helmut Kallmann, Laura Murray, and Grace Pincoe. Ottawa: Canadian Library Association, 1967.

List of Helmut Kallmann's Writings

LP jacket notes. Calixa Lavallée. *The Widow* [excerpts]. CBC International Service / RCA Victor Centennial Series Record 231. 1967. Reissued in 1986, Radio Canada International 231.

LP jacket notes. *Light Canadian Orchestral Classics / Les classiques de la musique d'orchestre au Canada*. CBC Winnipeg Orchestra. CBC International Service / Capitol Records (Canada) ST 6261. 1967.

LP jacket notes. Joseph Quesnel. *Colas et Colinette*. CBC International Service 234 / Select Records 24.160. 1968. Reissued in 1986, Radio Canada International 234.

"Weinzweig, John" and "Willan, Healey." *Die Musik in Geschichte und Gegenwart*, vol. 14. Kassel and Basel: Bärenreiter Verlag, 1968.

"Notes from the Canadian Music Library Association." Music Library Association *Notes* 25/2 (December 1968), 218–29.

"The CBC Toronto Music Library." *CMLA Newsletter* (December 1968), 6–10.

"Canada." *Harvard Dictionary of Music*, ed. Willi Apel. Second edition, revised and enlarged. Cambridge, MA: Belknap Press of Harvard University Press, 1969.

"Martin, Charles Amador." *Dictionary of Canadian Biography*, vol. 2. Toronto: University of Toronto Press, 1969.

"Report from Canada." [RISM] *Fontes artis musicae* 16/1–2 (January-June 1969), 21.

"Composers in a New Land: Musical Composition in Canada from 1867 / Compositeurs d'un monde nouveau; La création musicale au Canada, depuis 1867." *Musicanada* 20 (June 1969), 5–9, 14–16.

Review of *Historical Sets, Collected Editions, and Monuments of Music*, compiled by Anna Harriet Hyer. *Canadian Library Journal* 26/6 (November-December 1969), 486.

"Music." *Canadian Annual Review 1968*. Toronto: University of Toronto Press, 1969. 464–78.

"Historical Background." *Aspects of Music in Canada*. Edited by Arnold Walter. Toronto: University of Toronto Press, 1969. 26–61. [Revision of HK's essay written for *Music in Canada*, 1955.] French version published as "Aperçu historique." *Aspects de la musique au Canada*. Translated by Maryvonne Kendergi and Gilles Potvin. Montreal: Centre de Psychologie et de Pédagogie, 1970. For the French edition, HK also prepared the section "Bibliographie." 311–16.

*"James Paton Clarke, Canada's First Mus.Bac." *The Canada Music Book / Les Cahiers canadiens de musique* 1 (Spring-Summer 1970), 41–53.

"Notes." *Scene: National Arts Centre Orchestra*. Concert program. Ottawa, 24 July 1970.

"Music." *Canadian Annual Review 1969*. Toronto: University of Toronto Press, 1970. 445–59.

"Canadian Tasks for Musicology." Typescript prepared for the Canadian studies session at the joint meeting of the American Musicological Society and the College Music Society. Toronto, 7 November 1970.

"Music: An Introduction." *Rare and Unusual Canadiana: First Supplement to the Lande Bibliography*. Lawrence Lande Foundation for Canadian Historical Research, no. 6. Montreal: McGill University, 1971.

"Music Division / Division de la musique." *National Library News* 3/1 (January-March 1971), 3–7. [Unsigned.]

"Canadian Music Council, 7th Annual Conference." *CMLA Newsletter* (May 1971), 3–4.

"Canada's Musical Heritage a Concern of the National Library / La Bibliothèque nationale du Canada et l'héritage musical canadien." *The Music Scene / La Scène musicale* 259 (May-June 1971), 4, 21.

"Canadian League of Composers, 20 Years, 1951–1971, Chronology / La ligue canadienne des compositeurs, 20 ans, 1951–1971, chronologie." *The Canada Music Book / Les Cahiers canadiens de musique* 2 (Spring-Summer 1971), 81–90.

"Beethoven and Canada, A Miscellany." *The Canada Music Book / Les Cahiers canadiens de musique* 2 (Spring-Summer 1971), 107–17. Reprinted with slight changes in *German-Canadian Yearbook* 4 (1978), 186–94.

"Music." *Canadian Annual Review 1970*. Toronto: University of Toronto Press, 1971. 552–64.

"A Letter: To the Canadian Members of IAML." *CMLA Newsletter* (August 1971), 2–3.

"CMLA Centennial Project: Report up to June 1971." *CMLA Newsletter* (August 1971), 6.

"IAML Report 1970–1971: Prepared for CMLA Annual Meeting." *CMLA Newsletter* (August 1971), 7.

"Preface/Préface." *Healey Willan Catalogue*. Edited by Gilles Bryant. Ottawa: National Library of Canada, 1972. 6–9.

"Toward a Bibliography of Canadian Folk Music." *Ethnomusicology* 16/3 (September 1972), 499–503.

"Barbeau, Marius," "Beckwith, John," "Bernardi, Mario," "Kallmann, Helmut," and "von Kunits, Luigi." *Riemann Musik Lexikon*. Ergänzungsband, Personenteil. Vol. 1. Mainz: B. Schott's Söhne, 1972. [All entries unsigned.]

"Brauneis, Jean-Chrysostome (junior)," "Clarke, James Paton," "Dessane, Marie-Hippolyte-Antoine," and "Humphreys, James Dodsley." *Dictionary of Canadian Biography*, vol. 10. Toronto: University of Toronto Press, 1972.

"Music." *Canadian Reference Sources: A Selective Guide*. Edited by Dorothy E. Ryder. Ottawa: Canadian Library Association, 1973. 57–59. [Selections by Helmut Kallmann.]

List of Helmut Kallmann's Writings

"Who, What and Where in Canadian Music / Du nouveau sur la musique canadienne." *National Library News* 5/2 (March-June 1973), 4–6.

"Music and Criticism in Canada: A Preface / Musique et critique au Canada: une préface." *The Canada Music Book / Les Cahiers canadiens de musique* 7 (Autumn-Winter 1973), 69–73.

"Albani, Emma," "Brott, Alexander," and "Champagne, Claude." *Die Musik in Geschichte und Gegenwart*, vol. 15. Kassel and Basel: Bärenreiter Verlag, 1973.

"Canada." *Fontes artis musicae* 21/1–2 (January-August 1974), 24. [Part of the RIdIM Report No. 3, Fall 1973.]

"Weinzweig, John." *Dictionary of Contemporary Music*. Edited by John Vinton. New York: E.P. Dutton, 1974.

"Coron, Charles-François." *Dictionary of Canadian Biography*, vol. 3. Toronto: University of Toronto Press, 1974.

"Introduction." *Colas et Colinette*. Words and music by Joseph Quesnel. Reconstitution by Godfrey Ridout. Vocal score. Toronto: Gordon V. Thompson, 1974. 2–4. [In English and French, revised and adapted from the LP jacket notes of 1968.]

"Canada." *Guide for Dating Early Published Music: A Manual of Bibliographical Practices*. Chapter 17. Compiled by D.W. Krummel for the International Association of Music Libraries. Kassel and Basel: Bärenreiter, 1974. 243–44.

"Centennial 'Data Sheet' Project of CAML—Annual Report 1973-1974: Canadian Music Published up to 1921." *CAML Newsletter* 3/2 (September 1974), 21-22.

"Canadian RISM Report for 1973-1974." *CAML Newsletter* 3/2 (September 1974), 22.

"Heinz Unger Scores Donated to the National Library / Don des partitions de Heinz Unger à la Bibliothèque nationale." *National Library News* 7/1 (January-February 1975), 11-12. [Unsigned.]

"Music." *Canadian Reference Sources: Supplement*. Edited by Dorothy E. Ryder. Ottawa: Canadian Library Association, 1975. 26-27.

*"The Music Division of the National Library: The First Five Years." *The Canada Music Book / Les Cahiers canadiens de musique* 10 (Spring-Summer 1975), 95-100. Reprinted in *Musikbibliothek Aktuell* 2-3 (1976), 67-73.

"Dimitri Shostakovich." [Short obituary.] *The Canada Music Book / Les Cahiers canadiens de musique* 11/12 (Autumn-Winter 1975), 81.

"The German Contribution to Music in Canada." *German-Canadian Yearbook* 2 (1975), 152-66. Revised and translated by HK from his article "Der deutsche Beitrag zum Musikleben Kanadas" (1957).

"Lavallée, Calixa," "Mercure, Pierre," "Molt, Theodore," "Parlow, Kathleen," "Quesnel, Joseph," "Somers, Harry," and "Willan, Healey" (supplement to

HK's earlier article on Willan). *Riemann Musik Lexikon*, Ergänzungsband, Personenteil. Vol. 2. Mainz: B. Schott's Söhne, 1975. [All entries unsigned.]

"Canadian Music Publishing." *Papers of the Bibliographical Society of Canada* 13 (1975), 40-48. [Talk given at Colloquium on Canadian Bibliography, Toronto, 3 November 1973.]

"Coates, Richard," "Nordheimer, Abraham," "Perrault, Joseph-Julien," and "Wugk, Charles-Désiré-Joseph (Charles Sabatier)." *Dictionary of Canadian Biography*, vol. 9. Toronto: University of Toronto Press, 1976.

"A National Music Collection / Une collection musicale très accessible." *Musicanada* 30 (November 1976), 7, 12.

"Music." *Ontario Library Review* 60/4 (December 1976), 231-32. [Part of a reading list titled "Canadian Materials on the Arts".]

"Foreword / Avant-propos." *Canadian Music: A Selected Checklist 1950-73 / La musique canadienne: une liste selective 1950-73*. Edited by Lynne Jarman. Toronto: University of Toronto Press, 1976.

"Subject Bibliography—Music." *National Conference on the State of Canadian Bibliography, Vancouver, Canada, May 22-24, 1974: Proceedings*. Ottawa: National Library of Canada, 1977. 212-31.

"RISM." *CAML Newsletter* 6/3 (August 1977), 12.

"Union Catalogue of Canadian Sheet Music to 1950." *CAML Newsletter* 6/3 (August 1977), 13-14.

"The National Library: New Acquisitions / Bibliothèque nationale: acquisitions récentes." *Musicanada* 37 (November 1978), 11.

"Beethoven and Canada: A Miscellany." *German-Canadian Yearbook* 4 (1978), 286-94. Reprinted with slight changes from *The Canada Music Book* 2 (1971).

"Eckhardt-Gramatté, Sophie-Carmen," "Fricker, Herbert Austin," "Hambourg, Michael, Mark, Jan, Boris, Clement, Klemi," "Harriss, Charles Albert Edwin," "Kallmann, Helmut," "MacMillan, (Sir) Ernest Alexander Campbell," "Morawetz, Oskar," "Pelletier, Wilfrid," "Somers, Harry," and "Walter, Arnold." *Die Musik in Geschichte und Gegenwart*, vol. 16. Kassel and Basel: Bärenreiter Verlag, 1979.

"Le Fonds Claude Champagne à la Bibliothèque nationale du Canada." *Compositeurs au Québec 11, Claude Champagne*. Montreal: Centre de musique canadienne, 1979.

"The Mysteries of 'O Canada' / Les mystères d' 'O Canada.'" *Musicanada* 43 (Summer 1980). Abridged and reprinted as "Mystery Surrounds First Edition of 'O Canada'." *The Recorder* 23 (Fall 1980), 34-35.

"Clarke, James Paton," "Codman, Stephen," "Fricker, Herbert Austin," "Harriss, Charles Albert Edwin," "Jehin-Prume, Frantz," "Lavallée, Calixa," "Molt, Theodore Frederic," "Quesnel, Joseph," and "Vogt, Augustus Stephen." *The New Grove Dictionary of Music and Musicians*. Edited by Stanley Sadie. London: Macmillan, 1980.

List of Helmut Kallmann's Writings

"Historical Setting." *Music Resources in Canadian Collections*. Chapter 2. *Research Collections in Canadian Libraries*, no. 7. Ottawa: National Library of Canada, 1980. [Unsigned.]

"The Music Division / Division de la musique." *National Library News* 13/3 (March 1981), 4–7. [Unsigned.]

Review of *Canadian Music of the Twentieth Century* by George A. Proctor. *CAML Newsletter* 10 (April 1981), 8–13.

Encyclopedia of Music in Canada. Edited by Helmut Kallmann, Gilles Potvin, and Kenneth Winters. Toronto: University of Toronto Press, 1981. Published in French as *Encyclopédie de la musique au Canada*. Montreal: Fides, 1983. In addition to his work as the chief editor responsible for content, HK wrote more than 175 articles, alone or as co-contributor, signed or unsigned. A complete list is in *Musical Canada: Words and Music Honouring Helmut Kallmann* (1988), 321–23.

"Panneton, Charles-Marie." *Dictionary of Canadian Biography*, vol. 11. Toronto: University of Toronto Press, 1982.

"Preface/Préface." *Alexis Contant Catalogue*. Edited by Stephen C. Willis. Ottawa: National Library of Canada, 1982. iii–v.

"Periodicals Selected for Priority Indexing. II, North America—Canada." *Periodica Musica* [Newsletter of the Répertoire international de la presse musicale du XIXe siècle] 1/1 (Spring 1983), 4.

"The German Contribution to Music in Canada: A Bibliography." *German-Canadian Yearbook* 7 (1983), 228–33.

Directory of Music Research Libraries, Volume 1: Canada and the United States. Second revised edition. General editor, Rita Benton. Directory for Canada compiled by Marian Kahn and Helmut Kallmann. Kassel and Basel: Bärenreiter, 1983. Includes "Introduction—Canada" by HK.

"Major Music Acquisition by the National Library / Acquisition d'une importante collection musicale par la bibliothèque nationale." *National Library News* 16/6 (June 1984), 1–2. [Unsigned; about the acquisition of the Sir Ernest MacMillan papers.]

"Music Division Acquires Quentin Maclean Library and Papers / Acquisition des documents et de la bibliothèque de Quentin Maclean par la division de la musique." *National Library News* 16/9–10 (September-October 1984), 7. [Unsigned.]

*"The Canadian League of Composers in the 1950s: The Heroic Years." *Studies in Music from the University of Western Ontario* 9 (1984), 37–54. Reprinted in slightly abridged form in *Célébration*. Edited by Godfrey Ridout and Talivaldis Kenins. Toronto: Canadian Music Centre, 1984. 99–107.

"Music Materials Fund Yields First Acquisition / Première acquisition fait grâce au fonds pour documents musicaux." *National Library News* 17/2 (February 1985), 6, 8. [Unsigned; on the Edward B. Moogk Memorial Fund.]

List of Helmut Kallmann's Writings

"Music in Upper Canada." *The Shaping of Ontario: From Exploration to Confederation.* Compiled by Nick and Helma Mika. Belleville: Mika Publishing, 1985. 220–27.

"Canadian League of Composers," "Music History," and "Robb, Frank Morse." *The Canadian Encyclopedia.* James H. Marsh, editor-in-chief. Edmonton: Hurtig Publishers, 1985.

"Griebel, Ferdinand (Frederick)." *Dictionary of Canadian Biography*, vol. 8. Toronto: University of Toronto Press, 1985.

"Istvan Anhalt Papers / Documents d'Istvan Anhalt." *National Library News* 18/2 (February 1986), 7. [Unsigned.]

"RISM." [Report.] *CAML Newsletter* 14/3 (December 1985), 15–16.

Review of *Student's Dictionary of Music* by Wayne Gilpin. *CAML Newsletter* 15/1 (March 1986), 10–12.

"Canadian Music Publications to 1950: Report for 1985–86," and "RISM: Canada Report for 1985-1986." *CAML Newsletter* 15/2 (August 1986), 10.

"300 Years of Canadian Composition: Exhibition." *National Library News* 18/9 (September 1986), 11. [Unsigned.]

"Canada and the Music of the Grand Siècle / Le Canada et la musique du Grand Siècle." *Musicanada* 58 (December 1986), 3–4.

"Lavallée, Calixa." *The New Grove Dictionary of American Music*, vol. 3. Edited by H. Wiley Hitchcock and Stanley Sadie. New York: Grove's Dictionaries of Music, 1986.

"Music Librarianship." *Careers in Music: A Guide for Canadian Students.* Edited by Thomas Green, Patricia Sauerbrei, and Don Sedgwick. Oakville, ON: Frederick Harris Music, 1986. 80–88.

"Le Répertoire international de la presse musicale (RIPM)—II. Les sources canadiennes et le RIPM." *Les Cahiers de l'ARMuQ* 8 (May 1987), 20–21.

"Frédéric Glackemeyer: des données nouvelles sur sa vie et son style musical." *Les Cahiers de l'ARMuQ* 8 (May 1987), 86–92.

"Brauneis, John Chrisostomus" and "Mechtler, Guillaume." *Dictionary of Canadian Biography*, vol. 6. Toronto: University of Toronto Press, 1987.

"The Conservatory Remembered." *Performing Arts in Canada* 24/1 (June 1987), 9–11.

"Appassionata." Review of *Music from Within: A Biography of the Composer S.C. Eckhardt-Gramatté* by Ferdinand Eckhardt. *Canadian Literature* 115 (Winter 1987), 267–70. Reprinted, with German summary by HK, in *Brückenschlagen/Bridgebuilding 1902–1992: Festschrift für Ferdinand Eckhardt.* Edited by Claus Pese. Nuremberg: Hans Carl, 1992. 175–79.

"The Music Collection of the National Library of Canada." *Fontes artis musicae* 34/4 (October-December 1987), 174–84.

"Music at the National Library: Dr. Helmut Kallmann Reminisces about the Music Division." *National Library News* 20/2 (February 1988), 1–5. [Interview.]

"Conductors and Conducting," "Music History," and "Music Publishing." *The Canadian Encyclopedia*, 2nd ed. James H. Marsh, editor-in-chief. Edmonton: Hurtig, 1988.

Letter to the Editor. *Canadian Folk Music Bulletin* 22/1 (September 1988), 32.

Compiler, with Ruth Pincoe. *Glenn Gould 1988: Exhibition Held in Ottawa from April 14, 1988 to September 15, 1988.* Exhibition catalogue. Ottawa: National Library of Canada, 1988. [HK also wrote the "Introduction," in French and English, pages 11–15.]

"Music in Canada 1986–87." *Yearbook of the Great Soviet Encyclopedia.* Moscow: Sovetskaya Enciklopediya, 1988.

"Canada's Musical Past: A Forgotten Heritage Recalled." *Music Magazine* 12/3 (June/July 1989), 14–17.

Review of *Glenn Gould: A Life and Variations* by Otto Friedrich. *CAML Newsletter* 18/3 (December 1989), 7–12.

Editor. *Music for Orchestra I.* The Canadian Musical Heritage, vol. 8. Ottawa: Canadian Musical Heritage Society, 1990.

"Smith, Charles-Gustave," and "Jehin-Prume, Frantz." *Dictionary of Canadian Biography*, vol. 12. Toronto: University of Toronto Press, 1990.

Review of *Glenn Gould: A Life and Variations* by Otto Friedrich. *University of Toronto Quarterly* 60/1 (Fall 1990), 204–6.

"Shaping the Policies of the Music Division of the National Library of Canada." *Association for Canadian Studies Newsletter* 12/3 (Fall 1990), 22–23.

"Guest Editorial: To Hear and Remember." *SoundNotes* 3 (Fall/Winter 1992), 32–34.

Co-Editor. *Encyclopedia of Music in Canada / Encyclopédie de la musique au Canada*, 2nd ed. Toronto: University of Toronto Press, 1992 / Montreal: Fides, 1993. New articles by HK: unsigned articles—"Arrangers" (with Mark Miller); "Benjamin, William E."; "Calderisi, Maria"; "Canadian Musical Heritage Society"; "*Canadian University Music Review*"; "Colonial Harmonist"; "Delmar Music Co."; "Maloney, S. Timothy"; "Willis, Stephen"; signed articles—"Berry, Wallace"; "Doolittle, Quenten"; "Exhibitions"; "Geddes-Harvey, Roberta"; "Hall, Frederick A."; "Hund, Frederic"; "Johnson, Edward L."; "Lower, Thelma Reid"; "*La Lyre, revue musicale et théâtrale*"; "MacKenzie, William Roy"; "McElheran, Brock"; "Piccinini, Marina"; "Roman, Zoltan."

Letter to the Editor. *Classical Music Magazine* 16/2 (April 1993), 6.

Die Musik in Geschichte und Gegenwart, 2nd ed. Edited by Ludwig Finscher. Kassel: Bärenreiter / Stuttgart: Metzler, 1994–2008. *Sachteil* (by subject) in 9 vols. with an index vol. (1994–99), *Personenteil* (biographical), in 17 vols. with an index vol. (1999–2007). *Supplement* (2008). HK was the sub-editor responsible for Canadian entries and wrote the entries "Kanada" (*Sachteil* vol. 4: cols. 1653–77); "Clarke, James Paton" (*Personenteil* vol. 4: cols. 1186–87) and "Lavallée, Calixa" (*Personenteil* vol. 10, cols. 1351–53).

List of Helmut Kallmann's Writings

*"The Making of a One-Country Encyclopedia: An Essay after an Encyclopedia." *Fontes artis musicae* 41/1 (January/March 1994), 3–19.
"MacMillan Exhibition Review." *National Library News* 26/4 (April 1994).
Letter to the Editor. *SoundNotes* 7 (Fall/Winter 1994), 4.
Review of *Sir Ernest MacMillan: The Importance of Being Canadian* by Ezra Schabas. Music Library Association *Notes* 52/2 (December 1995), 493–96.
*"Music in the Internment Camps and after World War II: John Newmark's Start on a Brilliant Canadian Career." *German-Canadian Yearbook* 14 (1995), 181–91.
Editor. *Ex-Internees Newsletter*. 10 issues. September 1996 to February 2004.
"The German Contribution to Music in Canada, Supplementary Bibliography." *Canadiana Germanica* 91 (September 1996), 1–3.
"CMLA/CAML: 15 Plus 25 Years of Flourishing." *CAML Newsletter* 24/3 (December 1996), 9–10.
*"Taking Stock of Canada's Composers: From the 1920s to the *Catalogue of Canadian Composers* (1952)." *A Celebration of Canada's Arts 1930–1970*. Edited by Glen Carruthers and Gordana Lazarevich. Toronto: Canadian Scholars Press, 1996. 15–26.
"Canadian Music Council"; "Dett, Robert Nathaniel"; "Jesous Ahatonia"; "The Maple Leaf For Ever"; "Os-ke-non-ton." *The 1997 Canadian Encyclopedia Plus*. CD ROM. Toronto: McClelland and Stewart, 1996.
*"Mapping Canada's Music: A Life's Task." *Music in Canada: A Collection of Essays / La Musique au Canada*, vol. 1. Edited by Guido Bimberg. Kanada-Studien Band 25. Bochum: Universitätsverlag Dr. N. Brockmeyer, 1997. 11–34.
With S. Timothy Maloney. "Canadian Composer's 'Lost' Manuscripts Rediscovered." *Classical Music Magazine* 20/3 (September 1997), 14. Reprinted in *CAML Newsletter* 27/1 (April 1999), 27.
"Brahms, Mendelssohn and Schubert: Shaking Loose the Stereotypes." *Classical Music Magazine* 20/3 (September 1997), 20–22.
"Lucien Poirier's Contribution to Canadian Musical Heritage Society / Société pour le patrimoine musical canadien." *Les Cahiers de la Société québécoise de recherche en musique* 2/2 (November 1998), 41–44.
Editor. *Piano Music III: Marches and Dances*. The Canadian Musical Heritage, vol. 22. Ottawa: Canadian Musical Heritage Society, 1998.
Editor, with others. *Historical Anthology of Canadian Music*, 2 vols. Ottawa: Canadian Musical Heritage Society, 1998.
"Témoinage: Gilles Potvin." *Les Cahiers de la Société québécoise de recherche en musique* 4/1 (June 2000), 91–92.
"The Glenn Gould Fonds of the National Library of Canada: From Acquisition to Exhibition." *GlennGould* 6/2 (Fall 2000), 72–74.
*"The Matter of Identity." *Outlook, Canada's Progressive Jewish Magazine* 39/4 (July/August 2001), 15–16; online at http://www.vcn.bc.ca/outlook/library/

articles/culture/p05Identity.htm. Translated and reprinted as "In Sachen Identität." *Berlin Aktuell, Zeitschrift für exilierte Berliner* 69 (June 2002), 19–21.

"The Istvan Anhalt Fonds at the National Library of Canada." *Istvan Anhalt: Pathways and Memory*, ed. Robin Elliott and Gordon E. Smith. Montreal and Kingston: McGill-Queen's University Press, 2001. 342–54.

"Glackemeyer, Frederick." *The New Grove Dictionary of Music and Musicians*, 2nd ed. Edited by Stanley Sadie and John Tyrell. London: Macmillan, 2001. Also revisions of the articles "Clarke, James P."; "Codman, Stephen"; "Fricker, Herbert (Austin)" [with H.C. Colles]; "Harriss, Charles (Albert Edwin)"; "Jehin-Prume, Frantz"; "Lavallée, Calixa"; "Molt, Theodore Frederic"; "Quesnel, (Louis) Joseph (Marie)"; and "Vogt, Augustus Stephen."

Review of *Louis Applebaum: A Passion for Culture* by Walter Pitman and *Niki Goldschmidt: A Life in Canadian Music* by Gwenlyn Setterfield. *Literary Review of Canada* 11/5 (June 2003), 29.

"National Anthem." *The Oxford Companion to Canadian History*. Edited by Gerald Hallowell. Toronto: Oxford University Press, 2004. 424–25.

"My Evening with Glenn Gould." *Institute for Canadian Music Newsletter* 3/2 (May 2005), 14.

Index

Page numbers in italics indicate illustrations

A

Adaskin, John, 50, 172
Adaskin, Murray, 83, 167, 175
Adaskin, Naomi, 4
Albani, Emma, 36, 76n1, 85
Amtmann, Willy, 127–30, 133–34, 200
Apel, Willi, 183–86
Applebaum, Louis, 89, 96
archives and libraries, 11, 49, 54, 192, 195, 197–98, 202. *See also* CBC Toronto Music Library; National Library of Canada, Music Division

B

Ball, Peter (classmate of HK), 3, *141*, 237–38, 252
Bannerman, James, 7, 198
Barbeau, Marius, 40
Baum, Gregory, 125, *146*
Beckwith, John, 96, 105, *145*, 194, 200–201, 203–5
Beethoven, Ludwig van, 19, 68, 159, 186; and Theodore Molt, 5, 36–37, 151, 189–90
Berlin (Germany), *137–38*, *143*, 217, 223–62
Bimberg, Guido, 189
Blachford, Frank, 211n2
Blume, Helmut, 130, 133

BMI Canada. *See* Canadian performing rights societies
Bray, Kenneth, 27, 32
Bridle, Augustus, 170–71
Brochu, Lucien, 6, 200, 207
Brott, Alexander, 40, 132

C

Calderisi, Maria, 9, 14n16, 82, *144*, 202
Canada Council, 96–98
Canadian Association of Music Libraries, 6–7, 20, 23n2, 61–64, 198–200
Canadian Broadcasting Corporation. *See* CBC
Canadian Federation of Music Teachers' Associations, 181n9
Canadian League of Composers, 87–102, 196; age policy 93–94; *Catalogue of Orchestral Music*, 7, 95; concerts, 94–95; early members, 92–93; foundation, 88–89, 101n2; *Fourteen piano pieces by Canadian composers*, 95; predecessors, 89–90
Canadian Musical Heritage Society, 11, 23n2, 61, *145*, 199, 205
Canadian Music Centre, 95–98, 105, 179

Index

Canadian Music Council, 6, 90, 95–96, 101–2n5, 104–5, 196
Canadian musicians, earlier, 11, 46, 171, 174, 177–78, 197, 205–6. *See also* Canadian Musical Heritage Society; Clarke, James Paton; Quesnel, Joseph
Canadian music in international reference sources, 9, 39–42, 66, 76n1, 170, 185–86, 196–97, 203
Canadian Music Journal, 8, 96, 102n11, 196
Canadian Music Library Association. *See* Canadian Association of Music Libraries
Canadian music periodicals, 36, 84, 158–59, 184, 196
Canadian music publishing, 49, 61–64, 68–70, 80, 90–91, 95, 121, 151, 155, 181n9, 198–99, 202
Canadian performing rights societies, 88, 90, 173, 179
Canadian sheet music, 61–64, 69, 80, 84–85, 174, 198–99, 213n26
CAPAC. *See* Canadian performing rights societies
catalogues of Canadian music, 61–64, 82, 98, 170–72, 178–80; *Catalogue of Canadian Composers*, 6, 39, 95, 167, 172–79, 191, 194–95, 198
CBC, 7, 90, 93–94, 97, 132–33, 161, 186; *Ideas*, 13n1
CBC Toronto Music Library, 6, 20, *142*, 173, 194–95, 198
census, Canadian, 217–18
Centennial projects (1967), 7, 61–64, 81, 198–99
Chalmers, Floyd S., 9, 105, *144*, 203–4
Champagne, Claude, 83, 90, 93–95
Charlesworth, Hector, 66, 69–70
Chesterman, Robert, 186
Children of Peace, 199–201
Clarke, Hugh Archibald, 66, 69, 74, 77n13, 77n15
Clarke, James Paton, 63, 65–77, 151, *152*, 197–98
Couture, Guillaume, 89, 156, 197

D

Dessane, Antoine, 11
Diamond, Beverley, 47–48, 208
Duncan, Chester, 167, 176
Dunelyk, Leonard, 27, 32

E

Elliott, Robin, 123n7
Encyclopedia of Music in Canada (EMC), 9–10, 13, 17, 21–22, 103–24, *144*, 158, 167, 179, 202–4, 206–8, 210

F

Feldbrill, Victor, 18, 200
Ford, Clifford, 11, 61, *145*, 205, 215n50
Forsyth, W.O., 171, 174, 178, 197

G

Gagnier, J.-J., 172, 175
Gould, Glenn, 133, 232; papers, 14n13, 79
Goulet, J.J., 156
Grove's Dictionary of Music and Musicians, 9, 39–42, 66, 170, 201

H

Hall, Frederick A., *145*, 201, 205
Halpern, Ida, 132, 162
Harriss, Charles A.E., 50
Harvard Dictionary of Music, 183–86
Hitler, Adolf, 219–20, 226, 228, 239, 244, 246
Homburger, Walter, 18, 128, 133, *146*

Index

I

immigrant musicians, 17–18, 45–46, 209. *See also* refugee musicians
International Association of Music Libraries (IAML), 7, *146*, 197; RISM, 84, 207
International Composers' Conference (1960), 96, 101n4
International Society for Contemporary Music (ISCM), 89–90, 95–96, 101n4
internment camps, 2–4, 12, 125–35, *140–41*, *143*, *146*, 190, 217–18, 225, 241, 248
Iseler, Elmer, 27, 32, 200

J

James, Frances, 167
Jeanneret, Marsh, 21, 24n10
Jocelyn, Gordon, 27, 32, *141*
Johnston, Richard, 1, 27, 29–30

K

Kallmann, Arthur (father of HK), 2, 4, *137*, 223–34, 236, 238, 241, 243–58
Kallmann, Eva (sister of HK), 2, 4, *137*, 224–25, 234–36, 249, 253–57
Kallmann, Fanny (mother of HK), 2, 4, *137*, 224–25, 228–29, 232–34, 238–40, 243–44, 246, 251–52, 255–57, 259
Kallmann, Helmut: awards and honours, 1, 9–10; childhood friends, 3, *141*, *143*, 219, 229, 236–38, 258; education, in Berlin, 2, *137*, *139*, 223, 235–37, 252; education, university, 1–2, 5, 27–33, *141*, 190; Jewish identity, 2, 18, *139*, 217–21, 224–25, 242–43, 248; obituaries, 15n24; papers, 13, 19, 183; retirement, 10, 12–13, 217, 219; in Toronto, 4, 7, 131. *See also* CBC Toronto Music Library; internment camps; *Kindertransport*; Nazis
Kallmann, Helmut: as historian, 19, 22–23, 195–96; as librarian. *See* CBC Toronto Music Library; National Library of Canada, Music Division; melodic similarities project, 12–13, 19, 151; as pianist, 1–5, 11, 13, 18, 95, 130, *141*, *145*, 229, 237, 239, 241, 253
Kallmann, Helmut: on Canadian musical identity, 18, 21, 37, 44–46, 63, 108–9, 193–94, 208–9; on politics, 2, 12, 188, 221, 236; on scholarship, 17–20, 30–31, 35–38, 43-48, 113, 168, 201, 205–10
Kallmann, Ruth Singer (wife of HK), 7–8, 12, *143*
Kander, Gerhard, 127–30, 134
Kane, Jack, 18, 27, 32
Keer, Dawn, 13n1
Keillor, Elaine, *145*, 205
Kindertransport, 2, 218, 253–54
King's College. *See* University of Toronto
Koch, Eric, 125
Koerner, Michael, 105–6, *144*
Kraemer, Franz, 133
Kraus, Greta, 4, 133, 161

L

Laine, Mabel, 123n7
Lapierre, Eugène, 41, 57
Laughton, Wallace, 27, 32
Lavallée, Calixa, 40–41; "O Canada," 8, 85
Lavender, Jean, 6
League of Composers (United States), 89

279

Index

Lefebvre, Marie-Thérèse, 205
Library and Archives Canada. *See* National Library of Canada, Music Division
Lucas, Clarence, 11, 171, 174, 178, 197, 205

M

MacMillan, Sir Ernest: as musician, 5, 21, 27–28, 31, 41, 175, 194; as writer, 36, 47, 70, 159–60, 171–72, 196; papers, 79
MacMillan, Keith, 9, 105, 201, 204
Maloney, S. Timothy, 10
Mathieu, Rodolphe, 171, 177, 205–6
Mazzoleni, Ettore, 40–41, 94, 131
McCaul, John, 68–70, 73
McNeill, Ogreta, 6–7, 200
McPhee, Colin, 177, 206
Mercure, Pierre, 97
Miller, Mark, 22, 123n7
Misener, Erland, 6, 173, 195
Molt, Theodore, 5, 36–37, 151, 190, 193, 210
Montreal, 52, 154–57
Moogk, Edward G., 9, 81–83, 124n9, 202
Morel, François, 95, 97
Mráček, Jaroslav, 27, 32
Die Musik in Geschichte und Gegenwart, 6, 18, 196

N

National Library of Canada, Music Division: Canadian music collections, 61, 179, 198–99; history, 8–10, 23n2, 79–86, 198, 203; other collections, 128, 161; staff, 86n3, 144, 202
Nazis, 2, 217–20, 224–62
New Grove Dictionary of Music and Musicians. See Grove's Dictionary of Music and Musicians

Newman, Peter C., 183, 187–88
Newmark, John, 4, 125–34

O

opera in Canada, 37, 50–58, 117, 155, 193

P

Papineau-Couture, Jean, 93
Parlow, Kathleen, 134, 191
Pelletier, Wilfrid, 93
Pentland, Barbara, 96
Pohland, Günter (classmate of HK), 229, 238, 258
Poirier, Lucien, 145, 205
Potvin, Gilles, 106, 144, 202–4
PROCAN. *See* Canadian performing rights societies

Q

Quebec (province), 18, 174, 193
Quebec City, 54–55, 107, 151–54, 190
Quesnel, Joseph, 202; *Colas et Colinette*, 49–60, 195, 198; *Épitre à M. Généreux Labadie*, 51, 57; *Lucas et Cécile*, 54–56

R

refugee musicians, 125–35, 190
Ridout, Godfrey, 49, 54–56
Rosevear, Robert, 2, 27, 29–30
Royal Conservatory of Music (Toronto), 40–41, 190

S

Sale, David John, 76n7
Salter, Liora (daughter of HK), 8
Schafer, R. Murray, 5–6, 49, 198
Scholes, Percy A., 8; collection, 80, 85
Schubert, Franz, 75, 131, 149–65; *Rosamunde*, 154, 156–58

Schubert Choir (Brantford), 158
Sharon (Ontario), 199–201
Slonimsky, Nicholas, 42n2, 196
Smith, Leo, 27, 30, 73, 83
SOCAN. *See* Canadian performing rights societies
sound recordings, 29, 80–86, 90, 97–98, 100, 121, 161, 169, 202
Symposium of Canadian Contemporary Music (1950), 91–92

T

Telgmann, Oscar: *Leo the Royal Cadet*, 50, 63, 117
Ten Centuries Concerts, 7, 49, 198
Thompson's International Cyclopedia of Music and Musicians, 40, 67, 192, 196
Toronto, 37, 65–77, 153, 157–58
Toronto Conservatory of Music. *See* Royal Conservatory of Music (Toronto)
Toronto Symphony Orchestra, 41, 128, 133–34, 156, 160, 198
Torrington, Frederick Herbert, 40, 65, 73, 154
touring performers, 51, 117, 154–56, 193

U

Unger, Heinz, 5, 18, 40, 82, 132
University of Toronto, 66, 68, 70–71; Faculty of Music, 1–2, 5, 18, 27–33, 190
University of Toronto Press, 10, 21, 43, 115

V

The Varsity, 1, 5, 35
Versailles, Claire, 123n7
Vézina, Joseph, 40
Victoria (B.C.), 155, 157
Vogt, Augustus Stephen, 40, 63, 65, 89–90

W

Waddington, Geoffrey, 173
Walter, Arnold, 4–5, 27, 90, 102n11, 132, 196; papers, 83
Wardrop, Patricia, 123n7
Weinberg, Traute, 13, *147*, 217, 223
Weinzweig, John, 17–18, 87–89, 91–94, 96–97, 102n8
Welsman, Frank, 211n2
Werner, Erna (friend of HK's family), 242, 258–59
Willan, Healey, 41, 50, 73, 90, 93; as teacher, 27, 30–31; papers, 9, 79, 81, 203
Willis, Stephen C., 9, 82, *144*, 202
Winters, Kenneth, 9, 106, *144*, 202–3
Wolff, S. Drummond, 27, 31
women in music, 153, 193, 209
women's musical clubs, 157–58
writers on Canadian music, earlier, 36, 42n4, 47, 171–72, 180–81n6, 185, 192–93

Z

Zvankin, Peter, 167, 176

www.ingramcontent.com/pod-product-compliance
Lightning Source LLC
Chambersburg PA
CBHW072149070526
44585CB00015B/1058